THE
7
KEYS TO
COMMUNICATING
IN
MEXICO

An Intercultural Approach

OLIVIA HERNANDEZ-POZAS
ORLANDO R. KELM
DAVID A. VICTOR

Georgetown University Press | Washington, DC

The publisher is not responsible for third-party websites or their content. URL links were active at time of publication.

Library of Congress Cataloging-in-Publication Data

Names: Kelm, Orlando R., 1957– author. | Roble Hernández Pozas, Olivia del, author. | Victor, David A., 1956– author.
Title: The Seven Keys to Communicating in Mexico : An Intercultural Approach/Orlando R. Kelm, Olivia Hernandez-Pozas, and David A. Victor.

Description: Washington, DC : Georgetown University Press, 2020. | Includes bibliographical references and index.
Identifiers: LCCN 2019009099 (print) | LCCN 2019980310 (ebook) | ISBN 9781626167223 (hardcover : alk. paper) | ISBN 9781626167230 (pbk. : alk. paper) | ISBN 9781626167247 (ebook)
Subjects: LCSH: Business communication—Mexico. | Business communication—United States. | Business etiquette—Mexico. | Intercultural communication—Mexico. | Communication and culture—Mexico. | Mexico—Social life and customs—21st century.
Classification: LCC HF5718.2.M6 K45 2020 (print) | LCC HF5718.2.M6 (ebook) | DDC 395.5/20972—dc23
LC record available at https://lccn.loc.gov/2019009099
LC ebook record available at https://lccn.loc.gov/2019980310

21 20   9 8 7 6 5 4 3 2   First printing

Printed in the United States of America.
Cover design by Connie Gabbert.
Text design by click! Publishing Services.

CONTENTS

Figures

Tables

PHOTOGRAPHS

ACKNOWLEDGMENTS

Every author knows that many colleagues and friends help bring a book to completion. This is only intensified when three authors who live far from each other collaborate in the endeavor. Bear with us as we try to express our thanks.

In chapter 8 of this book, you will read the story of Marta Nieves, a bilingual and bicultural lawyer who works for Hutchison & Vaile LLP, a law firm that specializes in international trade and cross-border acquisitions. In actuality, we changed the name of the company, the people, and the location of the events. However, the vignette does tell of "Marta's" real work experience. We thank her for sharing her story, even if we do not publicly mention her by name. Suffice it to say that she knows who she is; thank you again, Marta.

We can and do recognize our guest executives who commented on the case study. We thank Juan Creixell, Rodrigo Ruy Gutiérrez Hernández, Ryan Jones, María Angélica Pech Ortega, Alfonso Padilla, and Mitchell Slape for making an awesome contribution to the case study in chapter 8. Each added a unique style, which added a personal touch and a rich perspective to the vignette. As readers review the case study, your individual perspectives and recommendations add a sense of reality to the vignette.

There are a number of photographs in this volume, and we hope that readers find them helpful in illustrating the topics. We literally had friends running to butcher shops, infiltrating *maquiladoras*, celebrating family reunions, knocking on doors for Posadas, cheering at soccer games, buying roses for mothers, and modeling for nonverbal gestures. Thanks to all—Adriana Bonilla-Hernandez, Vanessa Bonilla-Hernandez, Heriberto Bonilla Rios, Roberto Bonilla Rios, Rosio Briones, Elva O.

Cavazos Espinoza, Emilio Durazo Rocha, Adriana Gonzalez Ramirez, Paulina Guzman, David A. Leith Ramirez, Ma. Del Socorro Lopez de Bonilla, Mayra Nieto, Jesus Enrique Portillo Pizaña, and Jair Velasquez.

This book is a third in a series in which we have applied the LESCANT approach to discuss the keys of intercultural communication. After completing our books about Brazil and Japan, Hope LeGro and her team at Georgetown University Press encouraged us to consider Mexico for the third book. We thank everyone at Georgetown University Press. It is stunning to see how the text, photographs, figures, and tables all come together, and how creative designers utilize their skills to prepare the manuscript for publication.

Thank you to our families. This book was completed during a time of personal family challenges but also particular family triumphs. These challenges and triumphs put into perspective for us what is really most important in life, which unsurprisingly is not this book. And finally, thank you to those of you who over the years have shaped our experiences with Mexico, both those from Mexico and those who, with us, have experienced Mexico. *Pues, no hay mejor espejo que el amigo viejo.*

This book is now the third in our series, "The Seven Keys to Communicating . . . An Intercultural Approach." We started with Brazil, then moved on to Japan, and this volume focuses on Mexico. Who would have guessed that this Mexico volume would be released at such a pivotal time when the relationship between the United States, Canada, and Mexico is at a crossroads. Politically, this publication coincides with a time when communication regarding Mexico centers on talk of walls, immigration, tariffs, drugs, and the renegotiations of the North American Free Trade Agreement. And from the Mexican side, this book comes out at a time when Andrés Manuel López Obrador beat out, with an outright majority, both the Partido Acción Nacional and Partido Revolucionario Institucional candidates, all with a new party and new promises to deal with corruption, violence, and economic progress. No doubt, this is a moment for improved communication.

The purpose of this book is to provide a guide for North Americans on how to conduct professional activities and otherwise interact culturally with Mexican counterparts. Although this book uses the United States and Canada as its point of comparison in discussing Mexico, we hope that the book will be useful for any number of other nationalities as well. We also hope that this book will be of value for Mexicans who are trying to understand North America. When we say that this book works as a guide for "professional activities," we mean this in the broadest terms. Academics who conduct research in Mexico, students who will study abroad in Mexico, executives who never leave their home office in Saint Louis but who conduct weekly video conferences with Mexicans, expatriates who are assigned to live in Mexico, government employees who set policy—for all these, the approach in this book is designed to enhance the ability to recognize and understand the cultural issues that affect cross-cultural communication. Throughout this book we sometimes use the terms "North Americans" and "Americans" to refer to people who are from the United States. We do so for convenience, knowing that Mexico and Canada are both part of North America. We considered using terms like "US Americans," but in the end that seemed redundant and ungrammatical. Please note that no offense or insensitivity is intended.

To give structure and focus to our analysis, we follow what is called the LESCANT approach. LESCANT is a simple acronym that represents seven key areas where intercultural communication may differ from one group of people to another; it was developed by one of our authors, David Victor, to categorize intercultural communication. The seven areas are

- **L**anguage
- **E**nvironment and technology
- **S**ocial organization
- **C**ontexting
- **A**uthority conception
- **N**onverbal behavior
- **T**ime conception

Using the LESCANT approach in this book, we provide you with seven keys to Mexican communication. We examine Mexico by following each of the seven letters of the acronym in successive chapters. Each chapter explores the characteristics that define Mexico and its people. Using examples that illustrate the key in question, we highlight points to remember and make recommendations for interacting with Mexicans. We hope the keys in this introduction to communicating with Mexicans unlocks a few doors for you.

Chapter 1 examines the **L** of the LESCANT acronym, Language, revealing the significant aspects of Mexican Spanish. The language barrier is perhaps the most easily recognized because Spanish is the language of Mexico. We start by looking at words in English that come from Spanish. We then explain some of the characteristics of Mexican Spanish, including the number of borrowings from indigenous languages and English. We also discuss the use of English in Mexico, and we address some of the challenges that affect communication in English in Mexico. Then we discuss some of the ways that Mexican Spanish sounds different from other dialects within the Spanish-speaking world. We end the chapter with specific recommendations about what to do when using Spanish or English in Mexico.

Chapter 2 discusses the **E** of the acronym LESCANT, the **E**nvironment and technology, and their effect on Mexican society. This chapter deals with the physical differences that exist, everything from weather and climate to the carpeting on floors and the air conditioning units in windows. In this chapter we examine the effects of the topography, altitude, and size of Mexico; its population density and wealth; the use and source of its water; and the architecture of its buildings and the use of space. We seldom consider the cultural effects of our physical surroundings, and this chapter seeks to serve as an aid so learning can be more observant of these very factors.

Chapter 3 investigates the **S** of LESCANT, examining the **S**ocial organization that gives structure to personal and professional interactions in Mexico. We define social organizations as the common institutions and collective activities that members of a culture share. These include such areas as family, views toward work, individualism (and collectivism), religion, education, sports, the role of women in society, and how we use our leisure time.

Many of the variables that we examine in this book operate without our even being aware of them. In the case of social organization, we generally are aware of differences from other cultures but often are not aware of the implications. Because these differences are readily observable, it is easy for us to be critical when others deviate from our own system of social organization. The reality is that such matters are neither right or wrong—just different. In this chapter, we begin by showing what is meant by Mexican *mestizaje*, the US melting pot, and the Canadian mosaic, all as a way to ascertain multiculturalism. We also take a look at how the caste system of previous eras led to the class systems of today.

Chapter 4 addresses the **C** of LES**C**ANT, **C**ontexting. Although we try throughout the book to keep away from using technical terminology, in the case of "contexting," there is simply no good equivalent term. The great cultural researcher Edward T. Hall coined this term to describe how much of what we say or do is understood directly or indirectly, and this by understanding the context surrounding the communication.

Hall used the term "high-context" communication to refer to cultures where speakers depend more on gathering shared information, which then does not need to be specifically stated because it is understood. By contrast, Hall described "low-context" communication for those individuals in which we depend more on the actual words and gestures, so we need to state them specifically. On the contexting scale, North American culture is on the low end, meaning that North Americans need to say and hear the actual words. Mexico ranks at the high end of the scale, and as high-context communicators, Mexicans gather shared information, which is then stored, eradicating the need to overtly state what then becomes obvious.

This chapter compares the principles of North American and Mexican contexting, adding to our knowledge base of communication. In this chapter we begin by explaining in what ways Mexico is considered to be more high-context than the United States and Canada. We then present examples of high-context Mexican communication by way of famous Mexican *dichos*, or proverbs. All these proverbs illustrate a high-context communication style. We then offer insights into the relationship between contexting and the perception of dignity, respect, and face-saving. Next we review the relationship between contexting and humor, and how this is expressed in Mexican culture. We end the chapter with specific recommendations for interacting with people who have a different contexting style.

Chapter 5 explores the **A** in LESC**A**NT—how **A**uthority and power are conceptualized in Mexico. This topic deals with how we define power and authority, who has power, and how power is shared or exchanged. This category brings up issues of leadership style, how decisions are made, and how titles are used to show status. We begin this chapter with a look at three spheres or levels of Mexican authority. First, we look at the microlevel, the outward and surface-level distinctions that are made to show respect for those in authority. Next, we discuss the notion of *patrón*, the relationship based on reciprocal power. We explain reasons to reject the old terms *patronismo* and *caciquismo* (given the negative connotations and misrepresentations), and substitute these with the new term "Patrón System," all to illustrate how people of unequal power build ties and relationships. Finally, we discuss the third sphere, Mexican corporatism, focusing on the shared power of government leaders and key people who develop institutionalized interest groups of authority.

Chapter 6 focuses on the **N** of LESCANT, the many aspects of **N**onverbal communication. The way we move when we speak, how we use our eyes, how we dress, and what our various symbols mean are all part of nonverbal behavior. We begin this chapter by sharing and illustrating a number of gestures that Mexicans use to communicate. These gestures are almost subconsciously performed and are nearly meaningless to people unfamiliar with Mexico. Then we explore affect display, how much our nonverbal behavior reveals emotions. Next, we cover oculesics, messages that are communicated with our eyes. We then touch on dress and grooming, including Mexican dress for professional situations, and we also include a section on the meaning behind traditional Mexican clothing. We close the chapter with observations about passive nonverbal communication, such as the significance of color and Mexican symbols, ranging from eagles to chocolate to *alebrijes*.

Chapter 7 explores the final key of the LESCANT categories, **T**, for the concept of **T**ime. Although we often think of time as something immutable and universal, in reality our views of time are actually shaped by our culture. We can see this most clearly when contrasting those cultures, such as Mexico, that have a flexible and relaxed view of time (called polychronic) and those such as the United States, Germany, and the Netherlands, which have a fixed view of time (called monochronic). In this chapter we examine the way in which, for Mexicans, the past informs the present. In Mexico there is a connection with the past that constantly merges with the present. This makes for an interesting topic and leads to practical recommendations.

In the eighth and final chapter of this book, we provide readers with a vignette, a cultural case study that exemplifies Mexican culture in a professional setting. In this vignette, we provide a story based on the experience of a bilingual corporate lawyer who works for a law firm that mainly represents US clients who expand operations in Mexico. She shares stories from her extensive experience in international trade and foreign investments.

Following the case itself, we provide opinions from three North American professionals who work with Mexicans and three Mexican professionals who work with North Americans. Each provides their response to what they found significant in the vignette. These executives give their own views, providing another level of understanding of US–Mexican realities. Following the executive commentary, we add a few perspectives of our own, and also offer some questions for further consideration.

When it comes to North American and Mexican interactions, our experience over the years is that these interactions are seldom hampered by difficulties related to accounting figures, financial data, principles of marketing, or even technical details related to trade and exports. It is with misunderstandings related to intercultural communication, however, where we find the most significant challenges and problems. By following the seven keys presented in the LESCANT model, our hope is that you will unlock a growing aptitude in understanding intercultural communication with Mexicans.

1

THE SPANISH
Language

A Beautiful Mixture That Defines Mexico

Perhaps nothing affects intercultural communication between North Americans and Mexicans more than our choice of language—the L in the LESCANT approach. Even in situations where all participants are bilingual, we still need to decide which language to use. Sometimes, this choice is forced on us when members of the team are monolingual. Other times, language choice relates to our effort to be polite. Still other times, the language we use results from an assertion of power by insisting that we use either English or Spanish to gain some advantage in negotiations. Seldom are all parties totally bilingual. Somebody is going to make a sacrifice by speaking, listening, or reading the other's language. In other situations, when neither party has any fluency in the other language, we are forced to use interpreters and translators, which brings additional barriers to communication. It is inevitable that the use of one's native language or the use of a local language will drastically affect intercultural communication.

When we look at Mexico and consider how language becomes an issue of intercultural communication, the first thing we note is Mexico's proximity to the United States. A quick look at a map of the United States offers a reminder that Mexico is a gigantic part of North American history. Consider the names of US states and cities. California is indeed a hot oven. Arizona is an arid zone. Colorado is colorful. Nevada does have snow in the mountains. Montana does have beautiful mountains. Florida can be flowering. Imagine how weird it would be to call the major cities of California by their English equivalents: The Angels, Sacrament, Saint James, and Saint Joseph! It is impossible to visualize Tony Bennett singing "I Left My Heart in Saint Francis"! If it were not for Spanish, we would not be able to tell the "lost wages" joke about Las Vegas because we would call the city "the meadows." Can you imagine if Texans in the city of "Saint Anthony" would have shouted "Remember the Poplars" instead of "Remember the Alamo"? (Even in this case, we are not always positive if *álamo* refers to poplars, cottonwoods, or some other type of tree.)

And it is not only place names where we can see Spanish in North American English. Our cowboys have their ranches, rodeos, lassos, corrals, and stirrups. And what would happen to Tex-Mex without the Mex? In our cantinas and cafeterias, we would have no tacos, burritos, enchiladas, quesadillas, salsa, serranos, habaneros, tomatoes, tomatillos, cilantro, or fajitas. As North Americans, we are connected with Mexico in ways that go beyond 2,000 miles of shared *frontera*. As we will discuss in subsequent chapters, at the end of the Mexican-American War, Mexico lost about a third of its territory. Before 1848, a gigantic part of the United States was, in fact, Mexico! Even today, officially, Mexico is part of North America. Central America begins south of the Mexican border.

According to statistics from the US Central Intelligence Agency's *World Factbook*, Mexico's population in 2016 was estimated to be 123,166,749.[1] This is the most populous Spanish-speaking country in the world. The second-most-populous one is Spain, which at 48 million has only 39 percent of Mexico's population—and we could argue that the United States has the second-highest number of Spanish speakers in the world. Additionally, based on Pew Research Center Data, between 1965 and 2015, more than 16 million Mexicans migrated to the United States.[2] When we consider the two countries' historical, geographical, and linguistic ties, it is clear that Mexico and the United States share important connections. No wonder our decision to interact includes a decision about language.

Before we launch into our discussion of English versus Spanish, we also remind readers that Mexico enjoys a rich mix of ethnic groups. We will discuss the social implications of this in subsequent chapters. Here, however, as related to language, note that only 10 percent of Mexico's population is European (per the *CIA Factbook*), with the vast majority being Amerindian–Spanish mestizo or Amerindian. Linguistically, the result is that Mexican Spanish enjoys a beautiful mix with indigenous languages (most related to Náhuatl and Mayan languages). It is this influence that provides us with precious gems like Tenochtitlán, Popocatépetl, Chapultepec, and Tlaquepaque. Even Spanish speakers from other parts of the world find it difficult to pronounce all the indigenous words that are part of Mexican Spanish.

We begin this chapter with a brief look at the use of English and Spanish in Mexico. We then provide a description of some of the characteristics of Mexican Spanish. We also touch on the role of other languages in Mexico, a notable difference because Mexico has far less immigration than does the United States or Canada. We conclude the chapter with recommendations on how to communicate with Mexicans, both when using English and when speaking Spanish.

THE USE OF ENGLISH AND SPANISH IN MEXICO

We often hear that English is the lingua franca of business and that the whole world conducts business in English. Although it is true that English is the world's most common second language, it is difficult to make a blanket statement about the English-language proficiency of everyone in Mexico. The English Proficiency Index ranks Mexico forty-third out of seventy-two countries, which puts it in the low category.[3] And indeed the index is lower than other Latin American countries, such as Argentina, the Dominican Republic, Spain, Uruguay, Costa Rica, and Brazil. This national average, however, is also tempered with the English proficiency of the upper-class, educated, and professional portion of the country. At these levels, many executives may exhibit higher levels of English-language proficiency. Outside these circles, however, actual proficiency drops off and the vast majority simply does not speak English.

English-language learning in Mexico is similar, in many ways, to the learning of Spanish or French in the United States. Thousands of Americans can say that they studied a foreign language at school, but relatively few claim to be fluent speakers. Similarly, many Mexicans can say that they studied English at school, with similar bilingual results. Many Mexicans are just as confident in their use of English as Americans are in their use of their high school or college Spanish.

Immigrant Speakers of Spanish in North America and Speakers of English in Mexico

There is a common joke around the world about the lack of foreign-language knowledge in the United States. We have heard this joke in many languages, and it usually goes something like this:

> What do you call someone who speaks three languages?
> *Trilingual*
> What do you call someone who speaks two languages?
> *Bilingual*
> What do you call someone who speaks one language?
> *An American*

Although this joke for the most part still represents a reality in the United States, this situation has been changing. A 2013 YouGov survey by Kate Palmer found that 25 percent of people in the United States are proficient in a second language—and 58 percent of these are fluent in Spanish, far and away beyond the next-highest language, French, at 20 percent.[4] However, we need to consider these statistics within the context of immigration. The Pew Research Center's statistical portrait of Hispanics in the United States indicate that among Hispanics age five years or older, 68.4 percent speak only English (or English very well). This implies that 31.6 percent is Spanish dominant, with the others having various levels of bilingual proficiency.[5]

The main difference between Mexico, on one hand, and the United States, on the other hand, is the source of fluency in one another's language. In Mexico, almost none of those fluent in English are immigrants or the children of immigrants from English-speaking countries. By contrast, in the United States, a large number of those fluent in Spanish are either immigrants or the children of immigrants. (For 2018, the US Census Bureau estimates that 7 percent of US citizens will be first-generation immigrants from a Spanish-speaking country.[6]) By comparison, almost no one in Mexico comes from a home where English is spoken as a mother tongue. This is because just 0.34 percent of Mexicans were born in English-speaking countries.[7] Even in Canada, where immigration from Spanish-speaking countries is relatively small, the share of Canadians speaking Spanish as a mother tongue is four times (1.2 percent) the share of Mexicans speaking English as a mother tongue.[8]

As a result, almost everyone who speaks English in Mexico has had to learn the language in a more academic fashion. As we discuss later in the chapter, this is tied to Mexico's very low rate of immigration relative to the rest of North America. Only 0.5 percent of Mexico's population is foreign-born (as compared with 20.7 percent in Canada and 13.9 percent in the United States).[9] Furthermore, with regard to the United States, even beyond immigration, Spanish is an important language. Kate Palmer's YouGov survey also found that 31 percent of Americans age eighteen and over claimed to have a "basic command" of Spanish. This was defined as "being able to have a brief conversation, order food, ask for directions." This ought to not take away from the fact that 51 percent of Americans claimed that they did not have even a basic knowledge of another language— but for almost two-thirds (63.2 percent) of those who did have some basic language, that language was Spanish.

How Mexicans React to Nonnative and Heritage Speakers of Spanish

To explain how Mexicans react to nonnative speakers of Spanish, we need to divide these speakers into two general categories: Heritage Speakers and Nonnative Speakers. We sometimes hear the term "Heritage Speaker" used to refer to those people who have learned how to speak the immigrant language at home, in the community, and among family and friends. These Heritage Speakers often speak their second language in ways that differ notably from first-generation immigrants, and they do so without formal training. This is not limited to Spanish speakers, but because we are dealing with Mexico here, this is our focus.

The number of Heritage Speakers of Spanish is large, including children and grandchildren of first-generation immigrants. A review of the data cited above from the Pew Research Center's Statistical Portrait of Hispanics in the United States indicates that children of immigrants represent almost 12 percent of the US population—roughly 38 million people. (To put this in perspective, the entire population of Canada is only 36.5 million.) Because 44 percent of immigrants speak Spanish at home, we can roughly estimate the number of second-generation immigrants growing up in a Spanish-speaking home at 16.72 million people, or over 5 percent of the entire US population.[10] This number does not include the grandchildren, spouses, or other relatives of the original immigrants. The bottom line is that there are many Heritage Speakers of Spanish in the United States, the majority of whom have ties to Mexico.

Heritage Speakers have the advantage of high levels of general oral fluency, especially within the context of daily family life. The disadvantage, however, is that their Spanish is labeled "nonstandard," and these individuals are often judged as being "border Spanish speakers." The sad and brutal truth is that these speakers often suffer bias from their Mexican counterparts. There are delicate and sensitive topics that arise when these Heritage Speakers work professionally in Mexico. We recall a specific instance when a Mexican executive directly told us that he would rather be "bossed around by some monolingual English-speaking American than to be told what to do by some border *pocho*"

(*pocho* is a pejorative term used among Mexicans to describe those who left Mexico and lost their culture and language).

The irony is that this same Heritage Speaker could represent a company when doing business in Peru or Chile, or any other Spanish-speaking country. There would be no negative repercussions. These issues come up only in Mexico. Our recommendation is, when sending Heritage Spanish speakers to represent your company in Mexico, check first to assess their comfort level. There may not be an issue, but there also might be. Just be aware that it is unwise to ignore potential implications. Remember, too, that not all Heritage Speakers of Spanish have ties to Mexico. There are also significant immigrant populations from other countries—for example, Cuba, Puerto Rico, the Dominican Republic, and El Salvador. Still, the Pew Research Center reports that nearly two-thirds (64 percent) of the US Hispanic population comes from Mexico, accounting for 11 percent of the total US population.[11]

The second category is the nonnative speaker of Spanish who learned Spanish without heritage ties. These are the people who learned how to speak by taking classes at school, learned the grammar rules, memorized the vocabulary, and over time developed various levels of proficiency. The irony, as compared with the Heritage Spanish Speaker, is that your Mexican counterpart will have greater tolerance for imperfect Spanish. Indeed, he or she may not expect the North American to be a Spanish speaker at all but will appreciate the effort to try. This holds true for Canadians as well as Americans.

It is also the case that for many Spanish-speaking North Americans, the benefits of Spanish fluency are experienced outside actual business activities. As a Spanish speaker, one is able to keep up on local news, follow local sports, understand the side chitchat that is happening on the street, read advertisements and billboards, watch television, read restaurant menus, socialize after hours, meet a broader mix of people, engage in cocktail party conversations, and enjoy many other opportunities that are simply not available to monolingual English speakers. We see the benefit of being a Spanish speaker in the expansive opportunities that open up, mainly beyond the mere business context.

The Use of English in Mexico

Especially at upper levels of management, Mexicans will most likely assume that their North American counterpart does not speak Spanish. There are many instances when they even expect business to be conducted in English. A 2015 survey by the British Council, for instance, found that "33 percent of Mexican businesses participating in this study use English as the main language of internal business communication, while 47 percent use English as the main language of external business communication."[12]

For example, reports and data might be tabulated in English, or the home office might use English as the company's official language. It might also be that even if you personally speak Spanish, other members of your team will not, which necessitates the use of English among all. In other instances, some Mexican executives simply feel more comfortable conducting business in English. It may be that they received advanced degrees in the United States or they have always used English in professional contexts. The general rule of thumb is if your work involves other North Americans, executives from upper management, or high-level reporting to home offices in the United States, English will be the language of business. If, however, your interaction brings you in contact with low-level management, workers on a factory floor, local distributors, or others in the community, the need for Spanish will become evident.

The Use of English as a Status Symbol in Mexico

Most Mexicans view the ability to speak English as a sign of education and sophistication. It is generally assumed that those in Mexico's elite—especially those from a younger generation, in business, engineering, the sciences, and higher learning—will speak English. The reality, however, is that English is far from widespread, even among its elite.

In a much-publicized 2015 press conference, Juan Pardinas Carpizo, director general of the Mexican Institute for Competitiveness (Instituto Mexicano para la Competitividad) expressed alarm that Mexico's poor level of English proficiency was actually undermining its competitiveness in the global economy. Pardinas declared that just 5 percent of Mexicans were truly fluent in English, while 83 percent of the country's exports were conducted in English.[13]

Not only does the ability to speak English convey status but there is also a clear economic advantage in speaking it. The Mexican Institute for Competitiveness found that Mexicans who are proficient in English can earn between 28 and 50 percent more. It is no wonder, then, that the British Council's study found that self-motivated English learning in Mexico is "substantial," with "around 20 percent of the population accessing English tutoring via public or private means." Moreover, the study found that 58 percent viewed English as "a skill needed for greater employability and 49 percent valued English as a pathway to a better job."[14]

On the plus side of this, with one in five Mexicans trying to improve their English on their own, if you are a fluent English speaker, you will likely find many who ask to practice English with you. On the down side, however, with the demand for English-speaking so high, many Mexicans have become adept at pretending to speak English better than they actually do. After all, their status, their promotions, and even just their ability to keep their jobs may depend on it. This leads to many uncomfortable situations where you as an English speaker are aware that your Mexican counterpart does not understand English enough to keep up, or possibly may not even understand English at all. How you handle this, however, becomes a delicate matter of respect and face saving.

Let us consider an example. You are in a sales situation with a Mexican counterpart who has given you the impression that she speaks English. You assume that she speaks English with good comprehension, but then you become aware that something is wrong. For example, you have the following exchange:

YOU: How many units do you need?
HER: Yes.
YOU: Do you understand?
HER: Yes.

The problem here is that "yes" cannot possibly be an answer to the first question. You know that she has not understood (and she is also aware that she has not understood). Now comes the real question—how do you respond? Asking her if she has understood accomplishes nothing. If she feels that you are questioning her competence in English, then you have become a threat. After all, her status—perhaps even her job—depends on her ability to speak English. There *are* ways to approach this. You can rephrase the question with different words, use visual cues, reinforce with written text, and the like. The point here is that you will need to take into account the issue of the loss of face if you directly address her lack of competence in English. Our recommendation is to not assume that everyone speaks English as well as they claim, and to assist them in understanding what you are talking about.

CHARACTERISTICS OF MEXICAN SPANISH

Without getting lost in a technical, linguistic description of Mexican Spanish, it is helpful to be familiar with some of the characteristics of Mexican Spanish. We remind readers that there is no such thing as a single standard version of Spanish that applies to all areas of the Spanish-speaking world. Regional varieties in Spain differ as much as English does between those from Scotland and Louisiana. For example, in the Americas, Spanish in Argentina differs from Caribbean Spanish to the point where even native speakers have difficulty understanding one another. Even in Mexico itself, people from Mexico City have a distinct accent and intonation. This differs significantly from Mexico's northern regions, Gulf Coast, or Yucatán regions. A speaker from Chihuahua will tell you right away that her Spanish is distinct from that of another person from Monterrey. When we hear a person from Veracruz, we immediately recognize sounds that resemble those of other Caribbean speakers. And when we listen to speakers from Yucatán, we soon learn of the indigenous influence of substrate Mayan languages.

The origin of regional dialects in the Americas is complex and in loose terms relates to the origin of the initial settlers, the period when cities were colonized, and the effects of the existing substrate indigenous languages. Mexico City, like Lima, was one of the earliest Viceroyalties in the Americas, meaning that it was governed and populated by those who came from the plateau regions and government centers of Madrid. Veracruz, in contrast, as a coastal city, appealed to people who were more accustomed to living by the sea. Indeed, even today, the speech of a person from Lima and Mexico City will share similar characteristics that are not common in Veracruz.

Fuerte Consonantismo

Laying aside these specific regional differences, in general terms we can say that Mexican Spanish is known for its *fuerte consonantismo*, meaning that Mexican consonants ring out loud and clear. Unlike English, where dialects differ mainly in their vowel sounds (think a Texan drawl), Spanish dialects differ more in the way that consonants are pronounced. For example, in most parts of the Spanish-speaking world, in casual situations a word like *nada* (nothing) is pronounced ['na.ða], where the /d/ is pronounced similar to the "th" of "mother" in English. However, this /d/ is also often reduced to the point that it almost disappears: ['na.a]. In Mexico this /d/ tends to remain, not always, but more than in other parts of the Spanish-speaking world. We hear this in a word like *abogado* (lawyer), where the /b d g/ are all pronounced with less reduction in Mexico: [a.βo.'ɣa.ðo]. In many parts of the Spanish-speaking world, a word like *cantado* (sung) reduces to [kan.'tao]; but in Mexican Spanish, the tendency is to preserve the /d/ consonant: [kan.'ta.ðo]. This is not a hard-and-fast rule, but simply a tendency. Mexican Spanish exhibits less consonant reduction than most other dialectal varieties.

We see another example of Mexican *fuerte consonantismo* in the way they preserve the /s/ sound in places where many other dialects eliminate it. A word like *estos* (those) is pronounced ['es.tos] in Mexico, instead of ['eh.toh], which is heard in many other locations. This strong /s/ sound is one of the most salient features of Mexican Spanish. When anyone from the Spanish-speaking world hears a Mexican speak, it is this /s/ sound that stands out—as in *nosotros tenemos muchas cosas* (we have a lot of things) [no.'so.tros.te.'ne.mos.'mu.tʃas.'ko.sas].

Indigenous Borrowings

A second salient feature of Mexican Spanish is the large number of borrowings from indigenous languages. Consider, for example, these subway stops in Mexico City: Pantitlán, Cuauhtémoc, Chapultepec, Juanacatlán, Cuitláhuac, Popotla, Xola, Tlatelolco, Coyoacán, Tezozomoc, Azcapotzalco, Mixcoac, Coyuya, Iztacalco, Apatlaco, Aculco, Atalilco, Iztapalapa, Chilpancingo, Mixiuhca, Tepalcates, Guelatao, Acatitla, Ecatepec, Nezahualcóyotl, Mexicaltzingo, Culhuacán, Zapotitlán, Tlaltenco, and Tláhuac. This is not just a challenge for native speakers of English who learn Spanish. Even native Spanish speakers from other parts of the world will have a difficult time trying to pronounce the names of these subway stations. One of the charms of Mexico City is that these subway stations are interspersed with other stops that have European sounding origins: Zaragoza, San Lázaro, Isabel la Católica, Salto del Agua, and Insurgentes. It is impossible to travel around Mexico City without constant reminders of its past and its origins, and we see this in the names of the cities and neighborhoods. The Canadian-born coauthor of this volume recalls an embarrassing experience when he was traveling on a regional bus to Ecatepec to watch a bullfight. When the ticket taker asked where he was going, he could not remember how to say the name of the city, and he tried a number of versions: Etequepac, Epatequec, Equepotec, Epotepac. Be patient; you will eventually learn how to pronounce the names of places that have indigenous etymologies.

At this point, we should point out that indigenous languages are still widely spoken in some parts of Mexico. Far from dying out, in fact, the number of indigenous language speakers in Mexico has been going up, from under 5.5 million in 1995 to about 7 million (6.95 million) in 2010 (we are still waiting for the 2015 figures). To put this in perspective, that is about the number of Mormons (6.59 million) or Jews (5.3 million) in the United States.

1.1 Indigenous Language Sign in the Mexico City Airport
Complaints sign in Spanish, Náhuatl, Mayan, Mixteco, and Mazahua.

Roughly 6.5 percent of Mexicans do not consider Spanish to be their mother tongue, and of those, the Instituto Nacional de Estadística y Geografía estimates that 909,356 do not speak Spanish.[15] To illustrate the attention that indigenous languages receive from the Mexican government, note in photograph 1.1 that a complaints sign posted in the Mexico City Airport provides information in Spanish, Náhuatl, Mayan, Mixteco, and Mazahua.

We are not suggesting that indigenous languages play a significant role in all business practices in all parts of Mexico. We do recommend, however, in terms of intercultural communication, that we respect the fact that in certain parts of Mexico, there is a large indigenous population. In nine of Mexico's thirty-two states, 10 percent or more of the population speaks an indigenous language. This is particularly the case in the southern states of Oaxaca, Yucatán, and Chiapas, where indigenous language levels are about 30 percent and are part of everyday life.[16]

English Borrowings

A third characteristic of Mexican Spanish is the large number of English borrowings that come from its northern neighbor. As such, Mexican Spanish often includes words like *troca* (truck)

1.2 Quiero Chamba
Looking for work? Try Quiero Chamba. Photograph courtesy of Quiero Chamba.

instead of *camión*, *parquear* (to park) instead of *estacionar*, *jonrón* ("home run") instead of *cuadrangular*, *yonke* (junk) instead of *desguace*, *lonche* (lunch) instead of *almuerzo*, or those that refer to the American Chamber of Commerce as the *Chamba* instead of the *Cámara*, and so on. In fact, the word *chamba* is particularly interesting in Mexico because the word has taken on the meaning of "work" in general. As such, one hears phrases like *Marcos consiguió una chamba en la fábrica* (Marcos got a job at the factory). Photograph 1.2 gives a nice example of this. It shows an advertisement on a car that promotes Quiero Chamba for those looking for employment.

At certain levels, these borrowings are accepted or rejected by other native speakers. At other levels, many Mexicans use these words without realizing that they were borrowed from English.

One final observation about Mexican Spanish is that North Americans often think of Mexican Spanish as "normal" Spanish, mainly because it is the variety of Spanish with which they are most familiar, or the variety that they most likely learned at school. They do so without recognizing how distinct these Mexican characteristics sound, for example, to native speakers of Spanish from other regions of the world, such as Spain, Argentina, and the Caribbean.

Given the issues discussed above, we offer the following insights for North Americans when they communicate with Mexican colleagues, both in English and in Spanish.

General Strategies When Speaking English

If you are not a Spanish speaker, there are several things you can do to help Mexicans understand your English. To begin, Mexicans will not understand many of the idiomatic and slang expressions that native speakers of English use. Avoid references that may be unknown to Mexicans. For example, even monolingual North Americans barely understand the reference to horses in phrases like "chomping at the bit." Imagine how proficient a nonnative speaker would have to be to understand such a phrase in English. Without knowing it, many times North Americans use phrases from pop culture in ways that nonnative speakers cannot follow. References to events, stories, phrases, and clichés from classic television series are often difficult for Mexicans to follow. Imagine, for example, how hard it is to relate Sheldon's bizarre observations if you are unaware of *The Big Bang Theory*.

Next, slow down. As native speakers, we do not realize how fast we speak. A Mexican is expecting to hear, for example, "Are you going to eat your chips?" but instead she hears "yah gunna iicher ships?" This is also true when introducing people and giving their names. As a native speaker of English, when we are introduced to a new person, we simply need to remember the name. When nonnative speakers of English are introduced to someone, they have to learn the new sound of a name and remember that actual name. For example, if you are unfamiliar with the given name Hugh and the family name Hollingsworth, imagine how difficult it would be to repeat such a name after hearing it fly by at light speed. We help them out by speaking a little slower, rephrasing our sentences with new words, and keeping our vocabulary simple. If our interaction with Mexicans is mainly in the form of presentations, be sure to use written support. Many times, Mexicans can read English better than they can understand it orally. It helps to have a written outline and visual examples of oral presentations.

When we find ourselves listening to Mexicans who are speaking English to us, there are also a few things that will help to increase our comprehension. First, the Spanish language has only five vowel phoneme sounds (pronounced i e a o u), whereas English has at least eleven (beet, bit, bait, bet, bat, bought, but, Burt, boat, put, boot). The implication is that native speakers of Spanish are sometimes limited to five vowels when speaking English. They do not pronounce all eleven of the English vowels. The result, for example, is that "beet" and "bit" both sound like "beet"; "bait" and "bet" both sound like "bait"; "bat" and "bought" both sound like "bought"; and so on. When we know about this tendency, we become more adept at understanding their English.

Second, Spanish speakers tend to "strengthen" consonants when they appear are at the beginning of phrase. For example, a word like ya (already) is pronounced [ja], but may also sound like [dʒa], similar to the English "jaw." This means that when speaking English, Mexicans may say "you" like "Jew," "yellow" like "jello," and "yes," like "Jess." Again, knowing this tendency makes it much easier to understand a person who has a stronger accent.

Other English sounds that prove to be difficult for native speakers of Spanish include "th," any r-sounds, and any consonant cluster, like "sp, st, sk." As a result, "this" sounds like [dis], "Roger" sounds like ['ro.xer], and "stop" sounds like [es.'top]. Indeed, this all creates empathy for the poor guy who has to say "strengths," which has to be one of the most difficult words for Spanish speakers to pronounce in perfect English. We mention all this simply to state that when we know a bit about these tendencies, we start to understand Spanish-accented English much better.

Another strategy when communicating in English is to be aware of words that have a Latin origin versus those of an Anglo-Saxon origin. This sounds technical, but it really is not. In English, we often have pairs of words that have a similar meaning, one that comes from Latin (usually via French) and one that comes from the Germanic side, Anglo-Saxon. There was a time when English borrowed many words from French, to give speech a bit of a high-toned, aristocratic, or elite feel. This was distinguished from the common words, those that had more of a Germanic Anglo-Saxon origin. For example, we can *descend* or *go down*, *ascend* or *go up*, *congregate* or *get together*, *enter* or *go into*, and so on. You will notice that even today, the Latin-origin words sound more formal, and the Anglo-Saxon words are shorter, often have a preposition attached, and sound a bit more informal. The takeaway of this is that Mexicans who have limited English-language skills will understand you better when you choose to use the Latin-based words over the Anglo-Saxon words. We might add that this is also one of the benefits of learning how to speak even a small amount of Spanish, where you will learn Latin roots that cause us to recognize cognates between Spanish and English—for example, *comenzar*, meaning "to commence," verde, meaning "verdant," and so on.

General Strategies When Speaking Spanish

Conversely, if you are learning Spanish, there are a few things to be aware of as you speak with Mexicans. First, as compared with other regional varieties of Spanish, Mexican Spanish has a formal or polite sound. For example, when deciding to use the formal *usted* or the informal *tú*, Mexicans tend to maintain *usted* in situations where you might expect them to use *tú*. From our North American perspective, we think of *usted* and *tú* in terms of formality, and we often prefer to be informal. Mexicans, however, think of *usted* and *tú* in terms of respect or keeping a distance between speakers. Their use of *usted* helps demonstrate that respect and distance. This is not to say that young executives will never use *tú* among colleagues. We are simply observing that you will hear Mexicans use *usted* more than what you might expect.

Beyond *usted*, again as compared with other varieties of Spanish, Mexican Spanish often has a very polite ring to it. We recall an experience years ago when our Canadian-born coauthor was looking for a building on the campus of the Universidad Nacional Autónoma de México (National Autonomous University of Mexico) in Mexico City. Upon asking a student, almost the same age, about the location of the building, his response was "*No podría decirle*" (I am not able to tell you). The phrase simply had an ultrapolite feel to it. This is typical of the way that Mexican speech sounds. Similarly, in Spanish, when a person does not hear you or does not understand what you said, it is common to ask ¿*cómo?* or ¿*perdón?* (excuse me). In Mexico one often hears ¿*mande?* which sounds overly polite to people from other Spanish-speaking countries. (We should add that we do not believe in the folk etymology that somehow Mexicans hold on to some colonial inferiority complex by saying ¿*mande?*) What we are saying is that Mexican Spanish comes across as sounding polite, respectful, and formal.

Second, be aware that native speakers of English often use the pitch of their voice to show emphasis: *She* is smart. She *is* smart. She is *smart*. Spanish speakers, conversely, usually demonstrate emphasis by changing the word order of the sentence, not the pitch of their voice. For example, if a Spanish speaker wants to emphasize that *she* is smart, he will say something like *Es inteligente ella*, placing the word *ella* "she" at the end of the sentence. Other times, Spanish speakers add the word *sí* (yes) in front of the verb of the sentence, and the effect is to emphasize the verb; *Ella sí es inteligente* implies that she *is* intelligent. The result of all this is that native speakers of English do not grasp the subtlety of these changes in Spanish. Even worse, if nonnative speakers of Spanish superimpose their English intonation patterns on the Spanish sentences, it gives the impression of being overly emotional. Mexicans will feel that you are angry, upset, or emotionally charged. Consider, for example, how in English we sometimes pronounce "thanks!" with a sing-song, high-pitched voice. If we pronounce *gracias* with that same sing-song high pitch, it sounds almost ridiculous. By the way, the opposite is also true. When Mexicans impose their flat Spanish intonation on English phrases, it gives the impression of disinterest or boredom.

Third, getting back to the different vowel sounds between Spanish and English, in English we tend to reduce all our unstressed vowels sounds to "uh". As a result, a phrase like "I am American" reduces to sounds like "uh"m uhmeruhkun."

The problem is, if we transfer this tendency into our Spanish, Mexicans do not understand our Spanish words. For example, Mexicans make a clear distinction among *pasar* (to pass), *pesar* (to weigh), and *pisar* (to step). However, if our nonnative Spanish sounds like "vamos a puhsar," Mexicans will not know which verb we are trying to say. If you do speak some Spanish, our recommendation is to focus on the correct pronunciation of the five vowel sounds, and this will do wonders to improve your Spanish.

Knowing That the Language We Use Is Tied to Emotions

It is good to remember that there is an emotional connection between our words and our feelings. For example, if a native English-speaking man looks into the eyes of a native English-speaking woman and says "I love you," there will be an emotional feeling that goes with that declaration. The man will feel the impact of those words, and the woman will sense the power behind them. She may be flattered, she may act coy, or she may think that the man is a nut, but she will feel the emotion of the phrase. The same emotional reaction is not true when we speak in another language. We need to obtain high levels of proficiency before we start connecting the emotions with the actual words that are said. To a nonnative speaker of Spanish, *yo te quiero* and *yo te amo* are simply two ways to say "I love you." However, to a Mexican, *yo te amo* conveys a deeper romantic connotation, while *yo te quiero* is more similar to what a mother says to her children. Be careful, because without realizing it, our words potentially sound extremely harsh, blunt, direct, and bold when speaking a foreign language. The effects of this are twofold. First, as nonnative speakers of Spanish, we need to be sensitive to how much bolder our statements might seem to our Mexican associates. Second, when our Mexican friends talk with us in English, we also need to realize that they may sound more forceful than what they intended.

In a similar way, be aware of how much, as native speakers of a language, we can subtly change our speech. If we want to sound more formal, show a little more respect, or indicate a little more seriousness, we can do so with minute changes in our language.

Notice, for example, the subtle difference in phrase like "I want to marry your daughter," "I would like to marry your daughter," "I was hoping to marry your daughter, and "If you have a moment, I was wondering if I might be lucky enough to consider marrying your daughter." When we are using our native English with our Mexican counterpart, we bring all this subtlety into our communication. This happens practically subconsciously. It may very well be, however, that our Mexican counterpart is limited to much less flexibility. Be aware of these limitations, and give the nonnative speaker a break. If you are learning Spanish, you will feel these limitations in reverse. You may eat the most delicious *tacos rojos* that you have had the privilege of tasting—it makes your mouth water, it fills you with happiness and a desire to shout from the rooftops. However, with your limited Spanish, you will look at your Mexican friend and simply say *bueno* (good).

Becoming a Mexican Insider
We often hear how speaking a language allows one to be considered a member of a group. Clearly, a person who can speak Spanish in Mexico will be able to participate in conversations, read public postings, and understand details about Mexican society in ways that are not available to those who do not speak the language. We recall pleasant experiences in the kitchen with Mexican friends. Mexican food is complex, and it takes hours to prepare from scratch. Nothing compares with the delightful hours chatting while cutting up ingredients, grinding them in a *molcajete*, and telling mother-in-law stories while the tortillas puff up. Indeed, it is true that proficiency in Spanish opens the door to experiences that would be impossible otherwise.

If you are going to work with Mexicans for any length of time, try to learn to speak at least some Spanish. The insights into Mexican thoughts that come from understanding their language are simply not available to those who never learn the language. We are not naive enough to believe that all business interactions will happen in Spanish. However, even if your Spanish-language skills are used more in informal and non-work-related contexts, you will be rewarded with new insights into Mexican behavior.

For those who do not know how to speak Spanish and who are thinking of learning, we offer a brief reality check. Often, people approach us with requests to learn Spanish. Sometimes these people say that their plan is to use their lunch hour at work to "learn some Spanish so that we can negotiate with our Mexican partners." It simply takes more time and effort to learn a language than what most people think. Experts claim that it takes about 500 hours of study for native speakers of English to gain an intermediate level of Spanish proficiency.[17] This still would not be enough to be involved in high-level negotiations in Spanish. Our experience is that many who learn Spanish underestimate how long it will take and how much effort is involved. The result is twofold. First, learners sometimes think that they are not good language learners, when the truth is that they have simply not put enough time and effort into the learning process. Second, learners get discouraged or think their money and effort have been wasted. By all means, we encourage you to learn to speak Spanish. However, temper your efforts with realistic expectations of how long it will take. You will become proficient, and it will be worth it, but it will take longer than what most people suspect.

LANGUAGE SUMMARY AND CHAPTER 1 HIGHLIGHTS

Mexico and the United States share a history together:

- Thousands of English words were borrowed from Spanish.
- Large portions of the United States used to belong to Mexico.

The use of English and Spanish in Mexico:

- Although at certain professional levels there are Mexicans who are proficient at English, most Mexicans cannot speak English.
- Using Spanish in Mexico can go beyond the simple issue of comprehensibility, especially when viewed through the lens of concerns about anti-Mexican sentiment among some Americans.
- Heritage Speakers of Spanish may encounter social difficulties when using their Spanish with Mexicans.
- Often, English is used in professional settings. This is especially the case when reports are tabulated in English, if other members of the team do not speak Spanish, or if English is the official language of the company.

- The use of English among Mexicans is often tied to status and work qualifications. Issues of face may be involved if you question someone's ability to speak English.

Characteristics of Mexican Spanish:

- There are many regional dialects of Spanish, and this is also true of regions in Mexico.
- Mexican Spanish is known for its *fuerte consonantismo*, where consonants are reduced less than in other areas of the Spanish-speaking world.
- Mexican Spanish is known for its preservation and high-pitched /s/ sounds.
- Mexican Spanish contains extensive borrowings from indigenous languages, such as Náhuatl and Mayan-based languages.

Strategies when speaking with Mexicans (both in Spanish and English):

- Slow down, repeat yourself, and use written aids to help in communication.
- Avoid idiomatic expressions and those that come from pop culture.
- Be aware of how different the vowel sounds are between Spanish and English. Spanish has only five vowel phonemes, and English has about eleven.
- Do not be too quick to jump into informal speech patterns when speaking Spanish. Mexican Spanish has a relatively formal and respectful sound to it.
- Be aware that English-language intonation patterns give the impression of being overly emotional when transferred to Spanish.
- Remember that emotions are tied to the words we use in our native language. This is not always felt when speaking in another language.
- Native speakers make subtle adjustments to the speech, which are difficult for nonnative speakers to do.
- If you decide to learn to speak Spanish, have a realistic expectation that it takes effort and time to become proficient, more than what most people suspect.

2

THE MEXICAN
Environment

A Cornucopia

The second feature of the LESCANT approach is the environment and technology. When we look at the physical world around us, we often take it for granted that the things we see are somehow universal. In fact, however, culture has shaped many of these physical objects. These can range from the decorations in a room to the room itself and how things in that room are laid out. Is there heat or air conditioning—and, for that matter, what is the climate normally like? Do people take the stairs or the elevator? How do people get around, and what is the lay of the land where they are trying to get around in the first place?

This is a very broad category, so it should be helpful to look at twelve factors related to the environment that have an impact on professional activities in Mexico. In the next sections, we discuss each of these as it relates to Mexico:

1. Population size and population density
2. Wealth, gross domestic product (GDP), and per capita income

3. Country size
4. Natural resources
5. Water (and its lack)
6. Topography
7. Climate and weather
8. Crime and safety issues
9. A sense of time and space
10. Architecture, buildings, and office space
11. Mexican views on technology
12. The Two Mexicos

POPULATION SIZE AND POPULATION DENSITY

Mexico is a population powerhouse. With 127 million people, it is the world's tenth-most-populous country. Compared with countries such as Canada, Mexico has no largely uninhabited regions. Even the large desert regions of the country's North support major cities and development. Even Baja California Sur, Mexico's least densely populated state, has about the same population as Nevada, the eighth least densely populated US state.[1] That said, Mexico's population is far from evenly distributed. One in every six Mexicans lives in the Mexico City metropolitan area.

Magnet Cities

Many Mexican urban centers have grown rapidly through in-migration from the rest of the country. These cities work like magnets, attracting people to their economic and educational opportunities as well as cultural offerings. But no other Mexican city's magnetism compares with that of the capital (see figure 2.1). In 1950, Mexico City's metropolitan area had 3.365 million people; by 1970, the city had four times that number, 8.831 million; and by 2010, six times that number, over 20 million.

During the same period, other magnet cities likewise swelled in population. Guadalajara, Mexico's second-largest city, barely broke the 400,000 mark in 1950. By 1980, its metropolitan area had over 1.5 million people; today, it has over 4.4 million people. In just thirty years, Greater Monterrey grew fivefold, from just

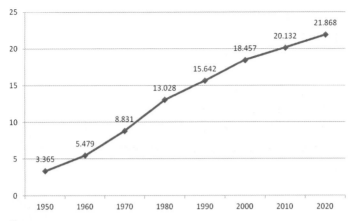

Figure 2.1

Mexico City's Growth Rate. *Source:* All data are from United Nations Department of Economic and Social Affairs, Population Division, "World Urbanization Prospects 2014 Revision, Highlights," (ST/ESA/SER.A/352), 2014, 336–37, https://esa.un.org/unpd/wup/publications/files/wup2014-highlights.pdf.

396,000 people in 1950 to over 2 million in 1980. Today, it has 5.35 million people.

Since the 1990s, other Mexican cities have become new magnets. With the influx of industry and foreign investment, Puebla, Querétaro, Torreón, and San Luís Potosí have all grown dramatically, joining the ranks of magnet cities.

Greater Mexico City

Mexico City is, by any measure, one of the world's largest conurbations. The United Nations uses two different measures: the urban agglomeration (i.e., the contiguous metropolitan area) and the city proper. In both respects, Mexico City is a giant. In the UN's most recent figures, Mexico City/Toluca is the world's seventh-largest agglomeration; the combined Mexico City–Toluca metropolitan area has 23.274 million people.[2] The city seems to go on forever, which is only hinted at in photograph 2.1.

Mexico City is the largest urban area in North America. As a point of comparison, the New York–Newark metropolitan area—the largest in the United States—ranked tenth, with 18.593 million. Toronto—Canada's largest city—ranked forty-ninth, with

2.1 Mexico City
Mexico City is North America's largest metropolitan area. Photograph courtesy of Richard Cawood.

5.91 million people. Until 2005, Mexico City, with a population of 19.276 million, was still the world's second-largest urban area, behind Tokyo. That said, today, Mexico City ranks seventh. As fast as it has grown, others have grown faster.[3]

The center of the Mexico City agglomeration is the Distrito Federal (DF), or Federal District. As with Washington and the District of Columbia, Mexico's DF is a capital district independent of the country's states. Also like Washington, DC, the DF is at the center of a much larger metropolitan area. The difference, however, comes in the sheer magnitude of the DF's scale. The District of Columbia has 681,000 people but a metropolitan area of over 6 million. The DF has 8.92 million people, and its encompassing, unbroken urban agglomeration has 21.157 million people.

Even if we just consider the 8.92 million people of the city proper on its own, the DF is North America's largest city, and the twenty-first largest in the world; New York City proper is twenty-fourth, at 8.55 million. The agglomeration consists of Mexico City proper plus forty-one contiguous cities. Many of these forty-one cities are major entities in their own right; twenty have over 100,000 people.[4]

In reality, the reach of Grea. :r Mexico City goes even farther, to what is called the Corona Regional del Centro de México—the Mexico City megalopolis.[5] This network of interconnected metropolitan areas includes the DF and the 41 cities of Metropolitan Mexico City, plus 131 other cities and towns. In all, the population of the Mexico City Corona is 29.73 million. By contrast, the entire population of Canada is only 35.15 million.

Mexico City's Corona has parallels with California's San Francisco Bay Area and the US Eastern Seaboard. As with the Corona's urban centers, both the Bay Area and Eastern Seaboard spread through multiple metropolitan areas, all of which keep their independent identities while still being tied together economically through transportation and telecommunications.

WEALTH, GDP, AND PER CAPITA INCOME

Mexico is one of only sixteen countries with a nominal GDP of over $1 trillion.[6] Moreover, Mexico has exploded in economic strength. In 1960, Mexico's GDP per capita was $360. Today, it is $9,807, a twenty-seven-fold increase in just under sixty years.[7] In short, Mexico's domestic market is important in its own right.

Although Mexico has come a long way, it still has just under one seventh of the United States' per capita annual income of $67,605, at purchasing power parity. Canada's per capita annual income of $46,260, at purchasing power parity, is likewise 4.7 times that of Mexico.

It is true that Mexico belongs to the Organization for Economic Cooperation and Development (OECD), which generally represents the "developed world." Still, Mexico ranks last among the thirty-four OECD member countries in GDP per capita income and far below the OECD average of $36,800.

Moreover, the gap between rich and poor in Mexico is dramatic. Among the OECD countries, Mexico again ranks last in terms of income inequality (in 2017 surpassing even Chile which had traditionally held the last position). If you are from the United States—which ranks fourth worst—this may not be as noticeable. If, however, you are from Canada—which ranks eighteenth—or most other OECD countries, the income gap may seem more striking.[8] Similarly, among the OECD member nations, the average annual income is $38,700. The United States ranks third, at $59,700; and Canada ranks twelfth, at $48,200; while Mexico ranks dead last, thirty-fourth, at $15,230 (well below Hungary's thirty-third and $20,667).[9] From this, we can say that though Mexico technically is in the wealthy nation category, it is just on the border of being otherwise.

COUNTRY GEOGRAPHICAL SIZE

Mexico is the world's thirteenth-largest country geographically, making it a relative giant compared with most other nations. It is important to remember that only when Mexico is compared with the world's geographically second- and third-largest countries—Canada and the United States, respectively—does the nation seem small.

Mexico is slightly over one-quarter the size in overall area of the contiguous United States.[10] Yet the two countries are nearly the same length from north to south. As figure 2.2 shows, when we overlay Mexico on the United States, its southernmost border starts at New Orleans and its northern border nearly reaches Spokane.

Mexico's northern border is far larger than its southern one. To the north, the US-Mexico border is the tenth-longest shared border in the world.[11] Yet to the south, the country tapers down to just 541 miles (871 kilometers) at its border with Guatemala. Mexico has another short border with Belize, jutting up north for 156 miles (251 kilometers) from the eastern border of Guatemala.

Because Mexico is shaped like a cornucopia, its geography can also be deceiving. At the end of its eastern curve up into the Gulf of Mexico, the Yucatán Peninsula swoops out 200 miles (320 kilometers) to the northeast, to almost midway along the length of the country. Indeed, Mérida, the capital of the state of Yucatán, is farther north than Mexico City. The Yucatán Peninsula itself is huge, covering roughly 76,300 square miles (197,60,0 square kilometers), larger than England and Wales combined.

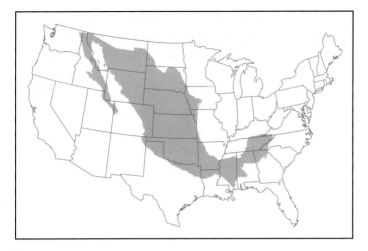

Figure 2.2
Mexico and the United States in a Geographical Size Comparison

Mexico also has a second peninsula descending from its West Coast. The Baja California Peninsula stretches 775 miles (1,247 kilometers) north to south, making it the second-longest peninsula in the world (after the Arabian Peninsula). Baja California is 5 miles longer than the US state of California (which itself is the longest state in the contiguous United States). To put this in global perspective, the Baja California Peninsula is 91 miles longer than the Korean Peninsula in Asia and 125 miles longer than the Italian Peninsula in Europe. Yet here, too, the geography may prove deceiving. For all its length, the Baja California Peninsula is very narrow, constituting just 7.5 percent of Mexico's overall area. At its widest, it reaches only 200 miles (320 kilometers), and at its narrowest, it runs just 25 miles (40 kilometers) across.

Like the United States and Canada, Mexico is so large that it has multiple time zones. These time zones correspond to those in the contiguous United States, although they have different names. Although multiple time zones are something the three countries have in common, this is actually quite unusual for most countries.

Most of Mexico is in the Zona Central, which corresponds to the US Central Time Zone. Quintana Roo on the extreme easternmost reach of the Yucatán Peninsula is in the Zona Sureste, which is equivalent to the US Eastern Time Zone.

A point of international confusion comes with the Zona Pacifica, in which are located the western Mexican states Chihuahua, Nayarit, Sonora, Sinaloa, and Baja California Sur. The Zona Pacifica corresponds to the US Mountain Time Zone. This is a point of some confusion, because the Mexican Spanish name does *not* correspond to the US English name (i.e., US Pacific Time is one hour behind the Mexican Zona Pacifica). Compounding this, one Mexican state—Baja California Norte—is in the Zona Noroeste, which *does* use what would be US Pacific Time. Confusion can arise when two people in, say, San Diego and Tijuana—which share a common time zone—unknowingly translate the time zone's name to the other language (i.e., Pacific Time or Zona Pacifica).

Daylight Savings Time also contributes to time zone confusion. This is because the United States and Canada differ from Mexico in the starting and ending dates for setting their clocks forward and back. In Mexico, all states observe Daylight Savings Time. Though this is true for all Canadian provinces as well, in the United States neither Hawaii nor Arizona observes Daylight Savings Time. This is particularly confusing in the case of Arizona, because it shares a border with Mexico. Throughout Mexico, Daylight Savings starts on the first Sunday in April and ends on the last Sunday in October. In the United States (for those states that observe it), Daylight Savings starts weeks earlier, on the second Sunday in March, and ends a week later, on the first Sunday in November.

NATURAL RESOURCES

Mexico is shaped like an inverted cornucopia, the horn of plenty (*cuerno de la abundancia* in Spanish), which in classical Greek mythology was the symbol of abundance and profusion. The tip of the horn begins where the Yucatán Peninsula juts out into the Gulf of Mexico. The horn then sweeps up to the west, where it opens along the Northwest states (where, some wits suggest, it then empties its riches across the US border). With regard to natural resources as well as agricultural production, the metaphor of Mexico as a horn of plenty is quite appropriate. Mexico is an agricultural powerhouse.

As might be expected, Mexico is by far the world's main producer of agave. Agave nectar is used in its own right as a natural sweetener. Agave nectar, however, is better known as the base source for two of Mexico's most famous alcoholic beverages: tequila (only from the blue agave plant grown in the region around the city of Tequila, Jalisco) and mezcal (distilled from the nectar of any other type of agave). It also leads the world in both limes (perhaps for those tequila-based drinks?) and avocados, both products that are heavily associated with the country. Mexico, however, also ranks among the world's top ten producers of a wide range of fruits, vegetables, and animals.[12]

In mining, Mexico is also a major producer. It dominates world silver production.[13] More than this, it is among the world's top ten producers of a dozen other significant mining products.[14]

WATER—AND ITS LACK

The resource with which Mexico is not so blessed is water—at least not uniformly throughout the country. A shortage of water, in fact, is one of the most serious problems facing the nation. Roughly 70 percent of Mexico is semiarid or desert. Although Mexico has a varied climate, with a great diversity of ecological zones, most of the country lacks adequate water for its needs, and much of what it does have is not suitable for human consumption.

Mexico City, in particular, is facing a water crisis. But it was not always so. When the Aztecs built their metropolis Tenochtitlán, the city was at the center of a lake with a series of canals. Once the Spaniards transformed it into Mexico City, the city's rapid growth essentially drained the lake and its underground aquifer, leaving it with no natural, replenishable source. Thus, the largest metropolitan area in the whole of North America has no natural source of water.

Mexico City is not alone in facing water scarcity. More than three-fourths of Mexico's people live in semiarid or desert environments. These regions support 90 percent of Mexico's irrigated land and 70 percent of its industry but receive only 20 percent of its rain. Mexico's northern states make up 30 percent of its territory but have only 4 percent of its water runoff.[15]

If you are from Canada or the United States (outside the Southwest), you will notice the effect of water scarcity right away. Water scarcity puts water quality at risk. People do not drink tap water.

You will notice that many people store water in rain collection cisterns on their roofs (and when those run dry, they have to be filled by water delivery). You will notice how much of the ground is brown and covered with scrub, cacti, and desert-friendly trees. You can see well-off areas demarcated by greenery and flowers. Where there is money for artificial watering and sprinklers in the courtyards of corporations and the grounds of golf courses, all is green with grass and foliage. As photograph 2.2 shows, where no water is provided, the scenery changes dramatically—often at the property line of the hotel where you are staying or the grounds of the company you are visiting.

Water Sources

Water shortages, as we have seen, are a major concern in Mexico. When it comes to rivers, however, resentments over political disputes with the United States compound the problem. In times of trade disputes and tensions between the two countries, the notion that the United States has unfairly taken Mexico's water has begun to resurface.

So what is this dispute about, exactly? Mexico lacks the great river systems available in the United States and Canada to build the sorts of reservoirs and irrigation systems used to compensate for the lack of rain and lakes. This is bad in itself, but it has been compounded by the limited access to rivers that Mexico does (or at least *did*) have, which is essentially gone. This is because both the Rio Grande River and Colorado River have been dammed and diverted to the US Southwest before they ever reach Mexico.

2.2 Where the Water Ends
Dramatic change when water is not provided. Photograph courtesy of Vanessa Bonilla-Hernandez.

Mexico has only one major inland waterway, which it shares with the United States at its northern border. In Mexico, this river is called the Río Bravo; and in the United States, this same river is known as the Rio Grande. Aside from this, Mexico has no major inland rivers, a problem exacerbated by the challenging growth of its population.

In English, this river's two names mean "Furious River" (Río Bravo) and "Big River" (Rio Grande). Today, neither name is accurate. This is because the Río Bravo/Grande itself has very little water left in it by the time it reaches Mexico. Much of the river's water is diverted directly before it ever reaches Mexico.[16] Agricultural use and population increase in Albuquerque, Santa Fe, and Las Cruces have resulted in major water diversion. As a result, most of the water is gone by the time Mexico's only major river flows out from the border where El Paso and Juárez meet. Yet this is the site of the biggest population boom of all. In 1960, Juárez had 261,000 people. By 2014 (the year of the latest available data), the city had just under 1.4 million, an increase of 436 percent.[17] The river frequently runs nearly dry below the Texas-Mexico border.

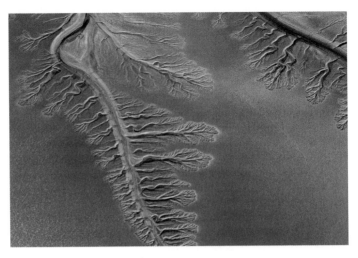

2.3 The Dry Colorado River Delta
View of the completely dry Colorado River Delta. Photograph courtesy of Pete McBride, US Geological Survey, January 12, 2009.

Along the internationally shared course of the Rio Grande/ Bravo, Mexico and the United States have established international treaties for shared use of its water. Together, the two countries operate two dams: the Amistad Dam (between Brownsville, Texas, and Matamoros, Tamaulipas) and the Falcon Dam (between Starr County, Texas, and Nueva Ciudad Guerrero, Tamaulipas). Both of these dams are run by the Binational International Boundary and Water Commission (Comisión Internacional de Límites y Aguas), which operates the reservoirs and hydroelectric energy installations at each site.

Although the Rio Grande/Bravo is by far the most significant waterway in the country, it is not the only one disputed with Mexico's northern neighbor. The Colorado River is 1,450 miles long (2,330 kilometers long), with almost its entire length in the United States. Still, it drains—or used to drain—into the Gulf of California at the tip of the Baja California Peninsula, where it borders the state of Sonora, just south of the US border at Arizona. Until the twentieth century, the Colorado River Delta on the Mexican side of the border was a lush marshland. But the damming and diversion of the river in the United States became so extensive that, at first, the Mexican portion of the river became too saline for use. Then, by 1960, as photograph 2.3 illustrates, it ceased to provide water at all.

This drying up of the Colorado River became a major point of contention between the United States and Mexico, especially because the diversion practices that caused it were in violation of a 1944 treaty between the two nations. In 2014, for the first time in sixty years (with the exception of a few strong rainfalls), water flowed into the Mexican section of the river. This was not due to natural causes, but rather to a 2012 agreement between the two countries to ensure that some usable water is released south of the Morelos Dam in Yuma, Arizona. A binational team of scientists devised a system for "pulse flow" of water south of the dam, guaranteeing a release of equivalent to 0.7 percent of the river's annual flow.[18]

None of the rest of Mexico's roughly 150 other rivers are particularly substantial. Consequently, Mexico has very few dams. This affects not only water availability but also hydroelectric power.

Mexico's river disputes with the United States are important in large part because (unlike the rest of North America) Mexico has virtually no major freshwater lakes. Mexico has just 2 lakes with a surface area of 100 square kilometers (38.6 square miles). For comparison, Canada has 561 and the United States has 44.

Mexico's largest freshwater lake is Lake Chapala, which is shared by the states of Jalisco and Michoacán. Lake Chapala has a surface area of 420 square miles (1,100 square kilometers). It is 3.5 times the size of Lake Cuitzeo, Mexico's next largest. By Mexican standards, both these lakes are massive. But to Canada and the United States, these lakes are negligible. To put this in perspective, Lake Chapala has roughly the same surface area as Lake Saint Clair, which is shared by Michigan and Ontario. At 430 square miles (1,114 square kilometers), Lake Saint Clair is about 10 square miles larger than Lake Chapala and ranks as just the United States' twelfth- and Canada's forty-fifth-largest freshwater lake. Mexico has almost no lakes of consequence, while Canada and the United States share the Great Lakes, the largest source of freshwater in the world. With so much freshwater at their disposal, it may seem difficult for Canadians and

Americans to even conceptualize how pressing a factor the lack of freshwater is in Mexico.

TOPOGRAPHY

It may be surprising to think of topography as a feature of cross-cultural communication, but the physical aspect of what surrounds us shapes the way we perceive our environment. Mexico exhibits extremes in altitude, mountains and beaches, earthquakes, and other climate-related phenomena. This is one of the most important elements of "Environment" in the LESCANT approach.

Altitude, Mountains, and the Mexican Altiplano

Most of Mexico sits at a high elevation. This is because much of the country is made up of an enormous highland plateau, the Mexican Altiplano. The entire Altiplano is cordoned off by three great mountain chains—the Sierra Madre Occidental to the west, the Sierra Madre Oriental to the east, and the Sierra Nevada to the south.[19] Even further south of the Sierra Nevada, running along the Pacific Ocean, is another mountain chain: the Sierra Madre del Sur. The mountains serve as barriers for water coming from the oceans, so the entirety of Mexico's North and Center consist primarily of arid, desert scrublands.

The high plateau averages roughly 6,000 feet (1,825 meters) above sea level and is nowhere less than 3,300 feet (1,005 meters). The effect of this on those traveling to Mexico are profound in terms of both adjusting to the lack of water (as discussed above) and dealing with potential altitude sickness (as we discuss below).

The Alitplano itself is divided into two giant mesas, the North Mesa and the Central Mesa. The North Mesa is the lower of the two; but even here, it averages 3,600 feet (1,100 meters) above sea level. To put this in perspective, the *lowest* point of the North Mesa is more than 3,300 feet (1,005 meters) above sea level, which is already at a higher elevation than the *highest peak* in nineteen of the United States' fifty states and five of

Canada's thirteen provinces and territories. In other words, even if you were at the top of Pennsylvania's tallest mountain—Mount Davis, at 3,213 feet, or 979 meters—you would find yourself at just under half the altitude of even San Luís Potosí's 6,070 feet (1,850 meters), let alone the other twenty-eight major Mexican cities at higher altitudes.

The geographic feature that most characterizes the North Mesa is the Chihuahuan Desert, which covers an area slightly larger than Germany.[20] This same desert extends into Texas, New Mexico, and Arizona in the United States.

The Central Mesa is even higher than the North Mesa. Given that it averages 6,600 feet (2,000 meters) above sea level, most visitors from sea-level areas find they need adjusting to the high altitude. For comparison, Canada's Banff (e.g., over 100,000 people) is a mere 4,537 feet (1,383 meters). In the United States, Denver, which famously bills itself as the "Mile-High City," has an elevation of 5,690 feet (1,731 meters) above sea level, which is less than the *average* elevation of the North Mesa. Colorado Springs, which has the highest elevation of any city with over 100,000 people north of Mexico, barely top 6,000 feet (6,035 feet/1,839 meters)—still below the *average* of the North Mesa's elevation.

Significantly, *most* of Mexico's population centers are located in these high-elevation zones. Mexico has more than thirty cities of over 100,000 people at an elevation above 1,850 meters (6,069 feet). The highest of these is Toluca, the capital of Estado de México, at 8,736 feet (2,663 meters). Toluca is in greater Mexico City, as are many of these thirty cities, with the DF itself sitting at 7,349 feet (2,240 meters), and with other major high-elevation cities in the states of Aguascalientes, Durango, Guanajuanto, Hidalgo, Jalisco, Puebla, Querétero, San Luís Potosí, and Zacatecas.

Altitude Adjustment and Altitude Sickness

Almost everyone from the United States and Canada visiting the Mexican Altiplano will reasonably expect to face some difficulty with altitude adjustment. Higher altitudes have lower air pressure than do lower elevations. The actual level of oxygen does not change, but the ability to process that oxygen seems to be affected.

When you go above 5,000 feet/1,500 meters, you can expect to notice minor symptoms such as getting tired easily and breathlessness. Feeling out of breath naturally leads to more rapid breathing, which leads to a dry mouth and nose. If you are already prone to nosebleeds, the dryness can increase them. Other common symptoms are headache, lightheadedness, a loss of appetite, increased gassiness, and insomnia—particularly, difficulty sleeping during the first night on arrival. Some people also may have a mild swelling of their face, hands, and feet. None of these are generally anything to worry about. Just take them as your body's way of telling you to take it easy for a day or two.

The most effective way to adjust your body to differences in altitude is to do so gradually. Driving over a few days is a naturally effective way to do so, to allow your body time to accommodate the differences over what is essentially a continuously uphill journey.

Driving the distance may not be too practical. Still, if you find yourself traveling between several cities, choosing to do so from lower to middle to higher elevations will help lessen the effects of altitude adjustment. For example, if you have business in several cities, you could schedule your travel according to elevation rather than distance. For instance, if you were traveling from the United States or Canada to Mexico, you would normally schedule trips in terms of distance for the following cities as, in order, Monterrey, Zacatecas, Mexico City, and Guadalajara. If you adjusted these for altitude, however, you would arrange them instead as Monterrey (1,770 feet/540 meters), Guadalajara (5,138 feet/1,566 meters), Mexico City (7,349 feet/2,240 meters) and Zacatecas (8,189 feet/2,496 meters).

Although most people can expect to experience some high-altitude adjustment, do not let it frighten you. Most symptoms begin to subside between 12 and 24 hours after arrival and disappear entirely within two days. Also, there are several easy things you can do to adjust. You can find these in table 2.1.

Because much of the Altiplano is above 6,000 feet/1,825 meters, you could naturally expect to experience some adjustment. This not only affects people living at or near sea level along the Atlantic Seaboard, the Maritimes, and the Great Lakes but

Table 2.1

Tips for Adjusting to High Altitudes

Tip	Explanation
Adjust altitude gradually	Changing altitude in stages gives the body time to adjust. If possible, try to move from a location with a middle-range altitude before going to a higher one.
Drink water throughout your stay	High altitude coupled with dry desert air leads to dehydration. Carry water with you and drink about twice as much as you normally would. Note that coffee, cola, and alcohol are dehydrating, so they do not count as water.
Avoid or reduce alcohol until you adjust	Alcohol is dehydrating, compounding the dehydration of high attitudes in dry climates. Avoiding alcohol before you adjust (the first night or two) helps.
Take ibuprofen	Studies show that taking ibuprofen 6 hours before arrival and then taking it every 6 hours during initial adjustment reduces the severity of symptoms. Ibuprofen also works for headaches associated with altitude adjustment.
Eat carbohydrates	Studies show that carbohydrates are more efficient at processing oxygen than fatty foods.

also even people from such high-elevation states as Colorado, Wyoming, and New Mexico.

Many people compare the feeling of altitude adjustment to a hangover, and like hangovers, it is hard to predict how different people will respond to the aftermath of the same night out. Bothersome symptoms can affect you if you change altitude quickly without giving your body time to adjust, but these usually are not dangerous. That said, some people might face worse symptoms than others. Still others may face serious reactions to altitude changes. This is a medical situation known as Acute Altitude Sickness (or Acute Mountain Sickness) or, in Spanish, Mal Agudo de Montaña.

Acute Altitude Sickness is common for those at very high altitudes (say, among mountain climbers above 18,000 feet/5,500 meters). It is uncommon *but not impossible* for locations below 7,900 feet (2,400 meters). Above this level, the risk increases as the elevation increases. Keep in mind that both Zacatecas and Toluca are major centers of industry and foreign investment and both are above this altitude. In addition, many smaller towns and villages may also be above this elevation. Again, it is unlikely that you will develop these symptoms at the altitudes involved in Mexico, but it is better to be aware and cautious just in case. If you have any suspicions, it is safer to assume that you have it than to ignore symptoms.

Coastal Lowlands

Not all of Mexico is at a high altitude. Mexico has two large coastal plains—one on the coast of the Gulf of Mexico winding into the Bay of Campeche, and one along the Pacific Coast. The contrast with the high-altitude areas is dramatic, given that most of these coastal regions are at or near sea level. The Gulf Coastal Plain is large, gaining only gradually in elevation for hundreds of miles from the coast until it reaches the mountains. The Pacific Coastal Plain, by contrast, is very narrow, ranging only from 40 to 70 miles (65 to 110 kilometers) before hitting the mountains.

Due to the dramatic contrast in elevation, both coastal plains have radically different climates from that of the Altiplano. In fact, Mexicans who are from the Gulf Coastal Plain often refer to their region as the *tierras calientes* (hot lands) and to the interior plateau as the *tierras templadas* (temperate lands). We discuss this more under climate below.

Coastlines and Beaches

For many in the US and Canada, Mexico's beaches are its best-known topographical feature. With around 5,797 miles (9,330 kilometers) of coastline, all in a warm climate, there is good reason for their fame.

The three particularly important resort regions for the Mexican beach tourism market are the Riviera Maya, Costa Maya, and Mexican Riviera. The northern section of the Caribbean coast of the Yucatán Peninsula is known as the Riviera Maya. This coastal stretch of 75 miles/120 kilometers has the largest coral reef in the Northern Hemisphere and includes the beach areas of Cancún, Punta Tachacté, Playa del Carmen, and Punta Allen. The southern section of the Caribbean coast has been marketed as the Costa Maya. This coast of Quintana Roo, which is 28 miles/45 kilometers long, is the least developed of the three, and has resorts interspersed with small fishing villages and less-developed areas. The earliest developed of the three is the Pacific Coast. It is also, by far, the longest, stretching southward from Mazatlán in Sinaloa for 2,200 miles/3,540 kilometers to Zihuatanejo in Ixtapa and to Acapulco in Guerrero. Its resort cities also include Puerto Vallarta in Jalisco and Manzanillo in Colima. These resorts cater to wealthier tourists, but the same beaches extend far beyond them.

As we have seen, most Mexican coastal regions are known for their beaches. One, however, is not. The Gulf Coast that runs from the Texas-Tamaulipas border to the Yucatán Peninsula is better known for its wetlands. Beloved by birdwatchers, this tropical coast is the wintering ground for waterfowl and other birds. When we say that birds fly south in the winter, this is where they go.

Earthquakes

Most of Mexico is fairly stable with regard to earthquakes. Just as most US earthquakes are concentrated in just a few states, so, too, Mexico's earthquakes are limited in area. In the US, the Pacific shores of Alaska and California are the locations of the vast majority of naturally occurring earthquakes, while most of the rest of the country is relatively stable.[21] Like the Alaskan and Californian coastlines, part of Mexico is in an earthquake belt. In fact, the tectonic plates that cause Alaska's and California's earthquakes are the exact same ones that hit Baja California. Additionally, Mexico's southern Pacific Coast is another earthquake zone. This is the one that resulted in both the disastrous 1985 Mexico City Quake and the 2017 Central Mexico Quake (centered just south of Puebla)—the two worst in Mexico's history.

Still, you should not feel particularly frightened of earthquakes. To put the frequency in perspective, from 2000 to 2015,

California *alone* had eight earthquakes over 5.0 on the Richter Scale. This is the same number as for the *entirety* of Mexico during the same period.

CLIMATE AND WEATHER

If you have watched tourist advertising for Mexico aimed at people in the US and Canada, you may assume that Mexico is sunny and hot all the time. Though this is good marketing, it is not actually true.

Although most of Mexico is arid, in parts of the country rain is plentiful. In fact, Mexico receives about 30 inches (760 millimeters) of rain annually, exactly the same average rainfall as Toronto or Omaha (or, for that matter, the United States as a whole). The difference is that most of Mexico's rain falls on limited parts of the country, where it is blocked by mountain ranges from progressing further.

Mexico has two seasons: a dry and a wet season. The deserts of the Baja Peninsula and northwestern states receive little rain even *outside* the dry season. That said, most of Mexico has a rainy season from May to September. This is especially the case for the lowland regions of the Pacific Coast, the Gulf Coast, and the Yucatán Peninsula. For example, Veracruz, the largest city on Mexico's Gulf Coast, averages 78 inches (2,000 millimeters) of rain annually, with the vast majority of it coming between June and late September. Mexico's famed Mayan Riviera tourist region along the Gulf Coast of Quintana Roo also shares the same hurricane season that batters the southeastern US from June to November.

Rain aside, Mexico has considerable extremes in climate. The climate is determined by elevation as much as latitude. An extreme example of this is the region of Huasteca. Huasteca is not a state but a geographical and cultural region reaching from the coast of the Gulf of Mexico to the edge of the Sierra Madre Oriental mountains. The mountains effectively block the rain from moving west. As a result, the lowlands east of the mountains are tropical jungles with some of the heaviest rains

2.4 Huasteca, Near Xilitla
The rich foliage near Xilitla in the San Luís Potosí Huasteca. Photograph courtesy of Pablo Rodriguez M.

in Mexico, while the highlands beyond the mountains are arid scrublands. A dramatic example of this is the state of San Luís Potosí, which is divided in half by the Sierra Madre Oriental mountains, as photographs 2.4 and 2.5 show. The rich foliage and rain in photograph 2.5 are typical of the region surrounding the town of Xilitla in the San Luís Potosí Huasteca. Xilitla receives over 100 inches (2,500 millimeters) of rain a year, with just under a quarter falling in September alone. The acacia, cacti, and arid scrubland shown in photograph 2.5 is seen from atop the mesa west of the mountains, near the region of the capital. The city of San Luís Potosí receives an average annual *total* rainfall of just 15 inches (392 millimeters). This is roughly equal to the amount Xilitla receives in December, its driest month. And this is all within the same state.

As we have discussed already, the high elevations of the Altiplano cover most of the country. At high and dry elevations, the temperatures are usually warm during the day and drop greatly at night. In the North Mesa, summer temperatures during the day regularly reach well above 100 °F (38 °C) but can easily drop

2.5 High Mesa Scrubland
Arid scrubland on a mesa near San Luís Potosí.

to 70 °F (21 °C) at night. On the Central Mesa, where the climate is less dry and the altitude is higher, the temperature is much cooler. Mexico City rarely goes higher than 80 °F (26 °C) during its hottest months (April and May), and it can actually get fairly cold in winter, with average lows in December and January of 43 °F (6 °C). In short, it is easy to forget that it can get quite chilly in the winter, and you may need a jacket, especially after the sun sets.

CRIME AND SAFETY ISSUES

Another area where the physical environment is seen in Mexican culture is the way that society handles security. The wealthiest neighborhoods of Mexico begin to resemble armed camps. Security guards and locked entrances are the norm for many apartment buildings. The same security holds with many university campuses and corporate offices. Photograph 2.6 shows a typical entrance into such a neighborhood.

Mexico evokes strong concerns about crime for people in most of the rest of North America. Some of this is with good

2.6 A Security Checkpoint
Security checkpoints like this one are common throughout Mexico. Photograph
courtesy of Vanessa Bonilla-Hernandez.

cause, but much of it is overstated. Many people from the United
States view travel to Mexico as dangerously crime-ridden. This
may surprise many Mexicans, who feel the same way about travel
to the United States (with concerns especially high about mass
shootings). In truth, however, Canadians have equal concerns
for travel to both Mexico and the United States, because both
have far more violent crime than does Canada (or most developed countries).

On the downside, it is true that Mexico has one of the world's
highest murder rates. Mexico ranks twenty-third worldwide in
the number of homicides, with a frightening 16.35 per 100,000.
This is the highest in the OECD. Even though the United States
ranks third (after number-two Latvia) in the OECD and ninety-
fifth in the world, the US rate of 4.88 is still only about a quarter
of Mexico's. For Canadians, the murder rate in Mexico is stag-
gering, at over nine times its own rate of 1.68 per 100,000.[22]

Of the world's fifty cities with the highest homicide rates
(in 2016), eight are in Mexico. On this list, Mexico ranked
second in the world only to Brazil (which had eighteen of the
fifty), though just barely so (Venezuela had seven). However,
the United States had four of the top fifty, tying for fourth (with

Colombia). Moreover, two Mexican cities fell among the top ten. Indeed, Acapulco in Guerrero had 113.24 murders, ranking second only to Caracas (with over 130). Ciudad Victoria in Tamaulipas ranked fifth, with 84.67. By contrast, the US city with the highest murder rate was fourteenth-ranked Saint Louis, with 60.37. The next highest rate in the US was twenty-sixth-ranked Baltimore, with 51.40.[23]

No other city anywhere in the OECD came close to making this list, and Canada's "murder capital"—Regina, Saskatchewan—had a mere 3.03—representing 8 murders in the whole year of 2016.[24]

Mexico did not always have a high homicide rate. For decades, Mexico was far safer than the United States. The shift came with the explosion of the drug wars—particularly with the rise of the Mexican drug cartels after the Mexican government's 2006 war on the cartels in the wake of the collapse of supply from Colombia beginning in 2007. As the United Nations Global Study on Homicide Report explains, "The sudden increase in Mexico's homicide rate since 2007 has come after a steadily declining trend, from comparably high levels in the mid-1950s." Though Mexico now has one of the world's highest murder rates, a direct correlation exists between where the drug cartels are located and this murder rate. And the same UN report just cited observes that "the presence of each additional cartel in a particular location results in a doubling of the homicide rate."[25] In short, homicide in Mexico is clearly linked to geography. Most of Mexico is actually comparable to what you would find in the United States.[26]

Indeed, robbery is the only main category of crime besides homicide where Mexico is notably less safe than the rest of North America. If you are in Mexico, it is true that you are almost three and a half times more likely to be robbed than in the US and five times more likely than in Canada.[27]

With regard to other types of crime, however, Mexico *is actually safer* than the rest of North America. That said, it is not possible to know how many crimes in any of the three countries go unreported. Nevertheless, the United States has three times and Canada over five and a half times the number of reported crimes in Mexico.[28] Burglaries are nine times more common in Canada and thirty-five times more common in the United States as in Mexico.[29] Auto thefts are three times more common in the United States and twice as common in Canada as in Mexico.[30] Finally, if you are in the United States, you are twice as likely to be raped as in Mexico (although Canada's rape rate is an eighth that of Mexico's and a sixteenth that of the US).[31]

So what does this all mean for you? First, do not let security measures concern you. This is just part of life at many companies, universities, and exclusive residential neighborhoods. They are designed to make you feel safe, not afraid. The security guards will likely want to copy your passport information. They will record your arrival and departure times, and perhaps even take your photo before you go through the gate.

Mexicans have less confidence in their law enforcement and judicial systems than their US and Canadian counterparts. This results in Mexicans giving attention to security concerns in ways that you may not see as commonly north of the border. For example, when you withdraw cash, you will notice that most Mexican automated teller machines (ATMs) are enclosed in a protected area. Though a few ATMs are unguarded in airports or malls, you will find far fewer on-the-street ATMs than in the US or Canada. Likewise, when you use your credit card at a restaurant, the wait staff will bring the machine to your table rather than taking your credit card where you cannot see it. In short, through these and similar actions, you will find that Mexicans simply give more *visible* attention to security measures than you commonly would find in the rest of North America.

Driving

Mexican driving is, by US and Canadian standards, often difficult. Mexicans are looser with traffic rules than their northern neighbors. Although not always the case, red lights often serve more like a stop sign and stop signs more like a yield. Squeezing past others, taking a short foray in the wrong direction on a one-way street, or double (even triple) parking (it is only for a minute) are all fairly commonplace.

Roads tend to be of varying quality. Beginning in 2007, Mexico committed to the National Infrastructure Program to modernize its roads. For those familiar with Mexican roads, say, in the 1990s, the improvements are remarkable. Though Mexican toll roads have almost always remained in excellent condition, it used to be fairly uncommon to have consistently good roads, at least outside the wealthiest areas. Public roads still largely depend more on how old they are and how wealthy the state is where they are located. Querétaro, for instance, takes pride in maintaining an excellent road system—but it is a comparatively wealthy state with considerable foreign direct investment, and a very small state area at that. The difference becomes evident when crossing the border between Querétaro and, say, its neighbors Michoacán and San Luís Potosí. If you are from the US or Canada, any expressways—especially older ones—have lanes that are much narrower than you might be used to driving.

Areas interlinked to the United States also tend to have fairly good road infrastructure. For example, Tijuana in Baja California south of California and Reynosa in Tamaulipas south of Texas have well-maintained roads that may not continue as such further south in their states. The great exception to this, however, is the Carretera Interamericana, the Mexican segment of the Pan-American Highway (Highway 85). Here, the contrast between free and toll roads is particularly noticeable. The portion of the highway running from Nuevo Laredo, Tamaulipas (south of Laredo, Texas, from where it continues north as Interstate 35), maintains well-kept toll roads and inconsistently kept free roads south through Monterrey, San Luís Potosí, and Pachuca, and into Mexico City.

Roads outside the larger cities pose their own risk. Dangerous curves are frequently unmarked and are more common than in the US and Canada. Despite considerable improvement in road quality, poorly maintained roads are common, particularly in less-populated areas. Moreover, signs marking construction areas are often poorly marked (or even absent). Also, wandering livestock and abandoned vehicles are common obstacles.

Finally, crime along some public roads—particularly those in areas where drug cartel violence is ongoing—may be a significant concern. Such road crimes are largely absent from toll roads.

Getting Around: Rideshares, Taxis, Rental Cars, and Public Transportation

There are a number of ways of getting around the country—including rideshares, taxis, rental cars, and public transportation. This subsection looks briefly at each one.

Rideshares. Ridesharing in Mexico is as reliable as that in the rest of North America. Uber, Cabify, and similar companies are considered App-Taxi services. Exactly as in the US and Canada, in Mexico the companies monitor their drivers, take payments through the app, and allow opportunities to rate the drivers.

Taxis. Mexico has two types of taxis, called *sitio* and *libre.* *Sitio* taxis are reputable and generally as safe as any in the US or Canada. *Sitio* taxis are radio-dispatched and cannot be hailed from the street or from a taxi stand. *Sitio* taxis have meters and are monitored by the government. They also often have set rates (paid in advance) for specific standard trips (e.g., from and to Mexico City's airport). By contrast, *libre*—or independent—taxis remain a gamble, especially in larger cities. Though many *libre* taxis—especially those in small towns—are reputable, many others are not. Some *libre* taxis are tied to organized crime rings. Others participate in scams. Some of these are minor, such as driving to destinations to which they have a personal tie. Others can be more serious, such as having one person place your luggage in the trunk after a driver lying in the front seat takes off with your belongings.

At this point, we should raise two things that are *not* scams (though they are often mistaken for them). First, in small towns and provincial cities, many (possibly most) legitimate taxis have no meters. In such cases, you must negotiate your fare before the ride begins. Second, when your taxi driver or rideshare driver gets lost in greater Mexico City and must stop to ask directions, this is generally for legitimate reasons. Mexico City and its surroundings are simply so large that many drivers are unfamiliar with areas outside their usual routes. Because the Global Positioning System is at times unreliable and many buildings are poorly marked, stopping to ask others may be the most reasonable way to find the location.

Rental cars. Mexico has most of the same rental chains as in the US or Canada as well as several Mexican local chains. Though small rental companies may be available, using the major chains is advised to ensure reliable vehicles. Just as in the rest of North America, you will need to have a valid driver's license, passport (if you have a non-Mexican license), and credit card. As elsewhere, you should inspect the vehicle for scratches or dents before taking the car.

The one major difference in Mexico from the US or Canada, however, is the need to purchase mandatory insurance. The price of insurance is rarely indicated in the advertised cost, and it is very high (often as much as the rental price, and sometimes higher).

Some concern has arisen in recent years regarding criminals targeting rental cars. Although the incidence of this actually happening is debatable, we note that the Canadian government issued a travel advisory to its citizens regarding the matter, which states: "Rent cars that do not have stickers or other advertisements for the rental company on them so that your vehicle blends in with those of the general population."[32]

Public transportation. By all means, if you are in Mexico City, ride the Metro (see photograph 2.7). It is an experience worth having. Though often very crowded, the Metro is safe, reliable, and very well marked (its stops use pictures so that those who cannot read Spanish can find their way easily). As with Canadian subways (the Canadian firm Bombardier is one of its builders), the Mexico City Metro uses rubber tires, making its trains much quieter and smoother-riding than trains with steel wheels, which are common in the United States. The Mexico City Metro is also extremely well-built; it survived the 1985 earthquake completely intact. The Mexico City Metro is the second-most-ridden and second-longest subway system in the Americas (both after New York City's), and is the ninth-most-ridden and eleventh-largest and in the world.

Mexico has two other cities with major subway systems: Guadalajara and Monterrey. Though not as large as Mexico City's

2.7 The Mexico City Subway
The daily commute on the Mexico City subway. Photograph courtesy of Ted McGrath.

subway, both are just as safe and reliable as the Mexico City Metro.

Airports

Mexican airports are generally well maintained and on level with any of those you will find anywhere else in the developed world. They vary in size from Mexico City International, the largest in all of Latin America, to smaller regional airports.

One difference you may experience at Mexican airports is the lottery system for inspection. The system consists of hitting a large plastic button at Customs, after which a light flashes green or red at random. The light flashes green for passing on without inspection or red for having your bags searched. Though some airports (Mexico City's Terminal 2 and the international airports in Los Cabos and Cancún, at least in part) have begun phasing this practice out, the lottery is still the practice for most airports.

A SENSE OF TIME AND PLACE

Mexico has grown through three eras, all of which blend together—the pre-Hispanic, the Colonial, and the Modern. Everywhere, Mexico's human-made environment reflects these three streams of Mexican history. Colonial churches stand next to cutting-edge modern office buildings. Giant Olmec heads decorate corporate courtyards and modern university campuses.

Because of this rich heritage, Mexico has the most UNESCO Cultural World Heritage sites in the Americas. With twenty-seven official sites, Mexico ties with India for the sixth-most UNESCO Cultural World Heritage sites in the world. Many places carry great symbolic meaning as well in Mexico. We will discuss the blending of historical eras and time in more detail in chapter 7. Here, we simply emphasize that the Mexican concept of place is more closely tied to both personal associations and shared historical memory than is commonly the case for the United States and Canada.

Murals

Mexican murals are the quintessential Mexican art form, and murals draw on the concept of historical memory we just described. Murals are a major feature of the Mexican human-made environment, adorning its buildings and public spaces. The mural is one of Mexico's most widely recognized art forms. Its masters include Jorge González Camarena, Desiderio Hernández Xochitiotzin, Juan O'Gorman, Victor Cauduro Rojas, Alfredo Zalce, Fernando Castro Pacheco, Arturo García Bustos, Gabriel Flores García, and the so-called Three Greats (Los Tres Grandes): Diego Rivera, José Clemente Orozco, and David Alfaro Siqueiros.

Mexican murals began to flourish in the 1920s, as they intended to unify the nation with messages of shared social and cultural values. Many of these murals blend multiple eras into one space, emphasizing the mixing of time periods in an ongoing present. Some famous examples of this (among many) can be seen in Diego Rivera's *History of Mexico* at the Palacio Nacional in Mexico City, Victor Cauduro Rojas's three-mural history of Mexico at the Casa Corregidora in Querétaro, Arturo García Bustos's *History of Mexico* and *History of Oaxaca* at the Palacio del Gobierno in Oaxaca City, Desiderio Hernández Xochitiotzin's *History of Tlaxcala and Its Contribution to Mexican Identity* at the Palacio de Gobierno in Tlaxcala, David Alfaro Siqueiros's *Dates in Mexican History or the Right for Culture* at the National Autonomous University of Mexico in Mexico City, and Jorge González

2.8 Jorge González Camarena's Mural at the Monterrey Tec Rectoría
Mexico is famous for its murals. Pictured here is Jorge González Camarena's *History of Mexico* mural at the ITESM Rectoría in Monterrey. Photograph courtesy of Vanessa Bonilla-Hernandez.

Camarena's *History of Mexico* mural at the ITESM Rectoría in Monterrey, as shown in photograph 2.8.

ARCHITECTURE, BUILDINGS, AND OFFICE SPACE

When it comes to office buildings, you may find that Mexicans have a more formal sense and use of space and privacy than you would expect. Mexicans do have cubicles, to be sure, but Mexican middle-level managers often have personal offices at a rank much lower than their US or Canadian counterparts. Relatedly, when in their offices, Mexicans more often close their doors, whereas Americans and Canadians are more likely to keep the door open. You should not interpret this as a sign for "do not disturb," as it would be in the rest of North America. Usually, the person inside is available but is simply working. Just knock. You will usually be invited in. One thing you may well notice is the way things sound inside buildings in Mexico. Mexican buildings rely much less on carpets and much more on stone and tile flooring. Walls, too, are often tiled.

Finally, you may find that Mexicans rely much more on open windows and natural air circulation than do their US and Canadian counterparts. Many government buildings, corporate offices, museums, and university classrooms have no air conditioning at all, and those that do use it much less frequently than you may be used to if you are from the rest of North America.

MEXICAN VIEWS ON TECHNOLOGY

Taken as a whole, Mexico is among the world's most industrially competitive nations. Mexico ranked twentieth among the thirty countries in the highest quintile of the 2018 *Industrial Development Report* of the United Nations Industrial Development Organization.[33] And though Mexico is well below the fourth rank of the United States, it remains fairly comparable with (if still notably lower than) eighteenth-ranked Canada.[34]

Mexico has advanced technologically at an extraordinary rate in the last thirty years. In the 1990s, roughly 10 percent of Mexicans had a telephone of any kind. Today, 80 percent of the population (over 100 million people) have a phone, and over 70 percent of those are smartphones.[35]

Mexico is the world's third-largest producer of commercial vehicles (after the United States and China), producing over 8.7 percent of those sold in 2017. It is also Latin America's second-largest[36]—and the world's ninth-largest—producer of passenger cars (roughly 2.6 percent of the world's supply).[37] Mexico has likewise grown to worldwide prominence in the aerospace industry. Begun only in 2006, with an investment by Canada's Bombardier in Querétaro, an entire aerospace cluster has grown around the city as French and Spanish firms have also built operations. By 2012, more than thirty related firms—Mexican and foreign alike—were operating in Querétaro,[38] and exports were over $6.3 billion.[39]

Such Mexican-based companies are world leaders in applying high-technology solutions to traditionally low-technology sectors. For example, by applying high-tech production methods and distribution tracking, Monterrey's Cémex became the largest cement company in the Americas and the fifth-largest in the world. Similarly, it has at least in part been through innovation applied to a traditionally low-tech industry that Grupo Bimbo has maintained its title as the world's largest baked goods company (known to Canadians as Canada Bread, Villagio, and Dempster's; and known to US customers for Sara Lee, Entenmann's, Thomas English muffins, Boboli, and more). As early as 1945, Grupo Bimbo, both to protect freshness and to allow consumers to check for moldiness, introduced the transparent cellophane bag for bread products that is now standard worldwide. This record of innovation continues, as evidenced by the introduction in 2012 of the company's Piedra Larga wind farm, powering its electric vehicle fleet, which as of this writing represents the largest conversion to renewable energy within not just the baked goods business but anywhere in the food industry.

A major factor contributing to the strength of Mexico's manufacturing and technology sectors comes with the high percentage of its students graduating with degrees in science, technology, engineering, and mathematics (e.g., STEM degrees). Though we discuss this in more detail in chapter 3, we note here that 25 percent of all Mexican bachelor's degrees are in STEM fields,[40] compared with just 15 percent in the United States,[41] and 18.6 percent in Canada.[42]

What is even more remarkable, Mexico until recently had the second-lowest gross domestic expenditures on research and development (GERD) of any nation in the OECD.[43] The average GERD for the OECD is 2.35 percent. Mexico, however, is one of only two OECD members to spend less than 0.5 percent (it spends 0.49 percent, underspent only by Chile, at 0.39 percent). By comparison, Canada (itself below the OECD average) has a GERD of 1.60 percent and the United States has one of 2.74 percent. At the top of the list, Israel spends 4.27 percent, more than eight and a half times what Mexico spends.[44]

Finally, many individual Mexicans have contributed greatly to the world's advances in modern technology. For example, Mario José Molina-Pasquel Henríquez and Guillermo González Camarena won the 1995 Nobel Prize in Chemistry for the discovery of the Antarctic ozone hole and the way to reverse it (the banning of chlorofluorocarbons), and Mexicans were among the main inventors of color television. Arturo Rosenblueth (along with Norbert Wiener and Warren McCulloch) was the cofounder of the field of cybernetics. José Hernández-Rebollar invented AcceleGlove, the first device for translating American Sign Language into spoken and written words.

As befits an earthquake-prone nation, it was a Mexican—Manuel González Flores—who developed earthquake-resistant foundations for buildings. And perhaps nowhere are Mexican contributors to technology as notable as in the field of medicine. Luis Miramontes famously (for a heavily Roman Catholic nation) invented the birth control pill in 1956. The Mexican dermatologist Fernando Latapí developed the first means to effectively treat leprosy. In the early twentieth century, Matilde Rodríguez Cabo Guzmán was among the leaders in the development of the field of child psychology, as well as a leading activist for women's rights and health issues. In the late twentieth century, the child psychiatrist Manual Isaias Lopez founded AMPI (Mexico's Child Psychiatry Association) and helped to cofound the New York–based IPTAR, the first child psychoanalytic training program. He was also one of the founders of the field of bioethics, in which he was heavily involved at the time of his death in 2017. The Hungarian-born Mexican George Rosenkranz was the biotechnologist who first synthesized the hormone progestin and was among the leading developers of therapeutic steroids. To market these, Rosenkranz founded Syntex Corporation in Mexico City, where he made his new product after fleeing Nazi persecution. Emilio Sacristan is one of the world's leading medical inventors with worldwide adoption of his innovations in stroke therapy, artificial hearts, and an aspiration condenser for anesthesia. It was researchers at the Tec de Monterrey's Biopharmaceutical Research Group, led by Mario Moisés Álvarez, who were credited with mass-producing a vaccine to stop the 2009 AH1N1 virus outbreak, among many other projects. The husband-and-wife team of Susana López Charretón and Carlos Arias Ortiz are generally considered the foremost experts in rotaviruses, and their work has annually saved an estimated 600,000 children from diarrheal illness—and has been recognized with UNESCO's Finlay Microbiology Prize (2001) and the World Academy of Science Prize (2008). López Charretón won the 2012 L'Oréal/UNESCO Award for Women in Science, as did (in 2011) another Mexican, María Alejandra Bravo de la Parra, whose work with bacterial toxins provided a powerful nonchemical insecticide. Other notable medical technology innovators from Mexico include the genetic engineer Francisco Gonzalo Bolívar Zapata and the immunochemist Reyes Tamez Guerra.

THE TWO MEXICOS

It is not really possible to speak of Mexican technology as a whole. This is because—at least in technological terms—there are two Mexicos. The one Mexico is middle class or wealthy and among the most advanced societies in the world. The other Mexico is poor and underdeveloped. Where people live and how wealthy they are has much to do with in which of the two Mexicos people find themselves.

This is an ongoing situation. In 1970, the Mexican Nobel laureate Octavio Paz described "the two Mexicos, one developed, the other underdeveloped."[45] Fast-forward to the present, and the issue still remains. A much-cited 2014 report from the McKinsey Global Institute carries the title "A Tale of Two Mexicos: Growth and Prosperity in a Two-Speed Economy" and contrasts a "modern fast-growing Mexico, with globally competitive multinationals and cutting-edge manufacturing plants, [which] exists amid a far larger group of traditional Mexican enterprises that do not contribute to growth. These two Mexicos are moving in opposite directions."[46] Similarly, *The Economist*'s 2015 article titled "The Two Mexicos" notes that "despite decades of reforms—at times half-hearted, at times full-throttled—Mexico has failed to bridge the gap between a globalised minority and a majority that lives in what Enrique Peña Nieto, the president, admits is 'backwardness and poverty.'"[47] In short, Mexico is one of the most advanced technological nations in the developed world but is simultaneously firmly entrenched in the less-developed world. This is due not so much to an inability to provide access to technology in the nation's less-developed parts as it is to the coexistence of two mind-sets: one embracing control of the environment via technology, and one resisting it.

It is possible to see all this as two Mexican cultures. The Mexico we have just described is alive and well in the well-educated and economically well-off classes of Mexico's industrial and educational centers. This is the Mexican culture that embraces the newest technologies and has propelled the nation forward as a technology leader. For most North Americans dealing with Mexicans at the industry, business, tourism, or educational level, this technologically advanced, current, and globalized worldview will often predominate.

That said, it is true that another culture is also widespread, which differs both in education level and economic well-being. This Mexican culture has a much more fatalistic view of technology and the environment, one in which people believe things happen to them that are beyond their control. Before explaining this in more detail, we want to express a concern here that we are not in some way reinforcing North American stereotypes of Mexicans as somehow lacking in motivation. They are not. They are, however, faced with an economic reality that may well be demotivating on an individual basis. When these individuals find themselves living in regions of Mexico where the majority of people around them also lack opportunity, the resulting fatalism becomes reinforced by the surrounding culture. As Carlos Coria-Sánchez puts it: "Fatalism is not inherent to Mexican culture but to social class."[48] This does not negate the cultural value of those who do feel less of a locus of control. This is equally *a* Mexican cultural view, if not *the only* Mexican view. This is arguably a Mexican culture with its roots not in the mestizo-dominant culture but the indigenous cultures. Santiago Ramírez explains its origins:

> The trauma that the conquest imprinted on the indigenous people was of such magnitude that their chances to overcome the new culture were almost nonexistent; the indigenous' defense mechanism and their strength come from accepting what they have, not to trust anything from the Spanish, the Criollo, or the Mestizo. Throughout several centuries of history, the indigenous people have learned that the aforementioned groups cannot give

them anything of value because if it were good, other cultural peoples would take it for themselves.[49]

It would be a mistake to overlook the widespread fatalistic cultural values of much of Mexico's lower socioeconomic groups and of its rural regions (for all groups).

Octavio Paz wrote that there is a dualism in worldviews in Mexico, which, he argued, cannot be fully reduced to the question of "whether or not the developed half will be able to absorb the underdeveloped."[50] Paz argued that this is the view of the developed Mexico (and we could add that this is likely the view of most development officials from outside Mexico as well). Rather, Paz argues that the issue instead is culturally based—with both cultures present in Mexico: one the culture of the developed Mexico, and one the culture of the rest of the country. Paz wrote that "the developed half of Mexico imposes its model on the other, without noticing that the model fails to correspond to [its] . . . historical, psychic, and cultural reality."[51]

Paz has suggested that only one of these two Mexican worldviews is "the cultural reality." We would suggest, however, that neither is somehow real or artificial, right or wrong. Instead, we suggest that the two worldviews coexist in Mexico.

RECOMMENDATIONS ABOUT AN ENVIRONMENT TO ENCOURAGE GOOD COMMUNICATION

The LESCANT category of environment is broad, but it does give observers an opportunity to focus on the "unseen," obvious reality that surrounds us. As related to Mexico, we offer these four recommendations. First, be willing to explore. Mexico is a varied country. The cosmopolitan dynamism and sheer size of Mexico City are worlds apart from sleepy rural towns. The industrial magnet cities each retain their characters, even as they grow into economic powerhouses. The jungles of the Huasteca and the deserts of the Northwest and Baja all have their charms—explore them all to get a fuller picture of the land and the people.

Second, be healthy. Climate and elevation are considerations. Do not take a high elevation for granted, and give yourself time to adjust. It is easy to get dehydrated in Mexico. High elevation is one reason, but so are the dry heat of desert and arid areas, the humid heat in the wetlands of the Yucatán, or just too much sun on the beach. Drink (bottled) water—and plenty of it. Finally, as with anywhere you travel, wash your hands often, especially before eating.

Third, be safe. Driving in Mexico is looser with the rules than the US or Canada—do not expect everyone to follow the rules. Big cities in Mexico have much the same sort of crime as in the rest of North America. Just as in Detroit, Toronto, Chicago, or Los Angeles, Mexican cities have parts of town that are usually safe and others that are more questionable. Crime from the cartels may be a factor in a few areas, so stay aware of what those areas are. In general, this is much overstated to ensure caution. Still, regardless of what country you visit, when traveling it is always good advice to check your government's travel warnings and to register with your embassy (US or Canadian).

Fourth and finally, be dubious about the hyperbole. Mexico seems particularly subject to exaggerated descriptions. Alarmist stories of crime, bad roads, or parched deserts are just that—alarmist. For that matter, gushing descriptions of Mexico's beach resorts, of Cancún or Cabo or the excitement of the Baja 1000s off-road racing, are not exactly all there is to Mexico either. Mexico is an easy place to misread and an equally easy place to enjoy.

ENVIRONMENT SUMMARY AND CHAPTER 2 HIGHLIGHTS

Topography and size:

- Thirteenth-largest country in the world.
- Cornucopia shapes mean that while one-fourth the size of the continental US, it is almost as long north to south.
- Much of the country is at high elevations.

Population size, density, and wealth:

- Tenth-most-populous country, with 127 million people.
- Mexico City is the largest in North America.
- Rapidly growing magnet cities.
- World's fifteenth-largest economy, with a GDP of over $1 trillion.

Crime and safety issues:

- Gated and fenced residences, universities, and businesses.
- No open automated teller machines.
- Cartel crime is a factor, but in some regions only.
- Cautious use of credit cards.
- Inconsistent road infrastructure.

Climate and weather:

- Climate affected by elevation as much as latitude.
- Both deserts and wetlands.

Architecture, buildings, and office space:

- Often no central air conditioning.
- Offices have formal use of space and privacy.
- Murals are a major art form.
- The senses of time and place are intertwined.

Natural resources:

- Agricultural powerhouse.
- Mining powerhouse.
- Water shortage.

Recommendations:

- Explore
  - Mexico is a varied country.
- Be healthy
  - Stay hydrated.
  - Adjust for high elevations.
- Be safe
  - Be vigilant in traffic.
  - Stay aware of troubled areas.
  - Remain wary of petty crime.
- Do not fall for the hyperbole
  - Mexico seems particularly subject to exaggerated descriptions, both good and bad.

3

M E X I C A N
Social
Organization

Mestizaje, Mosaic,
or Melting Pot?

Social organization in Mexico—the "S" of the LESCANT approach—is, in many respects, the result of historical circumstances. The language, religion, and rituals all demonstrate the relevance of the past. Although Mexicans acknowledge and learn from their past, they also live in the present with optimism and hope for a brighter future. Thus, Mexicans are proud of their ancient civilizations, their beautiful and diverse natural resources, their beaches, their Magic Villages (Pueblos Mágicos), their traditions, and their art and music as well as their characteristic food and drinks.[1] Mexicans are proud, more than anything else, of the graciousness of the people. And although they are recognized for their creativity and hospitality, in this chapter we address the reasons that they are also sometimes misunderstood.

Mexicans find strength to overcome the tragedies from the past in the people with whom they associate. They recover from the crises of the present by embracing those they love. And they use their belief in people to diligently work toward a promising future. Past, present, and future—all affect how Mexican society is organized. This is an important aspect of this chapter as well.

For those less familiar with Mexican culture, an understanding of the country's social organization is not an easy task. Often, it seems paradoxical. For example, how can Mexicans hold on to happiness when there are so many unresolved problems (e.g., inequality or poverty)? Or how is it that Mexicans celebrate the Day of the Dead with a parade and singing? Or why do Mexicans have so much faith in Our Lady of Guadalupe and have so many things intertwined with religion?

In this chapter, we explain the foundations of Mexican social organization. We start by comparing multiculturalism in the North American countries. We then review the caste system in Mexico that produced the unequal social classes of today. Then, we examine education, gender roles, family, kinship, and religion. We finish the chapter by elaborating on what Mexicans do with their leisure time. We trust that by reviewing all these topics, Mexican social organization contradictions can be better understood.

NORTH AMERICA'S THREE APPROACHES TO MULTICULTURALISM: MEXICAN, US, AND CANADIAN

Mexico is multicultural, meaning that the so-called Mexicanidad is a fusion of micro cultures. The best way to understand it is by observing its practices, habits, attitudes, values, behaviors, and institutions. During the twentieth century, Mexico's revolutionary nationalism created a united society and a homogenized culture of the country. At that time, those leading Mexico believed that in order to create a nation and to resolve conflict, Mexicans should have a unique identity. This concept—called *mestizaje*—reinforced the reason of being, and the rejection of other local cultural expressions.

Mexican culture has been strongly influenced by its indigenous groups and Spain but also by other European, African, and Asian ethnic groups. This evolution stems from a continuous blending of its people. Mexicans make sense of who they are by appreciating how they have combined, fused, and interchanged over time. Their identity with family, community, country, and humanity at large are all linked to this sense of heritage.

Mexico, the United States, and Canada are all thought of as "multicultural" societies. However, they each differ in how they perceive their multicultural development. For example, the counterpart to *mestizaje* in Mexico is a "melting pot" in the United States and a "cultural mosaic" in Canada. These three approaches present some of the clearest differences among the three countries. An understanding of these three self-concepts will go a long way toward helping us understand one another's ideals.

The Mexican *Mestizaje*

Mexico, as we mentioned, grew out of a cultural blending, or *mestizaje*. After its independence in 1810, Mexico began to emphasize its own self-identity as a hybrid identity of Spanish and indigenous foundations. This concept of a mestizo culture took on an even greater hold during and following the Mexican Revolution of 1910–20. Many thinkers, politicians, and artists advanced the concept of a new Mexican *raza* (race or ethnic identity) blended from its indigenous, Spanish, and new immigrant roots. Of these, however, José Vasconcelos was probably the foremost proponent of *mestizaje*. He proposed the notion of La Raza Cósmica, in his 1925 book of the same name, which laid the foundations for the mestizo culture that has a uniquely Mexican identity today.[2]

We should note that Vasconcelos's initial concept was intended to be universal (*cósmica*), but, somewhat ironically, it became in the end uniquely Mexican. Vasconcelos was among the greatest philosophers of Mexico's Revolutionary Period, and he influenced generations of Mexicans through his educational journal *El Maestro* (The Teacher), first as rector of UNAM (Universidad Nacional Autónoma de México [National Autonomous University of Mexico]), then as the founder and first secretary of Mexico's Ministry of Public Education, and then as a (failed) candidate for president in 1929.

Vasconcelos espoused the positive value of *mestizaje*—the idea of racial and ethnic groups intentionally blending together. This blending together, in turn, would give birth to a superior people who would result from "the fusion of the different contemporary races into a new race that will fulfill and surpass all the others."[3] (This was in sharp contrast to the European racial purity goals and social Darwinist claims of the same period in the 1920s.) For Vasconcelos, Latin Americans in general and Mexicans in particular had the opportunity to create a mestizo race that had not one origin but many—a new people. In Vasconcelos's words, Mexico had "the moral and material basis for the union of all men into a fifth universal race, the fruit of all the previous ones and amelioration of everything past."[4] We should clarify this by noting that in modern terminology, people refer to *mestizaje* in Mexico as pertaining to intercultural mixing more than the race-based language of Vasconcelos's original.

The American Melting Pot

Traditionally, the United States has approached its cultural diversity with the analogy of a "melting pot." The melting pot metaphor focuses on the assimilation of its immigrants. The underlying principle of this primarily US concept is that, whoever immigrants may have been in their previous lives, as newcomers to the country, they leave that life behind and become something new—a US citizen. The melting pot uses the image of the crucible, in which various materials are brought together and the combination results in something stronger than any of the originals. This image—for example, of how a steel alloy is stronger than the raw iron, carbon, nickel, and manganese—illustrates this image of a melting pot. Arguably, President Theodore Roosevelt is the person who helped popularize the US melting pot, which he described as "the crucible that turns our people out as Americans, of American nationality, and not as dwellers in a polyglot boarding house." He also argued against what he called "hyphenated Americans." Roosevelt was groundbreaking in his call for people of all backgrounds to have exact equality with everyone else, for it is "an outrage to discriminate against any such man because of creed or birthplace or origin," and he insisted that "this is predicated upon the man's becoming in very fact an American and nothing but an American."[5]

The Canadian Cultural Mosaic

Canada approaches its unique multicultural identity in what we call the "cultural mosaic," which focuses on the maintenance of the cultural heritage of its immigrants. The underlying principle of this primarily Canadian concept is that in becoming Canadians, whoever they may have been in their previous lives, newcomers as well as those already present (e.g., Canada's indigenous First Nations) maintain their way of life and add their own culture to the desired diversity of Canada. The concept uses the metaphor of the decorative art form mosaic, in which the artist combines small pieces of different materials (e.g., tiles or pieces of colored glass) to form a picture. In a mosaic, each tile adds to the picture as a whole without each part losing its individual characteristics. Canada is metaphorically the overall picture, and each person is a tile that adds to the picture. Although all Canadians adhere to the unifying rules of Canadian law, they also retain their own language, religion, and so on.

There are similarities and differences among the Mexican concept of *mestizaje*, the US melting pot, and the Canadian mosaic. Table 3.1 provides a quick overview of how these three systems compare and contrast.

Both Mexico's concept of *mestizaje* and Canada's cultural mosaic remain firmly entrenched as central to their respective country's national self-conception. Mexicans largely identify with the positive value of merged mestizo culture, just as Canadians widely identify with their society as a combination of discrete cultures. The acceptance of all groups regardless of religion, national origin, or race has from their beginning (the 1920s in Mexico; the 1970s in Canada) been a basic principle, both in theory and largely in practice. This widespread acceptance has not, however, been the case for the US melting pot—or at least not without considerable resistance. In this respect, both Mexico and Canada differ from the US position. In the United States, each generation seems to have struggled with groups that were prevented, to continue with the metaphor, from being placed in the melting pot.

Table 3.1

Three Views of Multiculturalism: The Mexican *Mestizaje*, the Canadian Mosaic, and the US Melting Pot

Aspect of Multiculturalism	Mexican *Mestizaje*	Canadian Cultural Mosaic	US Melting Pot
Widely held and firmly entrenched with national self-identity	YES	YES	Yes, but contested
Goal of a blended common culture	YES	NO	YES
Concept of a defining national identity	YES	NO	YES
Large-scale foreign immigration	NO	YES	YES
Assimilation and co-opting cultural contributions of others	YES	NO	YES
Acceptance in practice of all groups regardless of religion, race, or national origin	From beginning	From beginning	Recent

Until the mid-1960s, there were widespread discriminatory standards that overtly opposed the mixing of certain groups (limiting civil rights based on race, religion, national origin, and ancestry in 1964; prohibiting immigration based on race, national origin, and ancestry in 1965). After these legal changes, we might say that the US melting pot analogy became more aligned with the Mexican concept of *mestizaje*. However, even today this remains far from a universally agreed upon self-conception in the United States, and it is considerably more contested as a political and social issue in the United States than in either Mexico or Canada.

Another commonality between Mexico and Canada that is not shared with the United States has been mixing races. Mexico's *mestizaje*, as we have seen, is based on the concept of mixing races as a positive value. Canada has from its beginnings always allowed the mixing of races with no legal barriers, and since the mid–twentieth century has embraced such unions as a defining part of its cultural mosaic. The United States, by contrast, for most of its history has *not* shared this view of racial mixing. In this regard, the United States and Mexico were for centuries diametrically opposite from each other. The word *mestizo* has positive connotations in Mexico. Mexicans take pride in the blending of all races and cultures, and especially of indigenous and Spanish cultures.

By contrast, the direct translation of the Spanish word *mestizaje* is the English word *miscegenation*. Nevertheless, we use the original Spanish word throughout this book, because in the present-day United States, the English equivalent word *miscegenation* carries a more negative connotation. Miscegenation is inextricably tied to US laws prohibiting race mixing and is a loaded term in American English. Miscegenation carries with it the miscegenation taboos and formal laws that required racial segregation at the level of marital and intimate relations. *Mestizaje* does not have such a nuance in Spanish, and the term is completely positive.

In the US, miscegenation refers almost always to the criminalization of marriage between the races. At one time, forty-one of the fifty US states had formal antimiscegenation laws. At the beginning of the 1960s, twenty-one states still had such laws in place. The US Supreme Court overturned the last of these in 1967, with the *Loving v. the State of Virginia* ruling. At that time, sixteen of the fifty states still had such laws in place.[6] This is the exact opposite of Mexico's self-identity as a mestizo nation, where *mestizaje* was a goal to be desired.

Despite the linguistic nuance in terms, the Mexican *mestizaje* and the US melting pot analogies share similarities, in that both encourage the assimilation of immigrants to create a nationalized version of them. From the Mexican perspective, we hear this in northern Mexico's *norteño* music (based on Eastern European polkas) or the *son jarocho* of Veracruz and Tamaulipas—a fusion sound of African and Caribbean rhythms played on instruments of both Spanish (guitar) and African (*quijadas* and *güiras*) origin.

These different musical styles may have diverse origins but have been modified into "Mexicanized" versions. On the US side, we see this in the foods that Americans claim as their own. Hamburgers may come from Germany, pizza may come from Italy, and even tacos may come from Mexico, but they have all become standard US foods with their unique "Americanized" versions. By contrast, we do *not* see this assimilation in the Canadian cultural mosaic at all.

Within the Canadian ideal, there is no such thing as the "Canadianization" of anything. As the Canadian prime minister Pierre Trudeau put it in an often-quoted 1971 speech, "There is no such thing as a model or ideal Canadian. What could be more absurd than the concept of an "all-Canadian" boy or girl? A society which emphasizes uniformity is one which creates intolerance and hate."[7]

Mexico, however, unlike the United States and Canada, has not had the same volume of immigration from around the world. Although people have come to Mexico from all over the world, for the most part, the mestizo reality—if not the ideal—has come from two main sources: the indigenous people and the Spanish. Although Mexicans have had immigration from around the world, as of the 2010 Census, fewer than 1 million Mexicans were foreign-born, over 730,000 of whom were from the United States, with less than 223,000 from elsewhere, roughly 0.85 percent of its whole. By contrast, Canada in 2011 had just under 7 million foreign-born people, representing over 20 percent of its population, and the United States had roughly 40 million foreign-born people, or 13 percent of its population.[8]

MEXICO'S REGIONAL DIVERSITY

The definition of Mexican culture is additionally complicated because Mexico is regionally diverse. Regions in Mexico vary not only by culture and ethnicity but also by enormous differences in economic development. In Mexico, we see that different social classes coexist without integration. They have distinct values, beliefs, and practices, which together can form a completely different culture. Therefore, in order to clearly picture social organization in Mexico, we need to understand which characteristics differentiate one social group from another.

A close look at the gross domestic product (GDP) per capita of Mexico reveals the existence of remarkably different economic realities within the country. First, most states in the North possess a mechanized agriculture, a greater-than-national average GDP per capita, higher levels of literacy, more cities, and marginal indigenous populations (e.g., Tarahumaras in the mountains and the Yaquis or Huicholes isolated in the desert). Conversely, most states in the South have less mechanized agriculture, lower levels of literacy, more rural towns, and large indigenous populations. Also, we see that the states in the Center are the most populated. It is in the Center regions where the political power resides and where industrialization started. Therefore, the states in the Center are the ones where development has happened more quickly. These three groups have different habits, traditions, beliefs, and behaviors. When traveling across Mexico, one can observe regional differences in the food, the music, and in the way people use their free time, as well as in how people dress. One can also hear changes in the language or the pronunciation of Spanish. This includes specific words that only those familiar with the region will know.

Another way to understand differences in Mexico is by separating regions by those that are industrialized and those that are not. Ten out of thirty-two federal entities monopolize 69 percent of national manufacturing activities: Estado de Mexico (11.68 percent), Nuevo León (10.17 percent), Coahuila (8.10 percent), Guanajuato (8 percent), Jalisco (7.46 percent), Mexico City (6.53 percent), Veracruz (5.39 percent), Puebla (4.03 percent), Querétaro (3.88 percent), and Chihuahua (3.69 percent). In contrast, eight other states have very little industrialization, equaling 3.17 percent: Baja California Sur (0.10 percent), Campeche (0.10 percent), Colima (0.22 percent), Quintana Roo (0.27 percent), Guerrero (0.43 percent), Zacatecas (0.54 percent), Tabasco (0.74 percent), and Chiapas (0.77 percent).

In this section, we explain the caste system that was set up in colonial Mexico. This system normalized the social organization for many years. Later, independent Mexico abolished the caste system. However, the result is that the class system still prevails today in modern Mexico, and it exemplifies the hugely unequal distribution of income.

Before Mexico was an independent nation, it was known as the Viceroy of New Spain. At that time, there was a caste system, which dominated the political and economic life of the region. The caste, which was determined by the place where the individual was born and by his or her ancestry, conferred specific rights and obligations.

Those individuals with 100 percent Spanish blood, known as Peninsular People, were at the top of the system. At the beginning of colonization, everyone who arrived from Europe complied with this condition. In fact, European women who got pregnant in the new land often returned to Europe to have their children. By doing this, the European-born babies kept their position in the caste system, in contrast with those New World–born babies who received fewer privileges. These New World babies were known as *creoles*. Creoles constituted the second tier in the caste system. The mestizos were the children of European and indigenous populations, and they held the third position in the caste system. They enjoyed fewer rights than those of the first two groups. At the lowest level of the caste system were those who were born of pure or mixed indigenous and African blood. At that time, these individuals of mixed parentage were called mulattos (black/white), *zambos* (black/indigenous), and *cholos* (white/indigenous, e.g., mestizo). Today, most people in Mexico are either mestizos or a combination of mestizo with another group. The caste system no longer exists in modern Mexico, but its historical consequence, the class system, very much does in modern Mexico.

The caste system resulted in a clear social division. The initial consequence of this separation was the supposed supremacy of the Spanish and the lack of solidarity with those who were part of the less prestigious categories. And the result of this is that the political and social power rested in the hands of the privileged few. As the Spaniards forced creoles into inferior jobs, resentment from the less privileged groups grew. Consequently, another result was the huge inequality in the distribution of wealth and power. Mexico is not unique in this aspect, and this also happened in other Latin American and Caribbean countries.

Independent Mexico continued to reinforce this social structure in its class system. Those people who were in positions of power and influence continued to determine political and economic decisions. At the top of the system were aristocrats, the clergy, the military, miners, and wealthy foreigners. By the middle of the nineteenth century, there were gaps in infrastructure development (e.g., schools, roads, and communication), and there was a powerless middle class shaped by merchants, professionals, artisans, workshop owners, and employees in general. And at the bottom, there was a large majority population of the poor and the weak.

Over time, the differences in the regional concentration of wealth and production in Mexico continued to increase. In 1979, twelve of thirty-two federal entities (including Mexico City) represented 77 percent of total wealth. Thirty-six years later, by 2015, fifteen federal entities produced 76.21 percent of total GDP. More important, only six regions produced half of the national GDP: Mexico City (16.71 percent), Estado de Mexico (9.45 percent), Nuevo León (7.53 percent), Jalisco (6.83 percent), Veracruz (4.99 percent), and Guanajuato (4.46 percent). The North American Free Trade Agreement, which was signed in 1992, also benefited the states in the North of Mexico (e.g., Nuevo León, Sonora, and Coahuila); some in the Center (e.g., Mexico City, Estado de Mexico, Querétaro, and Puebla); and a few others like Jalisco in Western Mexico. Those in the South benefited less from the North American Free Trade Agreement. We see that the nationalization of banks in Mexico also benefited those in wealthier regions. Foreigners own some banks in Mexico (e.g., CitiBanamex from the US, BBVA Bancomer and Santander from Spain, HSBC from the UK, and Scotiabank from Canada). Other banks are owned by Mexicans (e.g., Banorte, Inbursa, and Azteca), and all these again represent the more developed states in the North and Center, causing the trend of disparity to continue. The result of all this is that the Mexican economy is best viewed not nationally but regionally. When looking at Mexican social organization, one should consider these economical regional disparities along with the existing social class system.

Beyond the role of the government, individual behavior shapes socioeconomic inequality. Those groups at the top of the class system behave in a way that is similar, or at least compatible, with those in other wealthy countries (e.g., Europe and North America). People at the top frequently travel the world, speak several languages, and hold university degrees. Many come from privileged families of the past. Those at the bottom, the majority population in the country, lack the resources to move up in the class system.

EDUCATION

In Mexico, the best way to move up through the class system is by education. Those individuals who hold a university degree earn 74 percent more money than those with a high school diploma. The return of investment of a university degree really varies depending on the type of degree and prestige of university, as well as other market variables. When comparing the educational system in Mexico, the United States, and Canada, we see significant differences at all levels of education.[9]

Compulsory education in Mexico, the United States, and Canada is very similar. In Mexico and Canada, it is eleven years; in the United States, it is twelve. However, the operation and results of educational efforts in these three countries vary considerably. The size of their economies, the educational models, and the administration of resources are very different. What follows is a presentation of salient indicators.

In Mexico, the annual expenditures per student from primary to tertiary education is one of the lowest among countries that belong to the Organization for Economic Cooperation and Development (OECD) and partner countries with available data.

Mexico ranks thirty-fourth out of thirty-six, in contrast to the US, which has one of the highest expenditure rankings, at second out of thirty-eight.

The challenge in Mexico is not in the amount of the public expenditures on education; as a percentage of total public expenditures, this is comparatively high (17.3 percent, ranking second out of thirty-four). Neither is the problem found in the lack of improvement in terms of expenditures on education. Between 2010 and 2012, the change in public expenditures on primary through tertiary educational institutions is large (with a 107 index, ranking 7 out of 28). The challenges for improvement in Mexico relate more to how the resources are used and what the educational models are.

Teachers in elementary schools face similar challenges. They spend a large number of hours at school, class sizes are large, salaries are low, and available resources are limited. The pupil-teacher ratio in primary schools in Mexico is 28.11, one of the largest among the countries that belong to the OECD. The ratio in the US is not much better, at 27. In addition, teachers in elementary and secondary schools of Mexico receive the lowest salaries of OECD countries—this even though their compensation represents up to 80.7 percent of total expenditures on education. In the US, teachers' salaries make up 55 percent of total expenditures, and those salaries are much higher than in Mexico. In the case of Canada, teachers' salaries make up 62.4 percent of total expenditures, and their salaries are generally higher than in US.

When we look at tertiary education, we find that the US and Canada have the highest percentages of young people who are expected to graduate from a short tertiary education program during their lifetime. Mexico, conversely, has one of the lowest percentages of young people expected to obtain a bachelor's or equivalent degree, and Mexico also has the lowest percentage of young people who graduate from tertiary education.

Disparities in the quality of education, as well as in the infrastructure of educational institutions, are still very common in Mexico—not only between the public and private educational sectors but also between those within the public and those within the private sector (see photographs 3.1 and 3.2).

3.1 The Infrastructure of a Private School
View of well-equipped and spacious rooms providing a variety of educational resources in a private school.

3.2 The Infrastructure of a Public School
View of a modest public school showing the disparities of infrastructure between private and public schools.

Given the general distrust of public education, we see that in Mexico those with means generally choose private education for their children. At the university level, enrollments in public universities in Mexico continue to dominate. In fact, enrollments in public universities have increased fivefold in the last twenty years. At the same time, enrollments in the private sector have grown by a factor of almost ten. Enrollment in the public sector is reaching capacity, and the trend is for private institutions to provide services for those who are willing to pay for them.

With regard to the breakdown in education by gender in Mexico, in the whole system 50.1 percent of current students are male and 49.9 percent are female. And as to university-level enrollment, in 2014 undergraduate enrollment in Mexico was divided into 51.3 percent male and 48.7 percent female. By comparison, at the elementary and secondary levels, 49 percent of students in the US are women, whereas at postsecondary levels, the share of women increases to 57 percent.

Keeping these figures in mind, we now turn to a brief discussion about gender roles in Mexico and how they compare with those in other North American countries.

GENDER ROLES

One of the ways to view the role of gender in society is to see how it plays out in the basic structure of employment, traditional norms, and how things have changed over time. In Mexico we see a gradual increase in the economic participation of women after 1950. The Global Gender Gap Index (GGGI) of the World Economic Forum shows that Mexico has improved markedly over the last decade in economic opportunity and participation levels among women. In the GGGI scoring, the higher the score (e.g., the closer to 1.000) the smaller the disparity between men and women regarding salaries, participation levels, and access to high-skilled employment.

When the GGGI was first published in 2006, Mexico's economic participation score was 0.480, placing it 98th among the 115 nations ranked and in the bottom 15 percent of all nations. By 2016, Mexico's economic participation score had jumped to 0.544, placing it 122nd among 144 nations, still near the bottom 15 percent but significantly improved overall. Still, this leaves a far greater gender gap in the economic sphere for Mexico than in either Canada (36th, at 0.732) or the United States (26th, at 0.752). When comparing overall scores today, Mexico looks better, at 66th, while the US ranks 45th and Canada ranks 35th.[10]

Traditional Roles

Beyond the basic structure of employment, another way of looking at gender roles in Mexico is vis-à-vis traditional gender roles. In Mexico today, most women are still responsible for domestic jobs and the care of children. Men constitute most of the labor force and are responsible for providing for their families.[11]

Within the traditional distribution of duties, when Mexican men are at home, there are specific tasks that they more readily accept (e.g., fixing the pipes, moving furniture, and painting the house). In today's world, these tasks may no longer be physically demanding, but they are still seen as something that men take care of. Interestingly, although women do a lot of the shopping, another task that is considered a man's job is that of choosing the good cuts of meat for an outdoor barbecue. It is not uncommon to see a number of men in front of the butcher, because they are the ones who will cook the meat. Photographs 3.3 and 3.4 illustrate this concept. Our Mexican-born woman author notes that she has received surprised looks from men when she demonstrates that she is able to pick out good cuts of meat for the outdoor barbecues.

Maquiladoras

In most cases where women work outside the home, this has come about as a response to an economic necessity. In 2015, women became not only the pillar of family cohesion but also the only economic provider of 29 percent of households in Mexico. This represents an increase from 24.6 percent in 2010. The *maquiladora* factories that dot the US–Mexican border often hire women as their main workforce.[12] Working conditions demand that workers are quick and have agile hands, which, accurate or not, are associated with women. Most of the time, these plants hire young and single women because others with family demands will find it more difficult to comply. However, because high employment turnover rates are common, and because the industry is growing, many *maquiladoras* have become more open

3.3 Men at the Butcher Shop
Often, men are the ones who choose the cuts of meat at the butcher shop before a barbecue is organized. Photograph courtesy of Roberto Bonilla Rios.

3.4 Men Preparing Meat
Usually, men put the meat on the barbeque for grilling, cooking, and cutting.

to hiring women with children. Photograph 3.5 illustrates a typical scene on a factory floor.

Despite the fact that men and women in Mexico share similar education levels, it is also true that women lag behind in salaries. Sometimes this is because of the nature of the employment, but

3.5 Women at a *Maquiladora*
Most *maquiladoras* hire women, who are considered to be quick, responsible, and agile. Photograph courtesy of Jesus Enrique Portillo Pizaña.

it also happens because of gender discrimination, unfair distribution of salaries, and job barriers for women. Data from 2017 show that 61.9 percent of those who were economically active in Mexico were men, compared with 38 percent who were women. Among the women who were not economically active, 70 percent stay at home to fulfill domestic chores. Another 20 percent are students, 3 percent are retired, 1 percent is disabled, and the rest fill other categories. By comparison, among males who were not economically active, 48 percent were students, 18 percent were retired, 6 percent fulfilled domestic chores, 3 percent were disabled, and the rest were subdivided into a number of other conditions. Women's average income level is equivalent to 80 percent with respect to men. Gender wage gaps vary depending on region and type of job, between 15 and 25 percent.

Another area where gender differences are evident in the workplace is in the average age of Mexico's workers. For men, maximum economic participation happens between the age of thirty and thirty-nine years. For women, maximum economic participation happens later, between the age of forty and forty-nine. Much of this is related to the fact that many women return to the workforce after their children have grown. In fact, Mexican values, beliefs, and norms related to family and kinship help explain this, an area where we now turn our attention.

FAMILY AND KINSHIP

It is of paramount importance to understand Mexicans' focus on family, the crucial building block of society. When a family member needs time and attention, Mexicans feel compelled to comply. In US culture, we sometimes refer to family and relatives. In Mexico, the notion of family combines the two. Family is more than the immediate family of parents and children. Family includes the wide circle of grandparents, uncles, aunts, cousins, grandchildren, and the like. In Mexico 28 percent of all family households include more than just parents and children. It is not uncommon for grandparents, uncles, in-laws, or cousins to live with the nuclear family. This is not to say that this does not happen in the US or in Canada; but in Mexico, this is the norm, and it is not thought of as anything that requires special sacrifice or planning. Photograph 3.6 provides a wonderful

3.6 A Party with an Extended Family
A party where "family" and "relatives" imply a large, extended group of people.

example of a family party, complete with lots of members of the extended family.

When we think of family in Mexico, we also include *los compadres* and *las comadres*. The simple translation of *los compadres* and *las comadres* is godparents, but the role they play in the family is much more involved. They share the guardianship of children. Parents invite close friends to be their children's godparents in Catholic sacraments, such as baptism, confirmation, and first Holy Communion. When couples get married, they will also have godparents to help. *Compadres* and *comadres* guide and support their godsons and goddaughters through life. This close relationship is one of the most respected traditions in Mexico. Those who are linked by this honor are expected to be loyal to each other. They are always invited to family events, and of course they receive preferential treatment. The *compadrazgo* bond is powerful. If the children or parents ever have problems, all know that they can go to their *compadres* for comfort, solidarity, or advice. Truly, the invitation to be a *compadre* is an honor, and one that is illustrated beautifully in photograph 3.7, as they pose with the new baby and her parents.

We often hear that Mexico values collectivist thinking as opposed to emphasizing individualism. This ties in to Mexico's

3.7 *Compadres*, the Guardianship of Children
Compadrazgo is one of the most respected relationships in Mexico.

identity with the extended family and the need to support and sustain family members. Where individualism expects people to fend for themselves, collectivism represents a preference for a tightly knit framework in society where people take care of family and other in-group members. It is not surprising that the well-known data from Hofstede put the US at the extreme end of individualism, at 91; Canada not far behind, at 80; and Mexico, far below, with a score of merely 30.[13]

Mexicans' collectivism also influences their need for harmony, not only within the family but also within society at large. Mexicans do not like to argue or cause others to look bad in public. As an example, consider the meaning of the word "discuss" in Spanish, *discutir*. According to the Real Academia Española, *discutir* means to say or to examine something.[14] However, in daily speech, Mexicans often associate *discutir* with a negative connotation. When they hear it, they immediately think of argumentation. In these cases, it is much better to use the verb *decir*, which simply means "to say" in Spanish. Figure 3.1 shows the results of a Google search of the words "*discutir*" and "discuss." Note the combative images that are associated with *discutir* and the conversational images that are associated with "discuss."

We see another example of the importance of family and the traditional roles of men and women in the way that Mexicans celebrate certain holidays. For example, it is common

Figure 3.1
Discutir versus "Discuss": The results of an online search for images related to *discutir* and "discuss," showing the negative versus positive connotations.

3.8 Mother's Day and Roses
May 10, Mother's Day in Mexico, is one of the most special celebrations. Photograph courtesy of Rosio Briones.

practice to celebrate Mother's Day (May 10) or Children's Day (April 30) by having programs, gifts, and free time from job and school. Father's Day does not receive much attention, but Mother's Day has become an extraordinary holiday. Unlike in the US and Canada, where it is celebrated on the second Sunday of May, in Mexico Mother's Day is always celebrated on May 10. This started in 1922, when the journalist Rafael Alducin advocated for its recognition. Children honor their mothers with a party, gift giving, singing with mariachis, preparing lots of food, and, most important, spending time with their moms. This time together is so important that if Mother's Day falls on a weekday, companies provide time off to working mothers so that they can properly celebrate with their children. Similarly, Children's Day in Mexico is celebrated on April 30. The celebration began in 1925, and today schools and companies invite parents and host special events for the children. There are no classes at school, and instead teachers organize activities with shows, face painting, storytelling, workshops, and games. Photograph 3.8 illustrates a classic scene of a Mother's Day celebration, complete with a bouquet of roses.

RELIGION

Another way to look at how society is organized is to consider the role of religion. In Mexico, the vast majority of people are Roman

Catholic (82.7 percent), and no other single religious group represents more than 5 percent of the population. Compare this 82.7 percent with that of the US, where 70.6 percent are Christian but only 20.8 percent are Roman Catholic; Canada has a similar distribution. It is simply the case the Catholicism—in its history, holidays, and traditions—affects daily life in Mexico.

Religion also played a crucial role in Mexico during the Aztec era. The Aztecs imposed their religious view of human existence on other indigenous groups before Mexico actually existed as an independent nation. When Hernán Cortés arrived in the new land, the indigenous people believed he was Quetzalcóatl, the Aztec god of wind and wisdom. The image of Cortés coincided with their notion of Quetzalcóatl. In his shield, Cortés had a cross, a pigeon, and a crosier. He arrived from the East, and he landed in Yucatán, exactly as the legend had foretold. At the time, the authority of a king deserved respect and obedience because it represented the wishes of the gods. This confluence of religious respect and political power resulted in much conflict.

Our Lady of Guadalupe

The story of Our Lady of Guadalupe and her appearance to Juan Diego is key to understanding the sentiment of faith that is associated with Catholicism in Mexico. Conquistadores and missionaries introduced Christianity to Mexico, and the Diocese of Mexico City was established as early as 1528. Juan Diego, a humble peasant, was one of the first Mexican indigenous persons to accept baptism and convert to Christianity. Official Catholic documents state that Our Lady of Guadalupe appeared to Juan Diego four times at Tepeyac, and then one more time to Juan Diego's uncle, Juan Bernardino. During colonial times, the image of Our Lady of Guadalupe became an extremely efficient instrument to evangelize. She resembled the Goddess Tonantzin—both had dark skin, and both represented a divine power.

On the morning of December 9, 1531, Juan Diego was on his way to Mass when he experienced the first apparition of Our Lady of Guadalupe. She spoke with Juan Diego in his native Náhuatl language (the language of the Aztec empire), and she identified herself as the Virgin Mary. She then asked that a

3.9 Juan Diego and Our Lady of Guadalupe
Juan Diego showing his *tilma*, with roses and the image of Our Lady of Guadalupe, to Fray Zumarraga. Photograph courtesy of Vanessa Bonilla-Hernandez.

church be built at that site in her honor. Juan Diego talked with Archbishop Fray Juan de Zumarraga and told him what had happened. The priest was compassionate, but initially he did not believe what Juan Diego had told him. However, Our Lady of Guadalupe, in subsequent apparitions, encouraged Juan Diego to keep on trying and to trust her, and she also informed Juan Diego that his uncle was recovering from an illness. She also told Juan Diego to not be discouraged, and she reassured him by stating, "Am I not here, who am your mother?" All this gave him strength to continue on with his duty. Then, following her instructions, he went up to the hill and collected flowers in his *tilma*.[15] These flowers were roses, like those grown in Castille, but foreign to Mexico. He then again visited Fray Zumarraga and showed him his *tilma*. In his *tilma*, there were not only the roses but also the beautiful image of Our Lady of Guadalupe. Fray Zumarraga wept at the sight and asked for forgiveness. He then took the *tilma* and laid it at the altar in his chapel. The Basilica de Guadalupe (today in a suburb of Mexico City) was built near the place of the apparitions. Photograph 3.9 shows a classic depiction of Juan Diego and Our Lady of Guadalupe at the Parroquia y Santuario de Nuestra Señora de Guadalupe.

The story of Juan Diego and Our Lady of Guadalupe, the joining of cultures, and the religious synchronism became synonymous with the Catholic faith and identity of Mexico. More than two hundred years later, during the independence era, Miguel Hidalgo, influenced by his Jesuit education, adopted the image of Our Lady of Guadalupe as the symbol of independence. After independence, Mexicans embraced their identity as a mestizo group. Our Lady of Guadalupe may have replaced Tonantzin in name, but Mexicans continue to adore the goddess. The religious traditions and festivals continue. Even today, during the first week of December, all across the country *matachines* dance in the streets on their way to church. Religious processions and festivities to celebrate Our Lady of Guadalupe are common in all parts of Mexico.

Día de los Muertos

Similar to the synchronism of European and indigenous beliefs in the story of Our Lady of Guadalupe, the celebrations of the Día de los Muertos (Day of the Dead), on November 1 and 2—the Feast of All Saints and the Feast of All Souls, respectively—is another example of the role of religion in Mexico. The basis for the Day of the Dead is the belief that death is a passage to another life, that we sometimes return to this life, and that we never actually leave those who loved us in this life. An excellent example of this belief is seen in many funeral celebrations in the southern part of Mexico. The celebrations are long lasting and include loud music. Relatives organize the events to honor their loved ones and to celebrate their passage to another life. It may be that non-Mexicans misinterpret this as macabre or as showing a lack of respect for the dead. In actuality, the intent is the exact opposite. Photograph 3.10 illustrates a Calavera Catrina, a female skeleton dressed elegantly, seen with other traditional depictions of skeletons, statues of Christ, a cross, and candles.

We also see the influence of religion in many other areas of Mexican life. For example, in the political arena, the first president of Mexico was José Miguel Ramón Adaucto Fernández y Félix. Truth be told, however, nobody knows him by that name,

3.10 A Traditional Day of the Dead *Catrina*
A Traditional *Catrina*, like those created by José Guadalupe Posada. Photograph courtesy of Mayra Nieto.

but rather by his religious name: Guadalupe Victoria. He chose this name to show followers his devotion to Our Lady of Guadalupe and to his sense of Victory.

As a final note about religion in Mexico, the balance between church and state has not always been without conflict. For example, the Cristero War (1926–29) was an anticlerical movement in Mexico. At the time, President Plutarco Elías Calles sought to eradicate the power of the Catholic Church and its affiliated organizations. These were times when the government suppressed religious celebrations, Mexicans were imprisoned for wearing religious items, and priests were forbidden to wear cleric robes in public. They were not allowed to express political opinions, not even in private conversations. Many Mexicans reacted to this oppressive time by taking up arms and shouting "Viva Cristo Rey [Long live Christ the King]!" The rebellion included more than 50,000 soldiers. After several years of fighting, the government made some concessions and the Catholic Church withdrew its support from the Cristero fighters, which brought the conflict to an end in 1929.

Indeed, each of the examples given above shows that religion plays a major role in the social organization of Mexico.

Our recommendation is that the more one learns to appreciate the historical development of religion in Mexico, the easier it becomes to see the relevance of holidays and traditions that professional, personal, and family life bring to its citizens.

LEISURE TIME

Another way to view social organization is to see what people do with their leisure time. This is the focus of the last section of this chapter. We begin with Mexican ferias, or town fairs and festivals. Mexico is famous for its town ferias—for example, the Mole Fair (La Feria del Mole) or the Craftwork Fair (La Feria de las Artesanías).[16] Perhaps the most famous of the ferias is La Feria de San Marcos, in Aguascalientes. Like many other fairs, here people buy handicrafts, embroidery, and other typical products of the region. Usually, each town organizes the fair to celebrate its patron saint, their *santo patrono*. In the case

3.11 Feria de San Marcos in Aguascalientes
A man looking from a balcony at the Feria de San Marcos in Aguascalientes.
Photograph courtesy of David A. Leith Ramirez.

of Aguascalientes, their patron is Saint Mark. The fair includes a playground, a merry-go-round, lottery, puppets, shows, and plenty of food and drinks. Some fairs last for several days or even several weeks. People love to spend time with their families at these fairs, and it is the perfect event at which to meet people from different social classes. Photograph 3.11 shows a man overlooking his balcony to the procession at the Feria de San Marcos in Aguascalientes that is going on in the streets below.

Charrería

The word *charro* comes from Andalucia and means "horse rider." When the Spaniards brought horses from the Old World, native people in Mexico were totally unfamiliar with them. They did not know how to ride horses or even how to take care of them. In fact, there were laws to designate who was permitted to keep horses. Over time, those laws changed, and the ability to ride horses flourished. The *charrería* started at the beginning of the sixteenth century in the *haciendas* (like a farm or ranch) in the Mexican states of Hidalgo and Estado de Mexico, and it then expanded from there. Initially, riders used military decorations

3.12 *Charrería* Competitions
A traditional *charrería* competition, which is practically the national sport of Mexico. Photograph courtesy of Paulina Guzman and Pasión Charra-Laura Patricia Fernández Garza.

called *charretas* to adorn the wardrobes of men in this region. As time went on, *charrería* became somewhat the national sport of Mexico. *Charros* need to demonstrate skills in nine events: *Cala de caballo* (reining), *Los piales* (heeling), *las colas* (tailing steers), *jineteo de novillos* (bull riding), *terna en el ruedo* (roping), *jineteo de yegua* (bareback riding), *manganas de caballo* (forefooting on horseback), *manganas a pie* (forefooting on foot), and *el paso de la muerte* (jumping from one horse to another). In addition, women participate in *escaramuzas* (skirmishes), highly choreographed sidesaddle riding competitions. Given that the equipment and upkeep of this sport are expensive, most *charros* come from those with financial means. Photograph 3.12 shows a picture of the *charrería*.

Mexican Cinema and Television

Between 1936 and 1959, Mexico experienced its Golden Age of cinema. Mexico produced movies that have become classics, and people enjoyed them for decades after they came out. In many ways, it is through these movies that Mexican culture was taken to the world. Through this internationalization, people beyond Mexico were exposed to Mexican songs and were introduced to such actors as Pedro Infante and María Félix. Photograph 3.13 shows a mural with classic images from Mexican cinema.

Television has also played an important role in the worldwide distribution of Mexican culture. Mexican television programs, especially soap operas, have been and continue to be exported to all parts of Latin America. One bit of interesting trivia: Color TV was invented by the Mexican Guillermo González Camarena. Beginning in the 1950s, television became one of the most influential forms or entertainment, and Mexico was no exception. It was also during this time when programs such as *El Chavo del 8*, and shows with such people as Jorge Negrete and Cantinflas, gained in popularity. *El Chavo del 8* was a situation comedy that took place in a small neighborhood, mixing commentary on social problems with lighthearted comedy. Jorge Negrete was famous for his amazing singing voice and for the dozens of movies in which he starred. Cantinflas, or Mario Moreno, was a

3.13 The Golden Age of Mexican Cinema
Mexico's Golden Age movies exposed the world to Mexican culture. Photograph courtesy of Vanessa Bonilla-Hernandez.

comic actor who was especially famous for his ability to play with language and his eloquent gift of gab. Photograph 3.14 provides a glimpse of these famous television stars, and photograph 3.15 shows figurines based on *El Chavo del 8*.

It was also in the 1950s and 1960s when a greater number of Mexican citizens started moving from rural areas to the larger cities. The urbanization in Mexico also implied an increased amount of time for leisure and entertainment. This transformed the structure of urban life. From 1940 to 2010, the population in Mexico grew from 19.7 million to 112.3 million people. From 1900 to 1940, urbanization in the country grew from 10.6 to 20.1 percent. Then, from 1940 to 1980, it increased again, to 51.8 percent. By 2010, the urban population in Mexico was already 62.5 percent. The pace of life in such places as Mexico City, Guadalajara, and Monterrey can be intense and full of stress. But life in the cities also implies that people have access to new restaurants, night clubs, and movies as well as time for entertainment—options that were less available in rural settings. It is not surprising to find that increased time with television and movies is part of urban dwellers' routine.

3.14 *Cantinflas* and Other Mexican Performers
The genius of Cantinflas and other Mexican performers. Photograph courtesy of Vanessa Bonilla-Hernandez.

3.15 Figurines Related to *El Chavo del 8*
The adventures and tribulations of the poor orphan boy El Chavo del 8. Photograph courtesy of Vanessa Bonilla-Hernandez.

Festivals

Seasonal festivals characterize another way that people interact with each other. We can divide festivals into three parts of the years. First, during the Christmas season, the Mexican *Posadas* are extremely popular. Las Posadas commemorate the difficulties that Joseph and Mary had before giving birth to the baby Jesus in Bethlehem. To celebrate Las Posadas, people get together with friends and family. As part of the celebration, the hosts of the party play the role of innkeepers in Bethlehem, those who deny Joseph and Mary a place to sleep. The guests play the roles of Mary and Joseph, singing songs in which they ask permission to stay. At the end of the song, everyone is welcomed as guests, and the festivities begin, with piñatas, tamales, chocolate, and fruit punch.[17]

It is also during the month of December that Mexicans celebrate what is called the "Guadalupe–Reyes Marathon." The marathon begins on December 12 with the celebration of Our Lady of Guadalupe, then continues with Las Posadas, Christmas Eve, Christmas Day, New Year's Eve, New Year's Day, and Three Kings' Day (The Epiphany). This series of celebrations is the perfect excuse to spend leisure time together with family and friends. Photograph 3.16 depicts the invited guests who arrive at the Posada and sing for entry into the house.

In addition to the events associated with the Guadalupe–Reyes Marathon, Mexicans enter into a second phase of festivities

3.16 People Singing in a *Posada*
Participants in a Posada carrying lit candles and singing Mexican Christmas carols. Photograph courtesy of Heriberto Bonilla Rios and Ma. Del Socorro Lopez de Bonilla.

3.17 A Mexican Carnaval
Dancing and partying in the colorful parade of Carnaval in Veracruz. Photograph courtesy of Jair Velasquez.

in the spring, beginning with Carnaval. The most famous celebration of Carnaval comes from Veracruz and Mazatlán. Initially, these celebrations had indigenous roots, including the parades with the wearing of ornaments and masks. Similar to most things in Mexico, these celebrations then merged with European traditions, adding to the syncretism with Catholic practices. Nine days before Ash Wednesday, the city of Veracruz becomes a paradise of colors, music, and parties. On the first day, people begin by burning away the bad mood; and on the last day, they bury Juan Carnaval. In Veracruz, *danzones* are always present (think a big band sound with a Latin beat), including artists, singers, and actors who participate in the celebration. Once again, Carnaval brings people together for celebrations, cultural and sports activities, and an excuse for family get-togethers. Photograph 3.17 shows the nighttime procession of the Carnaval in Veracruz.

A third time of year when national celebrations are held is in September. This begins on the night of September 15, with Independence Day and the famous *grito* "The Shout or Cry." The original *grito* of Mexican Independence occurred in 1810, which started a revolt against the Spaniards. The next day, Mexicans celebrate with parades, fireworks, parties, food, drinks, and flowers. It is also during this month that people decorate their cities with the three characteristic colors of Mexico—green, white, and red. Even if you speak limited or no Spanish, this is your opportunity to enthusiastically shout "Viva México" with everyone else in the crowd. Soon thereafter, we are back to the Día de los Muertos, and the cycle begins again.

Fútbol

We cannot end this chapter without at least mentioning one final essential part of Mexico's social organization: *fútbol*. Next to the devotion to Our Lady of Guadalupe and the pope, it is probably OK to say that next in passion is Mexico's love for soccer (or *fútbol*, as it is known in Mexico). Although soccer has its roots in Europe, already by 1902 tournaments were held in Mexico City. At that time, the teams had only foreign players and soccer was a sport reserved for the social elites. Today, however, it is for everyone, and the majority of the players on the professional teams are Mexican. When talking about Mexican soccer, we recommend that you learn the term *clásico*. The *clásico* is a game between two teams that are rivals. For example, the national *clásico* is a game between Chivas (from Guadalajara) and América (from Mexico City). There is also a *clásico* in the north between Rayados and Tigres (both from Monterrey). Our recommendation is that you take a side, and cheer as if you were really into it as well. Your Mexican friends will love you for it (or perhaps the opposite). (See photograph 3.18.)

3.18 *Fútbol*, Mexican Style
Goool! Mexican passions with intensity. Photo courtesy of Emilio Durazo Rocha.

The key to understanding and dealing with how Mexican society is put together is to be observant of what goes on around you. In this chapter, we have discussed the differences in how Mexico, the United States, and Canada perceive multiculturalism. Keep in mind that the foreign-born population of Mexico is very small. Many people in Mexico have relatively little experience in dealing with cultural differences between countries. Observe characteristics that differentiate one Mexican social group from another and adjust your behavior according to each subculture.

When doing business in Mexico, consider the regional differences. Keep an eye out for the development of manufacturing (mainly in the North) in those regions that are less developed but evolving. Observe also the variations in educational and vocational opportunities that people have. This is especially important when observing the role of women. Be aware of the responsibility for child care and what services are provided by companies that hire many women.

Observe how holidays and festivals are tied to religious beliefs, or at least religious origins. Enjoy the syncretism that resulted in today's celebrations. Our recommendation is to give value to those celebrations that are important to Mexicans, such as Mother's Day, Children's Day, and Our Lady of Guadalupe Day. The more one learns to appreciate the historical development of religion in Mexico, the easier it becomes to see the relevance of holidays and traditions, even for professional, personal, and family life among its citizens.

SOCIAL ORGANIZATION SUMMARY
AND CHAPTER 3 HIGHLIGHTS

Multiculturalism:

- Mexico, the US, and Canada differ in how they perceive multicultural development. For Mexico, it is *mestizaje*, for the US it is a melting pot, and for Canada it is a cultural mosaic.
- The Mexican concept of *mestizaje* reinforces the positive association of the blending of local cultures.

- Mexican culture has been strongly influenced by its indigenous groups and Spain. Even today, regional differences throughout Mexico are significant.

Mexican regional differences:

- States in the North of Mexico possess a higher level of mechanized agriculture, a higher GDP per capita, and higher levels of literacy but less of a presence of indigenous populations.
- States in the South have less mechanized agriculture, lower levels of literacy, more rural towns, and a larger indigenous population.
- Political power resides in the center states, and these are the ones where development happened more quickly.
- NAFTA benefited the northern and central states of Mexico more than those in the south.

The class system:

- Historically, the caste system put peninsular people with 100 percent Spanish blood at the top of the social scale; next, the Creoles represented whose who were born in the New World; then came the mestizos, who were children of European and indigenous groups; and at the lowest level were those born of pure of mixed indigenous and African blood.
- The caste system of the past gave way to the class system of today.
- Today, the best way to move up in the class system is through education.

Gender roles:

- In Mexico today, women are still the ones responsible for the domestic jobs and the care of children.
- Men constitute most of the labor force and are expected to provide for their families.

Family:

- The concept of family in Mexico encompasses a wide circle of relatives, including grandparents, uncles, aunts, cousins, grandchildren, and the like.
- Godparents, *compadres*, share in the honor of guardianship of children.

Important celebrations in Mexico:

- Mother's Day, May 10.
- Children's Day, April 30.
- Independence Day, September 15–16.
- The Day of the Dead, November 1–2.
- Our Lady of Guadalupe Day, December 12.

Leisure time activities:

- Mexican ferias and festivals.
- *Charrería.*
- Mexican cinema and television.
- Guadalupe–Reyes Marathon.
- Carnaval.
- *El Grito* "The Cry."
- *Fútbol.*

4

MEXICAN
Contexting

*The Hidden Wisdom
of the Proverb*

Chances are that we all know people who are master communicators. With minute changes in their speaking styles, they completely add new subtleties in meaning. It might be in the way they hint at something, a change in the pitch of their voice, or perhaps a way to soften a request or to show they are angry. The challenge, however, when dealing with someone in a completely new cultural environment, is that we do not always catch on to these subtle cues. This chapter focuses on these differences in style by using the concept of contexting—the "C" of the LESCANT approach. Edward Hall coined the term *contexting* to describe the cultural differences in how directly or indirectly people communicate.[1]

Hall set up a continuum from low context to high context. To reach meaning, Hall explained that we either communicate through reading "stored" information or "transmit" information through using words directly to explain what we mean. High-context communicators consider the setting of a message. For example, if a husband asks his wife, "Are you cold?" she might get up and turn on the heat, because she understands the implications of the question, assuming that her husband is cold. Low-context communicators simply consider only the actual words; they are, in other words, less inclined to assess the context. In such a case, the wife would simply respond, "No, I am not cold." If indeed the husband wants his wife to turn on the heat, he will need to specifically say so.

High-context communicators can communicate without even using words at all. In our example, the wife might move from a wooden chair to a specifically cushy chair near the heating vent. Her husband seeing this has "stored" information that this is what his wife often does when she is cold. The husband reads the stored information and, without asking, goes to the other room to turn up the heat. Even though the thermostat is out of sight, the wife knows that her husband has just "read" the unspoken message. When he comes back in the room, she may say, "thank you," even though no other words were spoken.

In general, Mexico ranks more within the high-context range of the continuum, with more indirect and implicit communication. The United States and Canada rank closer to the low-context range (with regional and ethnic group variation). Figure 4.1 shows Mexico and the United States along Hall's contexting scale.

The amount of stored information that Mexicans implicitly understand is considerably more than what those in the United States would typically be aware of (i.e., the area represented in white in figure 4.1). In turn, the amount of information that their

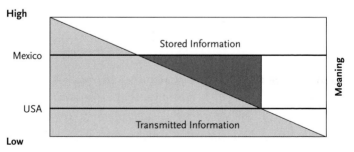

CHAPTER 4

Figure 4.1
Stored and Transmitted Information on High- and Low-Context Communication

US counterparts typically need to hear in actual spoken words is much greater than in Mexico (i.e., the area in gray in figure 4.1). The triangle in the middle of figure 4.1 represents the contexting gap between the two cultures, and it is a pretty big triangle. Above the top line, we see how much more Mexicans understand from stored information. Below the bottom line, we see how much more Americans expect a message to be overtly stated. When Americans do state things overtly, at least to a Mexican, it may come across as simply overstating the obvious or, worse yet, as being intentionally blunt and insulting. Conversely, when Americans do not actually hear the words, they may not get the message at all, because they were not told directly. From a US perspective, this Mexican reliance on stored information can come across as confusingly subtle. Worse yet, some Americans may misinterpret this indirection as being intentionally deceptive or even lying.

Hall actually described cultures as running along a continuum (rather than as an absolute either/or categorization). Thus, though Mexican communication is more highly contexted than the United States, we should keep in mind that several cultures are more high-contexted than Mexico or low-contexted than the United States or Canada. For our purposes, however, we are just going to talk about high-context and low-context as binary categories. Contexting always exists as a relative term. Mexicans seem high-context when compared with the United States; but Mexicans seem low-context when compared with, say, Japan.

WHY MEXICO IS CONSIDERED TO BE MORE HIGH-CONTEXT

High-context speakers use a holistic approach to communication, where the words are linked with context. It is for this reason that speakers may spend more time gathering initial information. In fact, direct and blunt messages are often seen as overstating the obvious, or even as face-threatening and unnecessary. In high-context cultures, the listener assumes much of the responsibility for understanding the real meaning of the message. In low-context cultures, the speaker takes on the responsibility to be absolutely clear in conveying the message, and this with specific details and unambiguous words, both written and spoken.

Let us draw from an example in an academic setting. When US and Canadian students from low-context cultures go to Mexico to study abroad, they often have different experiences from what they had expected. When the semester starts, North American students expect to receive a syllabus that has specific details about all assignments, due dates, requirements, grading procedures, and so on. Unlike their Mexican counterparts, these students also expect the professor to explicitly inform them of what is required during class sessions. The problem is that the professor, who comes from a more high-context orientation, fails to communicate any of these details explicitly. Because people from high-context cultures need to assess the environment, context, and situation, the specifics of many assignments can be finalized only after all these details can be assessed. There is more flexibility in how they will actually be carried out during the semester. This is not to say that the professor from the high-context culture is less organized, only that many details are finalized only after the situation has been taken into consideration. From a low-context point of view, North American students may feel that the Mexican professors are failing to communicate. From the Mexican professor's perspective, it seems that the North American students are being overly demanding about details. The same holds in the other direction. When Mexican students study abroad in the United States and Canada, they are often bewildered by the legalistic nature of the syllabus. The degree of details and the rigidity of the assignments, due dates, grading procedures, and other requirements seem unnecessarily impersonal and overly strict.

Our recommendation is that each side learn to understand the perspective of the other. Those from a low-context culture should realize that things will go unstated, and it is your job as the listener to take the hints. Those from a high-context culture should realize that blunt and direct communication is not rude, but simply focused on being informative.

One of the ways to appreciate the high-context communication style of Mexico is to look at some of the famous *dichos* (proverbs) that are sprinkled into everyday conversations. These *dichos* offer excellent insights into high-context communication styles. Let us look at a few representative examples.

Al buen entendedor pocas palabras

The popular Mexican saying *Al buen entendedor pocas palabras* (A word to the wise is sufficient) illustrates the idea of high-context communication style. This proverb explains that an intelligent person does not need a long explanation and can easily take a hint. The best way to become wise is to be a good listener, pay attention to the context, and gather information all around you. In Mexico, one cannot understand the meaning of messages without paying attention to the personal characteristics of the parties and the nature of the relationship. The physical environment and the type of event where communication takes place also matter. A word to the wise, be a good listener.

Mejor que digan que aquí corrió, que aquí murió

Keep in mind that Mexicans avoid direct confrontation. *Mejor que digan que aquí corrió, que aquí murió* is rendered in English with something like "It is better to say that he ran away from here than he died here." This proverb hints at the fact that Mexicans would rather keep some of their opinions to themselves, avoid offending others, and be cautious about saying the wrong thing. People think twice before challenging another person's statement, especially if that person holds a higher status. Notice that even the Spanish verb *discutir* carries a negative connotation that is much stronger than the typical English translation "to discuss." When people hear *discutir*, they immediately think that the conversation is going to be antagonist. Mexicans prefer to use softer words—such as *conversar, hablar,* and *platicar*—that mean something closer to "to talk." Similarly, in Mexico people accept that a compliment for doing well should be given in public, but a reprimand for doing wrong should be given in private. Again, it is important to avoid conflict. You will notice that Mexicans are careful to save face, maintain dignity, and promote harmony, and that this is especially true when interlocutors hold different hierarchical positions. We have witnessed numerous occasions when foreign managers in Mexico mistakenly think that punishing people in public will embarrass them enough to improve behavior. But quite the opposite happens; the shamed individual becomes a victim. A public reprimand does not resolve the problem, it only causes it to escalate.

The proverb *Mejor que digan que aquí corrió, que aquí murió* also implies that Mexicans are cautious to deliver a negative message. They prefer to give pleasant, respectful, and courteous responses, avoiding the confrontational ones. This style of indirect communication dramatically contrasts with the direct style of low-context communicators. However, from a Mexican perspective, directness is perceived as being almost rude or pushy. Courtesy is paramount.

Te digo Juan para que entiendas Pedro

Indirect communication includes messages sent to hidden receivers. The proverb *Te digo Juan para que entiendas Pedro* can be rendered in English as something like "I am telling you, Juan, so that Pedro understands." Mexican politicians often use this type of indirect communication when they give speeches, referring to one person, but sending the message to another. There is another similar proverb, *A quién le quede el saco que se lo ponga* (If the suit fits, wear it). Both proverbs emphasize this indirect style of communication, where the obvious does not need to be directly stated. In the corporate world, Mexican executives use these types of messages when they do not want to directly accuse someone of doing something wrong. Instead, they hint at the problematic behavior. If they want to stop the problematic behavior, they might say something like "Discrimination is not allowed in this company. Be aware, behave accordingly, and if the suit fits, wear it." Indirectly, the manager is acknowledging that there have indeed been discriminatory incidents in the company.

The culprits know the message was sent to them, even if they were not identified specifically. Nobody is overtly blamed by this message, and everyone saved face. When behavior in the company changes, indirect communication achieves its objective.

¿Te comieron la lengua los ratones?

The amusing proverb *¿Te comieron la lengua los ratones?* (Did the mice eat your tongue?) refers to the Mexican discomfort with silence. There is a certain irony that, in English, we hear the similar question, "Cat got your tongue?" The implication is that people wonder why another person does not talk. Remember that high-context communication implies the need for information, a need to understand the context of what is going on. This also means that good listeners need something to listen to. Silence may be a sign of trouble, which needs to be investigated.

Del plato a la boca, se puede caer la sopa

This proverb *Del plato a la boca, se puede caer la sopa* exemplifies the importance that Mexicans give to modesty. In English, this proverb translates as something like "On the way from the plate to your mouth, you might spill the soup." Things happen, so do not get cocky. There is a similar proverb, *Echarle mucha crema a los tacos* (Putting too much sour cream on your tacos). A person who exaggerates things to look good is putting excessive amounts of sour cream on his or her tacos. Mexicans use this phrase to show disbelief about what someone is saying. It can also apply to someone who is thought of as conceited. The implication of both proverbs is to be humble and modest, meaning that some things do not need to be directly stated. It is better to understate things. This goes counter to the low-context way of talking, where things must be explicitly identified. Thus, when communicating in Mexico, talk with modesty, *Ni tanto que queme al santo, ni tanto que no lo alumbre* (Not so much that you burn the saint, but enough to light him up).

The notion of modesty in Mexico relates to the strong link to religion and God's will. *Si Dios quiere* (God willing), is commonly added to many phrases. For example, when planning vacations,

4.1 *Tamal*
El que nace pa'tamal, del cielo le caen las hojas.

Mexicans may add *Si Dios quiere, el próximo mes viajaremos a Ciudad de México* (God willing, next month we will travel to Mexico City). If what happens to us is determined by God's will, then we should be humble enough to recognize His hand in what we accomplish. Note that many Mexican proverbs denote this idea:

- *El que nace pa'tamal, del cielo le caen las hojas* (The husks will fall from heaven for those born to be a tamale) (see photograph 4.1).
- *El que nace pa'maceta, del corredor no pasa* (He who is born to be a flowerpot will never go beyond the porch).
- *Lo que no es para ti, aunque te pongas. Lo que es para ti, aunque te quites* (If it's not meant for you, no way to make it happen. If it's meant for you, no way to run away from it).

THE HIGH-CONTEXT TENDENCY TO HINT AT THE DETAILS

Another characteristic of high-context communication is the tendency to hint at meanings and to allow the listener to understand the details. Rather than overtly state the obvious, speakers provide hints that suggest the meaning, allowing the listener to figure out the details.

The Mexican comedian Cantinflas often exclaims the well-known phrase *Ahí está el detalle* (That's where you find the details). Mexicans—at least relative to North Americans—are intuitive and learn how to read messages between lines. This indirect communication style is extremely convenient for Mexicans. It provides flexibility to the communicator, in case the situation changes later. For example, you will often hear a Mexican respond to a request with "Let's talk about it later." You may or may not talk about it later, but it leaves the door open for such a possibility. Truth be told, Mexicans are skeptical when it comes to planning for the future, as we see in the delightful proverb *El hombre propone, Dios dispone, llega el diablo y todo lo descompone* (Man proposes, God puts it into action, then along comes the devil and he spoils everything). Mexicans have learned that they do not have full control over events, and plans often change. One way to combat this is to avoid direct promises and instead hint at things with high-context, indirect communication.

These hidden messages also offer Mexicans comfort. For example, when Mexicans are invited to a party and they know that they will not be able to attend, chances are they will say something like "I don't know if I can make it, but I will try." Basically, the Mexicans who say this mean that they are not going to the party, but it would be too rude to bluntly say so. The Mexican counterpart understands that whoever says this will not attend the party. The low-context North American, however, literally thinks that the person is going to try to go to the party. Again, we see that high-context communicators keep the door open and avoid direct and blunt communication.

When listening to ambiguous responses like these, people in Mexico make an educated guess to decipher the message's real meaning. With so much practice on a daily basis, Mexicans have learned to manage with these hidden messages. We emphasize that in the Mexican mind, this is not done to lie or mislead others but simply not to commit or impose, just in case something happens. In the Mexican reality, something always happens, and one needs to be prepared. Thus, ambiguity pays off.

THE HIGH-CONTEXT TENDENCY
TO MAINTAIN DIGNITY AND SAVE FACE

It is not uncommon to see Mexicans celebrate with loud laughter, smiles on their faces, and boisterous music. Even if a person is sad on the inside, the tendency is to maintain a happy face. We have another *dicho* for this situation: *Al mal tiempo, buena cara* (In bad times, maintain a good face). High-context cultures emphasize the importance of preserving dignity and saving face, doing all they can to not shame others.

Another word of caution, to native speakers of English it may seem that *dignidad* and *respeto* are simply translated as "dignity" and "respect." However, in Spanish these words carry a strong connotation associated with self-worth, esteem, admiration, deference, and the like. It is similar to the East Asian concept of *face*. Recognize that an attack on a person's *dignidad* is a serious offense.

Traditional Mexicans songs offer excellent insights into this idea of intense emotions, despite the everyday difficulties around us. In fact, these songs give us the "context" to understand how Mexicans feel. For example, consider the well-known *corrido*, *Cielito Lindo*: *¡Ay! ¡Ay! ¡Ay! ¡Ay! Canta y no llores, porque cantando se alegran Cielito Lindo los corazones* (Ay! Ay! Ay! Ay! Sing and do not cry, because by singing Cielito Lindo, the heart becomes happy). This is more than just a song. It actually portrays an attitude, a way of thinking about life, that definitely influences the way Mexicans communicate with others. When you hear a Mexican sing *Cielito Lindo*, you will notice a level of passion and sadness in the *¡Ay! ¡Ay! ¡Ay! ¡Ay!* What a beautiful example of how Mexicans convert sadness into hope, when singing and laughing makes them feel happy. And by the way, they will not be singing with some timid, quiet voice either. On the contrary, everyone, absolutely everyone, will be shouting out at the top of their lungs with courage, determination, and happiness.

Mexicans have an ability to mock tragedy and death with humor and laughter. Talk about maintaining dignity—treat death with a humorist's attitude! We should emphasize that Mexicans do not actually laugh at death at a funeral; but consider what happens during the Day of the Dead celebrations. Part of the celebration during Day of the Dead is to write little rhymes to celebrate the death of your friends and loved ones. These *calaveritas*, "little skulls," are rhyming mock obituaries that make fun of people who already passed away or of people who are still alive (photograph 4.2). This playful tradition started in the nineteenth century in Mexico and had its origin in Europe. At the time, these funny poems appeared in newspapers. Today, Mexicans write these poems about others they know or about famous personalities. They do so to honor a person they love or to make fun of someone they hate. The *calaveritas* are written in metric verse and describe salient characteristics of the person or an event. Our Canadian coauthor recalls a time when he was invited to an international academic conference in Mexico City, which coincided with the celebration of the Day of the Dead. As the international guests arrived at the conference, there was a table set up with hundreds of personalized *calaveritas* for each of the conference attendees. Imagine the reaction of all the international guests as they searched through the *calaveritas* to find the one dedicated to them. Here is his *calaverita*:

Orlando mi amigo desde USA llegó,	My friend Orlando arrived from the USA,
pero luego viajó de nuevo porque la muerte lo llevó.	but soon he had to travel again because death took him away.

Humor can be like a weapon or a shield against misery. It is a way to disguise feelings. As an example of high-context communication, Mexicans appreciate the indirect way to convey pain, sadness, and frustration, converting them to laughter. The Mexican proverb *De broma, en broma, la verdad se asoma* tells us that "In every single joke, the truth can be seen." In April

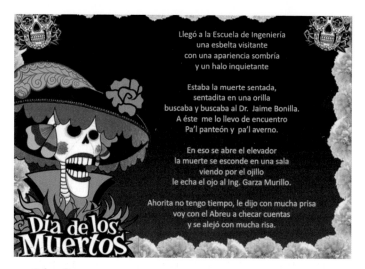

Llegó a la Escuela de Ingeniería
una esbelta visitante
con una apariencia sombría
y un halo inquietante

Estaba la muerte sentada,
sentadita en una orilla
buscaba y buscaba al Dr. Jaime Bonilla.
A éste me lo llevo de encuentro
Pa'l panteón y pa'l averno.

En eso se abre el elevador
la muerte se esconde en una sala
viendo por el ojillo
le echa el ojo al Ing. Garza Murillo.

Ahorita no tengo tiempo, le dijo con mucha prisa
voy con el Abreu a checar cuentas
y se alejó con mucha risa.

4.2 *Calaveritas*
Calaveritas, and little rhyming poems about death. Photograph courtesy of Elva O. Cavazos Espinoza.

2009 Mexico City experienced the devastating 5.7 magnitude earthquake and the H1N1 flu epidemic. What was the Mexican sarcastic reaction? *¿Qué le dijo México a la influenza? . . . ¡Ay sí! mira como tiemblo, mira como tiemblo!* (What did Mexico say to H1N1 . . . Oh sure! Look at me, I am trembling, I am trembling!) And be sure to add the appropriate sarcastic intonation to capture the impact of the hidden message, "We Mexicans are strong enough to overcome the H1N1 crisis!" Clearly, Mexicans were in pain at the time, but they needed to feel strong and united. Some people might think this joke was a disrespectful gesture to those suffering difficulties. However, for Mexicans the intent was to deal with the crisis, and humor brought people together.

A word of caution. Although humor is a common way for Mexicans to deal with life's challenges, jokes about Mexico made by foreigners are never well received. Mexicans get infuriated when foreign people joke about their country. Remember the importance of dignity in high-context cultures. Mexico has a long history of colonization and oppression, and there is a level of sensitivity regarding comments from outsiders that humiliates victims. Similarly, Mexicans do not relate to jokes about women who are dear to them (e.g., their mother, sister, wife, and the Virgin Mary). Our advice is to stay away from both these types of jokes.

The unbreakable principle here is that only Mexicans can mock Mexico. We recall the proverb *Sólo la cuchara sabe lo que hay al fondo de la olla* (Only the spoon knows what the pot keeps out of sight). Remember, only the one who lives the situation has the right to do something about it.

THE SUBTLE CONTEXT OF SPANISH-LANGUAGE DIMINUTIVES

In chapter 1, we presented a number of characteristics about Mexican Spanish. Let us add another one here. Mexicans frequently use diminutives in their speech, something that subtly changes the meaning. It is another high-context way for Mexicans to add indirect nuances to their communication. But caution should be used when trying to interpret the meaning behind diminutive forms of address. For example, when a Mexican mom says to her daughter *Hijita linda de mi vidita* (Little daughter of my little life), we see two diminutive forms, *hija-hijita* (daughter–little daughter) and *vida-vidita* (life–little life). In the first case, the purpose of using the diminutive is to show affection. Moms use the diminutive *hijita* independently of the daughter's age or size; it is endearing. Mexican daughters would never feel offended by the use of this diminutive, because all understand that it is a gesture of love. In the second case, the use of *vidita* can carry more of a sarcastic tone. It resembles more the sentiment of this poor, sorry, difficult little life of mine.

It is also true that diminutives in Spanish have Náhuatl corollaries. Náhuatl is an agglutinative language. In order to form words, one needs to add more words. Diminutives have many purposes for the Náhuatl-speaking indigenous group, the Mexicas (i.e., the Aztecs). For example, *tzin* is used in Náhuatl to show affection for a family member, and *ton* is utilized to show contempt for something. Today, in Mexico it is common to see a mix of Náhuatl words and grammatical rules with the Spanish language in a very original way.

Mexicans also use diminutives to soften command forms. For example, *hágase a un ladito* (i.e., *ladito* is the diminutive of aside) is the polite way to say "move aside." Likewise, *me pasas el salerito* (i.e., *salerito* is the diminutive of a salt bottle) is another polite way to say "pass the salt." This is courtesy taken to the extreme, but it fits within the mind-set of high-context communication.

Diminutives also help Mexicans mitigate the effect of unpleasant conversations. Such is the case when Mexicans talk about *malitos* (bad guys), using the diminutive of *malo* (bad). From the perspective of a American or a Canadian, it may seem strange to use a diminutive to describe criminals. They are bad people—and not just a little bad. However, for Mexicans, the use of the diminutive minimizes the negative effect of the conversation on those who listen. It is not intended to minimize the character of the bad guys. The mind-set is that the world is hard enough as it is, and if one adds a *poquito* of an "ito" (i.e., diminutive of *poco*, little), things seem less harsh. It can actually function as a psychological resource to reduce stress when talking or listening to unpleasant conversations.

Diminutives are also used to demonstrate compassion. For example, an expression like *pobrecito* (poor little thing) adds a sense of compassion to those that have had bad things happen to them. Mexicans may say it to show sympathy. (However, with a certain change in intonation, it can also sound sarcastic.)

And finally, the core meaning of diminutives is to refer to the size of something. However, even in this case, be aware of subtle changes in meaning. For example, when referring to the reduced cost of something, a Mexican may say *sólo unos pesitos* (i.e., *pesitos* is the diminutive of *pesos*) "only a few pesos." But again, this may not literally be a reduced price, but simply a term to use when haggling over the cost of an item. So be careful; it all depends on the context. For more Mexican sayings, see table 4.1.

RECOMMENDATIONS

The more we observe communication styles that exemplify low-context and high-context behaviors, the more we begin to

Table 4.1
The Use and Meaning of Mexican Sayings

Mexican Saying in Spanish	Mexican Saying in English	Meaning and Use
Ahí está el detalle	There it is where the detail is	To acknowledge someone found the contextual hint
El hombre propone, Dios dispone, llega el diablo y todo lo descompone	Man proposes, God decides, then comes the devil and spoils everything	To acknowledge that people do not have full control over events
Mejor que digan aquí corrió, que aquí murió	It is better to say here he ran away than here he died	To avoid challenging those with higher status or power
Te digo Juan para que entiendas Pedro	I tell you, Juan, so Pedro understands	To send a message to a hidden receiver
A quien le quede el saco que se lo ponga	Whoever the suit fits can wear it	To send a message to a hidden receiver
Al mal tiempo, buena cara	To bad times, good face	To cheer up someone
¿Te comieron la lengua los ratones?	Did mice eat your tongue?	To communicate discomfort with silence
Del plato a la boca se puede caer la sopa	The soup can fall from the plate to the mouth	To show modesty
Echarle mucha crema a los tacos	Put too much cream on the tacos	To prevent someone exaggerates or acts as conceited
De broma en broma la verdad se asoma	In every single joke, the truth can be seen	To communicate that jokes show the true
Chiquito pero picoso	Little but fiery	To communicate that in spite of size (or weakness), one can give hard time to the biggest one
Sólo la cuchara sabe lo que hay al fondo de la olla	Only the spoon knows what the pot puts out of sight	To communicate that only the one who lives the situation has the right to do something about it
Ni tanto que queme al santo, ni tanto que no lo alumbre	Not too much to burn the saint, nor too little not to light him	To practice moderation and modesty

Table 4.1 (cont'd)

Mexican Saying in Spanish	Mexican Saying in English	Meaning and Use
El que nace pa'tamal del cielo le caen las hojas	A person born to be a tamal from heaven the cornhusks fall to him	To show deference to predestination or God's will
Lo que no es para ti ... aunque te pongas y lo que es para ti ... aunque te quites	What is not meant for you ... not even if you do the line, and what is for you ... even if you run away from it	To show deference to predestination or God's will
Hágase un ladito	Move aside	To be polite
Me pasas el salerito	Pass the salt bottle	To be polite
Hijita linda de mi vidita	Little pretty daughter of my little life	To show affection (hijita) and to be sarcastic (vidita)
Malitos	Bad guys	To provide comfort when unpleasant conversations need to be told or listened
Poquito	Little	To reduce impact
Pobrecito	Poor guys	To show sympathy or use it in a sarcastic way (i.e., depending on context)
Pesitos	Few pesos	To haggle
Si Dios quiere	If God wants	To show deference to predestination or God's will
Gracias a Dios	Thanks to God	To show deference to predestination or God's will
Mande	Yes, what	To be polite when responding
Hablamos luego	Let us talk about it later	To leave the door open for possibilities
No sé si iré, pero trataré de ir	I don't know if I can make it, but I will try to go	To show appreciation

see significant differences between Mexican and US American and Canadian patterns. In this chapter, we have looked at everything from proverbs to *calaveritas* and from humor to diminutives. We have also mentioned how low-context communication focuses on what the speaker says and how high-context communication centers on what the listener picks up on.

If you find yourself identifying with low-context communication styles, we offer three recommendations when interacting to people who are more high-context oriented:

1. Become an active listener. Listen for the intent and not just to the actual words that are said. Be aware of pauses and of intonation. Think about what is not being said, and notice when people are trying to give a hint.
2. Do not focus exclusively on the literal meaning of the words, both written and spoken. You will appear overly aggressive and unreasonable if you oblige people to act on the exact words that they say. Things work both ways. Mexicans will try to avoid stating things too explicitly, but they will also provide hints to tons of details to give more context.
3. Play the low-context card. As a foreigner, there is an open door to ask lots of questions, ask for clarifications, request interpretations, and call for background information about everything that goes on around you.

If you find yourself identifying more with a high-context style of communication, we have three recommendations for you when dealing with people who are more low-context oriented:

1. Resist the urge to label the low-context speaker as rude or aggressive. There is almost something refreshing about not having to guess at what the speaker intends to communicate. Enjoy the direct, explicit communication style.
2. Help out the low-context speaker by providing written summary of your communication. Bullet-point summaries provide low-context communicators with a sense of the

most salient points. Use these types of lists and summaries to your advantage.

3. Realize that the strength of low-context speakers is not to read between the lines. Push yourself to express what you really mean, and do not assume that others will take the hint.

Whether you are more low-context or more high-context, when it comes to intercultural conversations it is important to actively listen. The more we consciously try to listen and try to understand, the greater the likelihood of a successful exchange.

CONTEXT SUMMARY AND CHAPTER 4 HIGHLIGHTS

Characteristics of high-context communication (typical of Mexico):

- Holistic approach.
- Words are linked with context.
- Listener assumes the main responsibility.
- Communicators rely on previous knowledge.
- Hidden cues are implicit.
- There is no need for explicit messages.
- Complies with social expectations and norms.

Characteristics of low-context communication (typical of the United States and Canada):

- Explicit verbal message, both in written and spoken forms.
- Speaker assumes the main responsibility.
- No assumption of preexisting knowledge.
- Message needs to be clear, logical, and persuasive.

Mexican proverbs:

- *Al buen entendedor pocas palabras*—A word to the wise is sufficient.
- *Mejor que digan que aquí corrió, que aquí murió*—It's better to say that he ran away from here than he died here.
- *Te digo Juan para que entiendas Pedro*—I'm telling you, Juan, so that Pedro understands.
- *A quién le quede el saco que se lo ponga*—If the suit fits, put it on to wear it.
- *¿Te comieron la lengua los ratones?*—Did the mice eat your tongue?
- *Del plato a la boca, se puede caer la sopa*—On the way from the plate to your mouth, you might spill the soup.
- *Echarle mucha crema a los tacos*—Putting too much sour cream on your tacos.

- *Ni tanto que queme al santo, ni tanto que no lo alumbre*—Not so much that you burn the saint, but enough to light him up.
- *El que nace pa'tamal, del cielo le caen las hojas*—The husks will fall from heaven for those born to be a tamale.
- *El que nace pa'maceta, del corredor no pasa*—He who is born to be a flowerpot will never go beyond the porch.
- *Lo que no es para ti, aunque te pongas. Lo que es para ti, aunque te quites*—If it's not meant for you, no way to make it happen. If it's meant for you, no way to run away from it.
- *El hombre propone, Dios dispone, llega el diablo y todo lo descompone*—Man proposes, God puts it into action, then along comes the devil and he spoils everything.
- *Al mal tiempo, buena cara*—In bad times, maintain a good face.
- *De broma, en broma, la verdad se asoma*—In every single joke, the truth can be seen.
- *Sólo la cuchara sabe lo que hay al fondo de la olla*—Only the spoon knows what the pot puts out of sight.

Other tendencies and characteristics of high-context communication:

- There is a tendency to hint at details.
- There is a tendency to maintain dignity and save face.
- Humor can be used to imply nuances that are not explicitly stated.
- Linguistic patterns, such as diminutives, provide subtle details to communication.
- The social context may be used to assess the appropriateness of certain speech patterns.

5

THE MEXICAN
Authority
Conception

Power Is Always Personalized

We now turn our attention to authority conception, the fifth category of the LESCANT approach. This topic deals with how we define power and authority, and how this differs in Mexico from the standards in the United States and Canada, particularly in the way power is shared or exchanged. This category also brings up issues of leadership style, how decisions are made, and how titles are used to show status. Finally, how people view authority and power is deeply embedded in culture, so we need to understand how authority and power are perceived among Mexicans in ways that differ from their northern neighbors.

THE SPHERES OF MEXICAN AUTHORITY

In this chapter we discuss authority in three spheres, each nested in the other, as shown in figure 5.1.

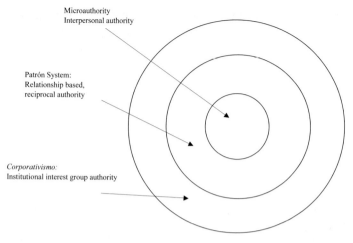

Microauthority
Interpersonal authority

Patrón System:
Relationship based,
reciprocal authority

Corporativismo:
Institutional interest group authority

Figure 5.1
Three Spheres of Mexican Authority

The innermost sphere in figure 5.1 is the interpersonal—or microlevel—sphere. Here, we look at the nature of authority on a microlevel as it plays out in Mexico relative to the United States and Canada. This microlevel explains the day-to-day way that authority affects how we communicate on a personal level.

The second sphere in figure 5.1 covers the realm of relationship-based reciprocal authority. This type of authority is highly personalized and depends on earned respect. Traditionally, authority in Mexican culture carries a sense of reciprocity based on the relationship built. This is not impersonal; those in power know you. In return for loyalty and respect, the person in power will look out for your well-being. Mexicans traditionally used the word *patrón* to describe the person in power in this personalized, reciprocal relationship. It is also a hierarchical network. Your *patrón* will usually show loyalty and respect to his or her own *patrón,* just as you are likely to be the *patrón* of someone lower than yourself. We are using the term "Patrón System" to describe the overall system of relationship-based reciprocal authority. As far as we know, Patrón System is a neologism (a word we just invented). We are using Patrón System, even though there already is a Spanish word for this: *patronismo.* We are intentionally using the combination Spanish/English phrase Patrón System to emphasize the positive meaning here and to avoid some of the negative connotations that the word *patronismo* carries. We explain later, in detail, some of the negative connotations of the word. The problem is that we have no better term—in English or Spanish—to describe this type of authority conception that actually is present on every level of Mexico. We will get to this later in the chapter, but for now we can think of the Patrón System as a Mexican mix of personalized networking, clientelism, and benevolent paternalism.

The third sphere in figure 5.1 covers what we call *corporativismo mexicano*. This is the uniquely Mexican version of corporatism, itself another highly nuanced concept, but for now we can think of this as the authority of the main institutionalized powers of Mexico as a whole. This is a sphere comprising the *patrones* of other *patrones*; thus, this third sphere of authority encompasses the other two and goes beyond. These are the leaders of business groups, labor and agricultural associations, educational experts and technocrats, and government leaders. These leaders work together—often under the surface—to find a consensus for governing the nation as a whole.

THE FIRST SPHERE: MEXICAN MICROLEVEL AUTHORITY

The interpersonal—or microlevel—of authority here is simply how and to whom we show respect, along with how we are expected to treat those above and below us in our own personal hierarchies.

Outward Respect for Authority

Generally speaking, Mexicans show considerably more outward respect for authority than do their northern neighbors. Much of this is on the surface level, but in terms of respect (as discussed in chapter 4), the surface matters a great deal when interacting with countries—such as Mexico—with a higher level of contexting.

In practice, Mexicans behave and speak more formally to their bosses, seniors, teachers, older people, public authorities, and any others viewed as being above them in the social hierarchy. For example, Mexicans, especially in public settings, may show respect through the use of honorific titles and the formal *usted* form in Spanish. They may refrain from interrupting or correcting those higher in the hierarchy. They may defer to the opinion of their bosses and in most respects avoid directly challenging authority. This formalized deference runs counter to US and Canadian tendencies to emphasize egalitarianism. Mexicans are often baffled by the grumblings of their North American counterparts. In the United States in particular, it is not uncommon to hear people claim "my boss is no better than me" or "I know better than my professors who are lost in their ivory towers." In Mexico, such things may be thought of, but those thoughts remain unstated.

We should note, however, that this deference to authority is *surface respect*. North Americans often mistake Mexican surface deference and respect for authority with submission or a lack of input. This is far from the truth. In fact, Mexican managers actively seek input and act on the consensus of their employees. North American egalitarianism is equally a *surface disregard* for authority. US and Canadian employees may call their bosses by their personal names, may correct their errors openly, and may even challenge them in meetings. But this deals only with the trappings of authority. What is interesting, however, is that those same US and Canadians are comfortable with—indeed even expect—their bosses to make the final decision.

Subordinates minimize the outward respect for authority in the United States and Canada while submitting readily to the individual decisions their bosses make. It is the boss or teacher or whoever is in authority who calls the shots; a consensus (if sought at all) is readily disregarded. In Mexico, the shots may on the surface appear to be the boss's call, but he or she generally does so only after securing—though *only informally*—a considerable consensus through networking under the surface. Subordinates emphasize the outward respect for authority while expecting that the decisions their bosses make will take into consideration the presumed consensus of the group as a whole.

Erin Meyer shares an interview conveying the frustration one Mexican manager felt in dealing with a society with little outward respect for authority:

I struggle with this every day. I will schedule a meeting in order to roll out a new process, and during the meeting my team starts challenging the process, taking the meeting in various unexpected directions, ignoring my process altogether and paying no attention to the fact that they work for me. Sometimes I just watch astounded. Where is the respect?

You guys know me. You know I am not a tyrant or dictator.... But in the culture where I was born and raised and have spent my entire life, we give more respect to someone senior to us. We show more deference to the person in charge.

Yes, you can say we are more hierarchical. And I don't know how to lead a team if my team does not treat me as their boss, but simply one of them. It is confusing for me, because the way they treat me makes me want to assert my authority more vigorously than I would ever want or need to do in Mexico. But I know that is exactly the wrong approach.[1]

The Effect of Class on Authority

In the last section, we said that Mexicans show outward respect to those they view as their superiors. When we listed examples of such people, we added the phrase "and any others viewed as being above them in the social hierarchy." This concept of "social hierarchy" is a touchy subject but one that represents a major difference between Mexico and its northern neighbors. Americans and Canadians are, generally speaking, very uncomfortable with visible class differences. Mexicans, if not particularly comfortable with overt class differences, are at least much more accepting of the reality of these differences.

Mexicans traditionally have accepted class differences as a fact of life. We have already discussed the duality of what Octavio Paz has called "the two Mexicos." Although Mexico has no equivalent to the formal British class system (and by extension that of Canada), Mexicans to a large extent show outward respect to the wealthy and powerful. In short, the richer or more connected that you are in Mexico, the more you can expect greater deference in how people treat you and how they speak to you.

We should, however, share that in the last decade, some have been challenging that respect. With the rapid growth of Mexico's middle class and with the influence of social media, deference for the elite is beginning to show some signs of change. This is especially the case with the entitlement expected from the children of the elite—known derisively in Mexico as the "Juniors." In 2013, *Nosotros los Nobles* ("We Are the Nobles") skewering Mexico's "Juniors" became the country's second-highest-grossing film of all time.[2] The abuses of the "Juniors" have received international attention—from the *Wall Street Journal*[3] to *The Economist*.[4]

Power Distance

"Power distance" is the term used to describe the degree to which people accept and expect differences in power within their societies. The Dutch researcher Geert Hofstede first coined the term in 1980, and he has conducted ongoing empirical studies of the relative power distance from one country to another.[5] Since then, numerous other studies have also looked at power distance.[6] In all, Mexico is shown to have a considerably higher power distance score than either the United States or Canada.

Although Mexicans consistently do have a greater degree of power distance than their US and Canadian counterparts in the broad terms of these studies, this does not mean that Mexican leaders are either more distant emotionally or that they lead in a more authoritarian manner with regard to receiving input from those below them. In fact, it is quite the opposite. One empirical study found six statistically significant personality differences between business leaders[7] from the United States and from southern Mexico.[8] After the data were corrected for relevant covariates (e.g., age, gender, and education level), the study found that "the Mexican leaders were significantly higher than their American counter-parts on warmth, emotional stability, social boldness, and openness to change. The Mexican leaders scored lower than the Americans on abstractedness and self-reliance."[9] Some of these terms merit a bit more explanation. For instance, Mexican leaders are measurably more "warm" than

US ones, but "warmth" is a culturally constructed norm. In other words, the US leaders probably do not view themselves as particularly "cooler" in personality in a general sense. It is only when US leaders would find themselves among Mexican leaders that they would be likely to see the contrast in their behavior. The same holds true in reverse. When Mexican leaders interact with their US counterparts, they would likely become aware of how much more attentive to others they seem relative to their US counterparts. The significance of the article by Ojeda and colleagues is that the study showed with data what many general studies of Mexico-US differences have claimed over the years.[10]

Authority and Corruption

Mexican authority conception is personalized at least in part due to the widespread level of corruption in the country as a whole. Many Mexicans presume corruption—or at least indifference—from authorities known only from a distance. By contrast, Mexicans generally feel a high degree of trust in authority for those in their own personal circles. Respect for authority in Mexico, in other words, is earned on an individual basis. To earn this respect, Mexican leaders need to interact with the groups that they lead. It is notable that Mexicans in the study by Ojeda and colleagues preferred more group orientation and affiliative, shared decision making than their US counterparts (who preferred solitary, self-reliant decision making). Notably, "warmth" was the personality scaled in the study where the data most greatly diverged between Mexican and US leaders' personalities. The impersonal decision making valued among US leaders is counterproductive in Mexico.

In Mexico, leaders who are cold are, with reason, distrusted. It may prove difficult for US and Canadian leaders to fully understand the cultural difference in the need for personalization. Cross-cultural preferences, however, are only part of why Mexicans respond best to personalized, "warm" leadership styles. The preference itself is intertwined with corruption.

The Berlin-based corruption-monitoring nongovernmental organization Transparency International (TI) scored Mexico 135th out of 180 countries. On TI's 2017 Corruption Perception

Index, Mexico scored a mere 29 out of a possible 100, by far the most corrupt nation belonging to the Organization for Economic Cooperation and Development.[11] Even in terms of its neighbors, Mexico is markedly more corrupt. In the whole of Latin America, Mexico tied with Paraguay, with only Guatemala, Nicaragua, and Venezuela ranking lower (and notably all three of these countries are undergoing significantly more social unrest than Mexico). Mexico fell well below even Cuba, Argentina, Brazil, and Bolivia, all Latin American countries often criticized for their corruption. By comparison, the United States ranked 16th, with a score of 75 out of 100; and Canada ranked 8th, with a score of 82 out of 100.[12]

Corruption is, in fact, so endemic in Mexico that the average citizen often expects little else from those in power. As Gabriel Zaid famously wrote in his book *La economica presidencial* back in 1986, *La corrupción no es una caracteristica desagradable del sistema politico mexicano: Es el sistema* ("Corruption is not a disagreeable characteristic of the Mexican political system: It is the system").[13] Far from improving in the thirty-plus years since Zaid made his often-cited observation, corruption in Mexico seems to have grown only worse. Rather, as Max Kaiser, of the Mexican Institute for Competitiveness, told the *New York Times* in 2017, "The decades of impunity have generated a level of audacity and absurdity that we have never seen in Mexico."[14]

This high level of corruption leads to the belief that you can trust your own web of connections but that others are corrupt. As Anabella Dávila and Andreas Hartmann put it, "Due to lack of proper institutions or the inability of the government to provide for the well-being of its citizens, companies have taken over a part of these responsibilities, if only for their own employees."[15]

THE SECOND SPHERE: THE *PATRÓN*, THE SPHERE OF RELATIONSHIP-BASED RECIPROCAL AUTHORITY

Mexicans run their lives through a deeply rooted system of interactions based on personal relationships, which are the basis of what we are calling Patrón System here. Power flows in two directions. This is called reciprocal power, and represents the middle sphere in figure 5.1. As Essabbar and colleagues eloquently explain, "Power is a reciprocal relationship between two actors.... No power is only unidirectional."[16] Reciprocal power is present in all societies, not just Mexico. That said, people in power in the United States and Canada rely considerably less on reciprocal power than their Mexican counterparts.

Reciprocal power is personalized in Mexico more than in the rest of North America. Mexican culture carries a sense that in return for your loyalty and respect, those in power will look out for your well-being. The relationship in the United States and Canada, by contrast, is largely impersonal. Mexicans leaders earn respect through personalization among those they lead. US and Canadian leaders practice an impersonal contractual exchange: You get what you agreed to receive in response for doing what you agree to do. The well-being in Mexico is more akin to that of a family (paternalism) than a quid pro quo exchange among what are (by Mexican standards at least) interchangeable job titles (i.e., strangers).

As mentioned above, the term *patronismo* is a heavily nuanced one, which is why we are using the Spanish/English term "Patrón System" in its place. *Patronismo* often has different meanings to different people. For many among the Mexican elite (as we explain below), *patronismo* is something that represents a past way of life or is present today only in rural settings. We explain this point of view in detail below. Other Mexicans blur the word *patrón* with that of the *cacique* or local strongman. But the two are very different.

Bearing this in mind, we are using Patrón System to describe the deeply personalized relationship network that is the positive side of *patronismo*. The Patrón System remains as a central (and actually quite positive) attribute of Mexican authority conception.

The Patrón System refers to the relationship where a person of influence—such as a boss, government bureaucrat, or personal mentor—has a variety of "clients" to whom he or she bestows favors. These favors are granted less in the form of material goods as much as in removing obstacles. The *patrón*, for example, can speed up the process of obtaining necessary permits or secure job interviews for others. In return, the clients give undiluted loyalty to the *patrón*, who then is in a stronger position to call on others to remove even more obstacles.

This form of authority conception is far from limited to Mexico. Indeed, it is widespread throughout almost all of Latin America and also in Italy, Greece, Cyprus, Portugal, Romania, Armenia, Haiti, Turkey, and most of the countries of the Arab world and Sub-Saharan Africa. Though the terminology used to describe this phenomenon differs from one place to another, the general concept of a patron–client connection affects family relationships, business, politics, and many aspects of day-to-day life.

In the English-speaking world, the word "patron" may carry a negative association, given such terms as "political patronage," which is a form of corruption. The English word "patron" in this context remains negative in a way that is absent from the Spanish equivalent word *patrón*. When a Mexican refers to someone as a *patrón*, the title carries only a positive connotation.

The reason that these words carry different meanings in the two languages is more than a matter of mere linguistics. There is simply no equivalent position to a *patrón* in US or Canadian culture. Because of this, the word does not translate to the same meaning when we refer to the relationship as "patron–client" in English versus *patrón–cliente* in Spanish. The closest thing English has would be in the art world, where someone might be considered a *"patron* of the arts," which actually *is* comparable to the Spanish term *patrón* because a "patron of the arts" carries little, if any, negative meaning. Some recent researchers writing in Spanish have begun to refer to the "patron" part of "patron–client" as *mediadores* (in English, brokers) to differentiate the sense of the English in describing the Patrón System.[17]

The Patrón System: *Patronismo* by Any Other Name

Up to now, we have explained that we are using Patrón System to explain a conception of authority that no longer has an acceptable name. At this point, we should explain why this is the case. For many in Mexico, the term *patronismo* is viewed as old-fashioned or outdated. This is particularly the view held by those who might describe themselves as more modern or cosmopolitan in their worldview.

There is also a geographic correlation to who accepts or argues against the influence of *patronismo*. In talking with people from the North of Mexico, many (perhaps most) people may at first deny that *patronismo* exists at all. For them, *patronismo* is often viewed as a thing of the past, or something that exists as a holdover in Mexico's less-developed areas (including, if pressed, the small towns of the North itself). The northern Mexicans are not alone in this denial. The business elites of the Valley of Mexico may argue that *patronismo* is something that—though admittedly present in the nation's governmental and political circles—is not something they themselves see as part of their lives. By contrast, in the Yucatán, in the South, and in the Western regions of the country, people are more likely to accept the term as uncontested.

The problem, however, is not with the concept of relationship-based reciprocal authority. Even the most urbane and worldly Mexican would likely accept that this sort of relationship, in its positive form, is a mainstay of their culture. Several scholars have attempted to describe the phenomenon of authority and earned loyalty without using the exact word *patronismo*. For example, Patricia Martinez discussed "Paternalism as a Positive Form of Leadership" (the term used in the title of her 2005 essay).[18] Over a decade later, the concept continues—without a name. Anabella Dávila and Andreas Hartmann, for example, refer to the "high degree of dependency on authority figures," which they call the "paternalistic-benevolent leadership," and which "fits well with the idiosyncrasy of the Mexican worker, who behaves as a subordinate expecting employment protection from the owner of the company or immediate superior in exchange for loyalty and compliance with instructions."[19] Therefore, in place of *patronismo*, we offer our solution, adopting the name Patrón System.

So what is going on here? Why did we need to invent this new term? At least two things may be at play. The first reason is regional. One possible reason why the term *patronismo* seems to have a geographic bias against its use could be connected to regional differences in development. At one time, *patronismo* referred primarily to the relationship on large agricultural estates (ranches, haciendas, and farms) between the workers and the estate owners (who, indeed, are still called *patrones* today). The owners of these ranches and farms treated their workers as a form of extended kinship or family tie. The *patrón* provided workers with more than simply wages and places to live. The relationship was highly personalized. The owners knew their workers individually, gave them advice on social and personal matters, shared celebrations together, and provided protection from the uncertainties of life outside the ranch (whether from questionable government officials or—especially in the northwestern states—the Mexican equivalent to the "wild west" of the frontier). As modern industry has supplanted the great ranches of Mexico's northern states, this may give the word *patrón* a sense of a bygone *vaquero* era in that part of the country more than in those parts of the country where such large farms still predominate.

A second (and probably more widespread) reason that some people deny the presence of *patronismo* may have more to do with the association of *patronismo* with corruption and boss machine politics. To a large extent, this sort of thing really is something of the past, especially among those classes and within those regions in which people most strongly deny that it exists. This does not, however, mean that the positive side of *patronismo*—the Patrón System—is equally something of the past. Moreover, in the less-developed areas where local government or political party bosses still do act as enforcers, they are more properly described as *caciques*, and the machine politics of which they are a part is called *caciquismo*. Below, we describe in detail the differences between *caciquismo* and *patronismo*.

Whether Mexicans choose to name it *patronismo* in Mérida or leave it unnamed in Monterrey, the Patrón System is very apparent to the US or Canadian visitor viewing Mexico from a foreigner's perspective. Mexicans run their lives through a deeply rooted system of interactions based on personal relationships, which are the basis of the Patrón System. This personalization of interactions woven into the fabric of everyday life in Mexico stands out to US and Canadian visitors precisely because it seems foreign even in social settings, let alone in workplace or government settings (apart from specific ethnic subgroups, that is). The Mexican concept of *jefe, director, executivo, licenciado, don/doña,* and, yes, *patrón* all suggest the personalized and interconnected sense of a protector, advocate, and relationship builder. Those who live in northern Mexico or those among some of Mexico's business elites may not accept that they have a *patrón* per se; but most Mexicans, wherever they live, would recognize that they are part of a web of intertwined and highly personalized loyalties. It is in this sense that we use the Patrón System in place of the word *patronismo* here.

How the Patrón System Works

The Patrón System's relationships act as a vast and complex system. Each *patrón* almost always depends on yet another *patrón* higher up. At the highest levels, the top *patrones* themselves interact with each other, forming alliances of favors given and owed as well. While *patrón*–client systems often include family ties (nepotism), the system reaches much farther than just one's relatives. Blood relatives are generally among the *patrón's* clients because a family relationship is assumed to guarantee loyalty. Nevertheless, in the *patrón*–client relationship, the *patrón* very often favors clients who are not related by blood. The Patrón System depends less on advancing one's own personal family than on those who owe loyalty. The end goal is in having the ability to smooth the way in getting things done. As a result, if a nonrelative is better able to accomplish a particular goal than a family member would be, the *coronel* will favor the nonrelative.

It bears repeating that in Mexico having (or being) a *patrón* is thought of as a good thing. In this sense, the Patrón System differs markedly from protectionist cronyism (*amiguismo* in Spanish). By contrast, most Mexicans condemn the Patrón System only when others use it, *but* (and this is a big but) the same system is good in the specific interaction of the individual Mexican with his or her own *patrón*. For most Mexicans, *amiguismo* is usually seen as a bad thing, even when you are practicing it yourself. Robert Kaufman was one of the first major observers (at least in English) of the positive side of what we are calling the Patrón System.[20] Kaufman noted that the *patrón*–client relationship is neither right nor wrong but only differently viewed across cultures. Kaufman explained that though the nature of this relationship changes often markedly from one society to another, where it does exist, three features characterize the system. The relationship is

1. between people of unequal power and status;
2. self-regulating and dependent on both patron and client reciprocally playing their part (and which ends if the favor owed is not honored); and
3. based on individual ties and relationships (particularistic) and private (rather than based on governmental laws or regulation).

Again, these three features describe fairly well how most Mexicans relate to the Patrón System. Note again that these definitions, as related to Mexico (or indeed most of Latin America), dissociate any negative or corrupt connotations. We emphasize here that the Patrón System is not the same as cronyism, although the two can be intertwined. Cronyism is the appointment of friends and relatives to positions of authority without regard for their qualifications. Unlike the Patrón System, cronyism has no reciprocal bonds and the recipient is not expected to perform well, if at all. Cronyism (*amiguismo* in Spanish) certainly does exist in Mexico. But cronyism is something separate from the Patrón System. In fact, many Mexicans view the Patrón System (reframed as "modern Mexican participatory management") as being in many ways the *antidote* of the poison of corruption.

Within a closed system among those you know well, you build up personal trust. Where there is personalization of trust, in which people feel that those above them have their best interests in mind, corruption falls by the wayside. Corruption is what happens when you deal with people you do *not* know well.

Knowing that to the Mexican the Patrón System is not associated with corruption, we also see better how it comes into play in a society where the rule of law and governmental oversight are unreliably administered over very long periods. The Patrón System enables people to get things done when they would not otherwise be able to do so. In a country where bribery and corruption are widespread, the Patrón System is actually a form of protection. Because the *patrón*–client system is by nature particularistic, the *patrón* ensures a hearing for those whose voices would otherwise not be heard. In this instance, many Mexicans view the *patrón* as their guarantor, a trusted framework against marauding elites and government bureaucrats.

All this is to say that though a *patrón* may not play a significant role in the United States or Canada, where most people see this personalized network as biased and unfair, this is not the case in Mexico. Our challenge is twofold. First, Mexicans relate to the Patrón System but do not always relate to the actual terminology. That is to say, they participate in it, but they do not attach any terminology—including the word *patronismo*—to it. Second, though people in the Spanish-speaking world have two variants of the general relationship (the negative *amiguismo* and the positive Patrón System), people in the English-speaking world generally have no real notion of how the system works, precisely because they have nothing comparable to it in their own culture. Thus, they frequently default to condemning the Patrón System as corrupt. We recommend that you recognize that in Mexico this framework works—at least on an individual basis—and that it is effective and efficient. When working with Mexicans, you will experience their efforts to put you in contact with people who can open doors and remove obstacles.

The Patrón System versus *Caciquismo*

Here we need to clarify one more set of related terms: the Patrón System and *caciquismo*. *Caciquismo* is the rule by local strongmen—*caciques*—for political parties In this regard, *caciquismo* is similar to what was called "boss machine politics" in the United States.[21]

It is easy to confuse *caciques* and *patrones* because both use their influence to provide assistance to their clients. There is a big difference, however; where the *patrón* acts as a benefactor, the *cacique* acts as the local party or government enforcer. *Patrones* build the loyalty of those they serve through earned respect. *Caciques* maintain their base primarily through fear.

Because most everyone views *caciquismo* as something negative, *caciques* often call themselves *patrones*; but they are not. All this has done is taint the word *patronismo*. Many Mexicans (especially those in rural areas) use the words *patrón* and *cacique* interchangeably. Even many among the Mexican elite confuse the negative *caciquismo* and the positive *patronismo*. When people among the business and elite classes of the advanced economic areas of Mexico City, Guadalajara, Monterrey, or the other magnet cities assert that *patronismo* is a thing of the past, they most likely are actually referring to *caciquismo*. And for them, this would be true. In fact, that is *why* we are using the term "Patrón System" here.

What is important to understand here, however, is that beyond the use of influence, authority conception in the Patrón System is almost the exact opposite of authority conception in *caciquismo*.

There is a big difference in how people feel about *patrones* versus *caciques*. People have an entirely different relationship between the *patrón* or *cacique* and those who owe them allegiance. People view their *patrón* positively. The *patrón* builds a relationship based on trust. In other words, you see your *patrón* as being on your side, providing assistance or help when you or your family needs it. In return, you pay this back with your unwavering loyalty and respect. People view *caciques* negatively. The *cacique* forces you to do what he or she wants. The "favors" he or she provides are often more in line with protection from harm (often harm that they themselves create), requiring those under their "protection" to pay protection money. Many (if not most) *caciques* accompany their loyalty with threats of (or actual) violence. As a result, as James Cockcroft explains, "Not surprisingly, most Mexicans today reject or resent their local or regional *caciques*."[22]

In the typical Patrón System, *patrones* have their own power base drawn from any number of sources. When *patrones* help you, it is because they choose to do so from their own resources, and by doing so they earn your respect and gratefulness. *Caciques*, by contrast, draw their power almost entirely from one source: political party backing. Because *caciques* have no power of their own, people view them as puppets of those above them. The *cacique*'s power rests on his or her ability to ensure (or enforce) loyalty to a political party. This has little to do with you personally, and is often not something that benefits you at all, because the party's policies are often against the interests of the less-developed or indigenous regions they control.

At this point, we should point out that it would have been simpler here just to have ignored the subject of *caciquismo*. After all, the continuing presence of *caciques* is an embarrassment to many (perhaps most) of the Mexicans readers of this book.

As elsewhere in this book, however, we are dealing with the duality, as previously mentioned, of what Octavio Paz has called "the two Mexicos." In the educated and prosperous world of the Mexican elite, it is easy to ignore the influence of *caciquismo*. For them, the subject, if addressed at all, should remain on the academic level.[23] At the same time—for rather obvious reasons—Mexican government officials and political party leaders downplay *caciquismo*.

And it is true that for the developed-world Mexico of the educated, prosperous, and the elite, *caciquismo* essentially does not exist. For that other Mexico, however, the Mexico made up of people who are economically struggling or for those who live in the country's rural or heavily indigenous regions, *caciquismo* remains a force to be reckoned with.

It would be simple to dismiss *caciquismo* as something unimportant or, at least, something that Canadian and US visitors would be unlikely to encounter when working with the Mexican elite in the country's most-developed regions. We agree that, though somewhat callous, this would be true most of the time.

The problem is that the two Mexicos are not really all that separate. First, the *caciques* occasionally do cross over into the "developed Mexico." For example, *caciquismo* received international attention in 2011 when in Guadalajara (clearly the "developed Mexico"), local *caciques* murdered five food vendors who had complained about paying extortion money to sell their goods near government-owned high schools. Public Radio International titled its story "Caciques, Not Cartels, Kill in Mexico This Time."[24] Likewise, *caciquismo* also remains widespread (if less publicized) elsewhere in the urban and highly developed areas of Mexico, as suggested by Ismael Solís Sánchez's 2016 study of *caciquismo urbano* (urban *caciquismo*) in Estado de México.[25]

THE THIRD SPHERE: CORPORATISM AND MEXICAN AUTHORITY CONCEPTION

The outer sphere shown in figure 5.1 is corporatism, the institutionalized interest group of authority.[26] Corporatism takes many forms. In each society where it is present, corporatism seems to take on characteristics that are unique to that nation. *Corporativismo mexicano*—Mexican corporatism—is distinct from that of other places, as one might expect.

We can roughly define corporatism as rule by interest groups.[27] These interest groups together (corporately) share nearly absolute power within their own functional area. The central concept behind corporatism is that a country recognizes its main interest groups, then gives them the authority to work out any conflicts they have through a consensus. Through ongoing negotiations, these interest groups jointly rule the country. In other words, corporatism is consensus rule by organized interest groups. Corporatism serves as "a mechanism for controlling change and keeping interest groups in line."[28] Corporatism's main interest groups include government leaders, various elite families, employer associations, trade associations, and labor groups.

Understanding *Corporativismo Mexicano*

How corporatism evolves in each country differs; but for our purposes, we focus on how corporatism functions in Mexico. For this reason, we use the Spanish phrase *corporativismo mexicano* to keep it separate from other countries' types of corporatism.

In the Mexican version of corporatism—*corporativismo mexicano*—those in authority share power. The key interest served in this power sharing are Mexico's elected leaders, institutionalized bureaucracy, key elite families and business groups, and leaders of labor and agricultural associations. Mexico's northern neighbors often criticize this as unrepresentative. It is not. Each key group has a say for its constituents. This type of representation just is not the same as the US and Canadian one-person, one-vote.

There is, however, accountability in *corporativismo mexicano*. No interest group leader is beyond the reach of control, because each of the key groups in Mexico holds power conditionally dependent on the support of its own members. In *corporativismo mexicano*, business leaders remain in power not by inherited position but only through maintaining the success of their economic interests. Key families hold power only as long as they succeed in their functional area (e.g., the economic success of their enterprises). When new businesses flourish, they too have a say. Mexico's president serves for only one term, and politicians do not inherit office.[29] Labor and agricultural association leaders too must be able to show that they are helping their members.

Finally, there is an understanding that a balance of power must be maintained to keep order in the country. The key groups are expected to personalize and nurture relationships not only among one another but also between those ruling and the ruled. Unlike the mechanistic system of power so common in the US and Canadian models of leadership and control, *corporativismo mexicano* requires a humanistic approach. Power is *personalized*, deriving from the nurturing of individualized relationships.

We can argue that the US and Canadian model of the ideal business or organization is that of a smoothly running machine. By contrast, the Mexican model of the ideal business organization is that of a family, with all its idiosyncrasies, exceptions, and messiness, but also—and this is the key distinction—with caring and even love.

If you are like most US or Canadian readers, that word "love" should seem out of place, especially in a business context. Love is not that far a stretch, however, if we keep in mind that Pope Leo XIII specifically developed corporatism as requiring personalization. The pope viewed corporatism as a counterbalance to the impersonal nature of either revolutionary and Marxist movements or profit-maximizing capitalism. Where both of these economic systems view individuals more as cogs in a greater plan or collateral damage in the growth of material success, corporatism has from its beginning addressed the individual needs of the people involved. In corporatism, those key groups ceded this power are expected to ensure the well-being and *personalization* of those over whom they hold that power.

In short, the relationship between the ruler and the ruled is based on the family or Church model of benevolent paternalism. If you think that "benevolent paternalism" sounds a lot like the Patrón System, you are right. It is just the Patrón System raised to the next level.

The Special Hold of Corporatism in Mexico

Corporativismo mexicano has its own characteristics that differentiate it both from *how* corporatism is practiced in other nations and also *why* corporatism in Mexico is so widely embraced as a positive force.

First, Mexico is a heavily Roman Catholic country, and corporatism has its origin in a papal encyclical. This fact gives corporatism—not only in Mexico but also throughout the Roman Catholic world—an aspect of moral and religious duty. In this sense, corporatism has a stronger hold in Mexico than do most other nations' business and political systems.

Second, and probably more important, corporatism came at just the right moment for Mexico. For Mexicans, corporatism was a compromise solving an otherwise unsolvable dilemma. The result was a uniquely *corporativismo mexicano*.

That unsolvable dilemma was the rift between the secular revolutionary liberal camp and the religious capitalist conservative camp. This led to the culture wars first of law (La Reforma) and then open fighting (the Reform Wars and the French Invasion). The very fiber of society seemed to have frayed to the breaking point. The fighting stopped only temporarily under the dictatorship of Porfirio Díaz, but the underlying divisions never went away, and the same issues burst into war again following the 1910 Mexican Revolution.

This time, however, the two sides had a tailor-made compromise solution: corporatism. Based on the pope's *Rerum Novum*, the compromise system allowed the elite, the state, and the

Church to continue in power on condition that they would help the poor and the needy by sharing power with labor and agricultural leaders. The result was *corporativismo mexicano,* Mexico's unique version of corporatism.

Corporativismo Mexicano as the Price for Peace

Corporativismo mexicano allowed stability. Although neither side in the culture wars got exactly what it wanted, Mexicans embraced the compromise system wholeheartedly. The suffering that the culture wars had wrought remained deeply embedded in the Mexican psyche.

Corporativismo mexicano to this day remains a continuing solution to the same issues that had led to the Reform Wars in the first place. Key families and business elites still see themselves as best able to make Mexico prosper, but the country's labor and agricultural organizations have a seat at the table of that decision making (with no less than the papal requirement of such). Where US and Canadian onlookers may see a problem, Mexicans recognize (or more accurately *deeply feel*) a solution in *corporativismo mexicano* to a deeply rooted problem that would resurface without it.

Misunderstanding *Corporativismo Mexicano*

Now that we understand what *corporativismo mexicano* is, let us take a look at what it is not—and why, as a concept, it is hard for so many North Americans to grasp. Corporatism—either in its Mexican or any other national form—is very difficult for those in Canada or the United States to understand, let alone accept. A big part of the problem is that neither Canada nor the United States has anything similar to corporatism.

On one hand, *corporativismo mexicano* has at its core the acceptance of rule through the compromise of interest groups. On the other hand, both the United States and Canada profess disdain for the influence of interest groups. Conceding power to special interests undercuts the concept of individual pluralism, which is so central to both countries' self-definition. Because the two systems are incompatible, the US and Canadian response has simplistically been to label *corporativismo mexicano* as corrupt.

To appear more acceptable to its northern neighbors, Mexicans have put in place formal rules of US-style democracy. These rules may appear similar to those of its northern neighbors, but this is only on the surface. As Grayson explains, "Relying on nominal written and rhetorical descriptions of Mexico's politics today will blind observers to the underlying distribution of power. While differences between the Mexican and US political systems have narrowed of late, especially through the adoption of the North American Free Trade Agreement . . . and other external influences, a huge gulf continues to separate the two systems."[30]

The illusion that the Mexican system matches the norms of the rest of North America is a dangerous one if we read only what appears on the surface. The US and Canadian political systems rely on democratic pluralism, in which differing groups fight it out to set the course for their country. *Corporativismo mexicano* relies on a negotiated consensus, in which the conflict among the key groups is not on the surface. When this surface does not match the reality, Mexico's northern neighbors cry foul. If you recognize echoes of differences in contexting, you are right.

American Projections onto Mexico and the "End" of Corporatism

For most Americans, views of Mexico as an equal partner replaced the overt racism of pre-1970s US governmental and business policy with a preconception (even a delusion) that Mexicans were becoming more and more "Americanized." This desire for Americans to see Mexicans as becoming—or even wanting to become—"Americanized" raises a very old and deeply ingrained pattern in US thinking toward Mexico. Little has changed.

This intractable desire somehow to "Americanize" Mexico often complicates the understanding of *corporativismo mexicano* for what it is (and, for that matter, what it is not). Americans in particular have a long and sad history in Mexico of looking down on the Mexican way of doing things, or, worse still, of imagining that they see their own value systems taking root in Mexico. As Mexico's Nobel laureate Octavio Paz famously put it in his *Labyrinth of Solitude* (1950), "In general, Americans have not looked for Mexico in Mexico; they have looked for their obsessions, enthusiasms, phobias, hopes, interests—and these are what they have found. In short, the history of our relationship is the history of a mutual and stubborn deceit."[31] This has not changed.

On June 16, 1865, the *New York Times* published an article titled "Can Mexico Be Americanized?"[32] Jump forward 144 years, to 2009, and we find that seemingly little has changed. "The Americanization of Modern Mexico" was the subtitle of *Newsweek*'s former Mexico City bureau chief Joseph Contreras's best-selling book *In the Shadow of the Giant*.[33]

The result has been an ongoing series of claims in the United States that Mexico's corporatism has died or is at least coming to an end.[34] The point is that recognizing the effectiveness of *corporativismo mexicano* is necessary for accepting Mexico for what it is rather than what Americans imagine it to be.

We are not saying here that *corporativismo mexicano* has remained unchanged at all. The Mexican version of corporatism has evolved to accommodate a host of factors—among which, clearly, are Mexico's joining the North American Free Trade Agreement, the influx of foreign direct investment, and the more open democratic institutions that allowed for the fall of the Partido Revolucionario Institucional (Institutional Revolutionary Party) after seventy-one years with the subsequent election of the National Action Party's (Partido Acción Nacional) Vicente Fox in 2000 and the Party of the Democratic Revolution's (Partido de la Revolución Democrática) Andrés Manuel López Obrador in 2018. Rather than being "Americanized" somehow, it seems just as likely that Mexico will "Mexicanize" these foreign influences. But this not a zero-sum game. As James Samstad explains, "The relationship between democracy and corporatism is far from simple; ... it cannot be assumed that one merely replaces the other over time. Indeed, the relationship between democratization and corporatist change can be reciprocal: not only can democratization reshape corporatist practice, but changes in corporatist structures can have a critical impact on democratic consolidation."[35]

One well-founded criticism of corporatism is that some who have embraced it—Mussolini's fascist Italy is the worst case—did so in very bad ways. In many others, the result has been positive. In short, corporatism takes on uniquely national characteristics in many of the countries where it has taken hold.[36] That is why we have specifically used the term *corporativismo mexicano* rather than corporatism alone.

That said, corporatism as it has played out in Mexico is generally viewed as something positive in general.[37] In short, those who criticize *corporativismo mexicano* do not do so due to associations with fascist Italy or the like. Rather, the main criticism of *corporativismo mexicano* comes from those (including quite a few US-educated Mexicans themselves[38]) desiring that Mexico be more like its northern neighbors; *corporativismo mexicano* muddies the waters of transparency needed to clean up corruption, makes power and authority overly dependent on relationships, and makes democratic pluralism (e.g., the US and Canadian model of government) seem unreachable.

In short, the critics of *corporativismo mexicano*, as viewed from a North American concept, argue only that it makes Mexico, well, too Mexican. We are all right with that. We urge you to be too.

TYING IT ALL TOGETHER: MEXICAN PERSONALIZATION OF AUTHORITY

We have now discussed Mexican authority conception in three ever-larger concentric spheres: the day-to-day level of interpersonal authority, the relationship-based reciprocal authority level of the Patrón System, and the uniquely Mexican version of consensus rule by key groups of *corporativismo mexicano*. What ties all these together is the personalization of authority.

In Mexico, what matters is the interaction between people. Indeed, all three of these spheres of authority have proven to be remarkably resilient, even in the age of globalization with the influence of US business practices. Some antiglobalization critics have argued that globalization results (to use Fredric Jameson's often-cited term) in the "Americanization" of those nations involved.[39] If any nation were to be "Americanized" as a result of globalization, Mexico, by mere proximity to the United States, would logically be the most likely to have felt that effect. Mexico is, however, in its own right, a global economic power and one of only fifteen nations (at the time of this writing) to exceed $1 trillion in nominal gross domestic product. Mexico has more free trade agreements than any other nation in the world. If globalization meant "Americanization," then it would stand to reason that the Mexican personalization of authority would have disappeared.

Instead, Mexican values have changed to adapt to global situations on the surface, but the essential nature of the nation's authority conception remains firmly entrenched with the humanistic personalization that characterizes the Patrón System in its most positive sense. In closing, it is worth noting here what the Mexican journalist Carlos Monsiváis has said: "We are still Mexicans, and proudly so, . . . but a different kind of Mexican."[40] For Monsiváis, the essence of Mexicanidad (Mexican-ness) is in what he called "cultural creation."[41] We suggest that the means for achieving this cultural creativity is this very ability of people to interact with one another on a *personalized* level as they grow together.

RECOMMENDATIONS

Given the issues related to authority in communication, we offer these three recommendations related to how people from the United States and Canada approach their interactions with Mexicans.

First, personalize your approach. Mexicans' authority derives from personalized relationships. US and Canadian counterparts are used to more impersonal interactions, especially in the workplace. Getting to know someone is not separate from the job— it *is* the job.

Second, rely on who you know. In the United States and Canada, people often complain about situations in which influence is involved. That complaint takes the form of the expression: "It's not *what* you know but *who* you know!" In Mexico, this makes little sense. Of course it is *who* you know as much as *what* you know. The two are in equal balance—or even a bit more tipped toward the *who* over the *what*. If authority conception relies on personalization, relying only on the *what* creates a damaging distance.

And third, *remember that personal networks are not innately corrupt.* Mexico has, as we have seen, a long way to go in terms of corruption. Ironically, the confusion regarding the nature of *patronismo* has led many from the United States and Canada to mistake corruption, cronyism, and *caciquismo* with the very system that insulates average Mexicans from the corruption surrounding them. Personalized ties between client and the *patrón* (or, if you prefer the term, benevolent paternalistic manager or authority) are the oil that keeps the machinery of Mexican authority relations running.

AUTHORITY SUMMARY AND CHAPTER 5 HIGHLIGHTS

Three spheres of Mexican authority:

- Microlevel: communication on a personal level.
- Relationship-based reciprocal: *patrón*.
- *Corporativismo Mexicano*: institutionalized powers.

Sphere 1—Mexican microlevel authority:

- Outward respect for authority.
- Surface level.
- Respect shown based on social hierarchy and class distinctions.
- Power distance.
- Strategy to combat corruption.

Sphere 2—The *Patrón*:

- Relationship-based reciprocal power.
- Rejection of old term *patronismo*, with negative connotations of corruption and boss machine politics.
- Rejection of term *cacique*, with negative connotations of local strongman.
- Adoption of term "Patrón System" to focus on positive connotations—
  - People of unequal power.
  - Self-regulating.
  - Individual ties and relationships.

Sphere 3: Corporatism and the Mexican concept of authority:

- Institutionalized interest group of authority.
- Corporatism, from the Latin *corpora*, meaning bodies, or special-interest bodies.
- *Corporatismo Mexicano*—
  - Share power between government leaders and key groups.
  - Govern under unwritten conditional social contract.
  - Personalize and nurture relationships.
- Interest groups together share a near-absolute power.

Recommendations:

- Personalize your approach.
- Rely on who you know.
- Recognize that personal networks are not innately corrupt.

6

MEXICAN
Nonverbal Communication

*Colorful, Bold, and
Making a Statement!*

Intercultural relationships rely on adequate verbal and nonverbal communication—the "N" of the LESCANT approach. In this chapter, we review nonverbal communication in Mexico as it contrasts to the most common norms in the United States and Canada. Even this statement merits explanation. As we discussed in chapter 3, Mexico is a much more homogeneous society than either of its neighbors to the north. Because nonverbal norms are tied deeply to culture, numerous studies have shown that these norms differ markedly by ethnic group within the United States and Canada.[1]

We refer to a wide range of topics, including how people show emotions (affect display) and facial gestures. We also address Mexican communication patterns that include how we use our eyes and how we touch as well as how close we stand or sit together. Nonverbal communication also includes customs related to dress and appearance as well as the way that Mexicans respond to color, signs, and symbols around them.

One of the challenges in discussing nonverbal behavior is that most of it is done unconsciously. Unlike many of the concepts discussed in other chapters, Mexicans are often unaware of their own patterns of nonverbal communication. Still, because Mexicans are high-context communicators, they have much experience interpreting others' messages. Those who are not familiar with the meaning behind these nonverbal signals in Mexico can easily become confused or misinterpret the ideas behind the communication.

KINESICS

We begin our review of nonverbal communication with a look at kinesics. Kinesics refers to the way people move their bodies to communicate a message. For example, gestures people make with their head, shoulders, arms, hands, legs, and feet are included in this category. People from the United States and Canada, just like those from Mexico, also move their bodies to communicate, but sometimes the same exact movements have different meanings.

Some movements, called regulators, have indirect meanings. For example, when people nod their head, it might mean "go on," but it might also mean "I agree." There is not always just one specific meaning attached to a movement, and these may differ from one cultural norm to another.

Other movements, called emblems, do contain messages that replace a specific verbal communication. For example, when someone shakes their head to replace the word "no," that is an emblem. Although emblems sometimes coincide from one culture to another, other times we fail to recognize the meaning or misinterpret the intent.

Here are brief discussions of typical Mexican emblems. We explain the meaning of each one and the context in which Mexicans use them.

6.1 The Thank-You Gesture
A raised hand to signify
thank you. Photograph
courtesy of Vanessa Bonilla-
Hernandez and Ariana
Bonilla-Hernandez.

The Thank-You Gesture

When Mexicans want to thank others, they demonstrate appreciation by showing the back of their right hand to those people
they want to thank. Sometimes they even move their right arm
back and forth, keeping the hand in the same position. Typical
occasions to use this gesture include those when a driver allows
a pedestrian to cross a street, or when a driver lets another driver
go ahead first. This gesture can also be used to show appreciation for doing some kind of favor. Thus, when making the
gesture with their hand, Mexicans often say *muy amable,* "very
kind of you" (photograph 6.1).

The "Yes" and "No" Gestures

To say "yes," Mexicans repeatedly flex their index finger. To say
"no," they move their index finger from side to side several times.
As to the facial expressions that Mexicans make that accompany these hand gestures, when saying "yes" with their hand,
as expected, they often smile to show agreement or approval.
Be aware, however, that they may also smile when saying "no."
If so, they probably believe that you are trying to outsmart them.
If, when saying "no" with their hands, they are showing a more
serious face, then they are probably reinforcing their message
of disagreement or reprimand. It is worth mentioning that these
two gestures for "yes" and "no" are rare in formal and business-
related meetings among adults. They are more appropriate
for informal gatherings, among friends, and for kids or young
people.

6.2 The Share-It Gesture
The *móchate*, or "give me some," gesture. Photography courtesy of Vanessa Bonilla-Hernandez and Ariana Bonilla-Hernandez.

The Share-It Gesture

When Mexicans want to split the check or when they want to share in something good that another person is getting, the emblem for this is to move their right hand across their chest diagonally, as if they were cutting it into two parts from their left shoulder to their waist. In the northern states of Mexico (e.g., Nuevo Leon, Chihuahua, and Tamaulipas) and in informal gatherings of friends, people might smile and add the popular expression *móchate, ¿no?* meaning "give me some, share it." People use this gesture in more of a lighthearted way, and when making a joke. People from Mexico City and southern states rarely use the verbal expression, and might not be familiar with it, but still use the nonverbal one. We recommend that the *móchate* gesture be limited to informal settings among friends and not be used in formal business meetings (photograph 6.2).

The A-Lot-of Gesture

In Mexico, holding both hands with the tip of their thumbs touching the tips of their fingers, as if making a tube shape, and moving their arms back and forth several times means "a lot." Mexicans can use this gesture to refer to a lot of food, many people, a lot of heat, and the like. It is common to see Mexicans

6.3 The A-Lot-of Gesture
That is a lot of food, and there are tons of people! Photograph courtesy of Vanessa Bonilla-Hernandez and Ariana Bonilla-Hernandez.

6.4 The Let's-Go-Eat Gesture
We're hungry and it's time to eat! Photograph courtesy of Vanessa Bonilla-Hernandez and Ariana Bonilla-Hernandez.

making faces and stretching out their mouths to reinforce the a-lot-of message (photograph 6.3).

The Let's-Go-Eat Gesture

The let's-go-eat gesture is similar to the a-lot-of gesture. It is made when the tip of the thumb touches the tips of the fingers, as if making a tube shape. The difference is that the let's-go-eat gesture is made with only the right hand instead of both hands.

When making this gesture, it should look as if the person is eating a taco. Thus, Mexicans make this gesture near the mouth (photograph 6.4).

The Fear Gesture

The fear gesture is similar to the previous two gestures; it starts with the tip of the thumb touching the tips of the fingers, again making a tube shape. The fear gesture can be made with one or two hands, depending on how much fear you want to communicate. Two hands communicate much fear. In this case, the hand(s) should be held out in front, opening and closing several times.

The Hurry-Up Gesture > The Expensive/Rich Gesture

When Americans or Canadians refer to an expensive item or a very rich person, they rub their thumb back and forth against their forefinger and middle finger, meaning a lot of money. However, in Mexico, people use the same gesture to encourage others to hurry up, often adding *apúrate*, "hurry up." The way to refer to an expensive item or a rich person in Mexico is to place your hand palm up, with the index finger and thumb in a "u" shape and the other three fingers forming a loose fist (photograph 6.5).

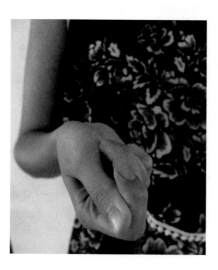

6.5 The Hurry-Up Gesture
Apúrate—meaning hurry up, and not the US and Canadian meaning of expensive. Photograph courtesy of Vanessa Bonilla-Hernandez and Ariana Bonilla-Hernandez.

The Stingy Gesture

The stingy gesture is typically used to signal a cheap person, someone who is not willing to spend any money. Mexicans rub their elbow several times to describe a stingy individual, a movement that means absolutely nothing to an American or a Canadian. Often, this gesture is used in jest to make fun of a friend. It is lighthearted and not meant to be taken as a serious offense. Still, we do not recommend that you use it in a professional or business context, unless it is made playfully to someone with whom a relationship is well established (photograph 6.6).

The *Más o Menos* Gesture

Mexicans use the *más o menos*, "more or less," gesture in situations when they do not know exactly how to describe or count something, or if they prefer to use approximations. It can also be used when giving directions—for example, "More or less far away from here." It is also used when describing a person, an object, or an event—as in "kind of pretty." We also see it when people talk about the price of something: "More or less 200 pesos." The gesture is made by holding the palm facing down, and then twisting the wrist from side to side several times (photograph 6.7).

6.7 The *Más o Menos* Gesture
I guess you would say that he is kind of smart! Photograph courtesy of Vanessa Bonilla-Hernandez and Ariana Bonilla-Hernandez.

The However Gesture

In Mexico, people hold up their index finger to say "However" or to stress part of the conversation. This gesture is similar to the "hold on a second" gesture in the United States or Canada, but it carries only the "however" meaning in Mexico.

The Cheated-On Gesture

With apologies to our Texas friends, the well-known "Hook 'em Horns" gesture of the University of Texas Longhorns carries a whole different meaning in Mexico. This hand gesture is made by extending the index and pinky fingers and then grabbing the second and third fingers with your thumb. In Mexico, this refers to someone who has been cheated on, such as the husband of an adulterous wife. Mexicans say *le pusieron los cuernos*, which can be both offensive and vulgar. Therefore, it is best to be avoided when in Mexico.

The Make-It-Short Gesture

Despite the fondness for the gift of gab, when someone asks you to cut the conversation short, move your index and middle fingers as if you were using scissors. Along with making this gesture, you will hear people say *córtale*, "cut it."

6.8 The I'm-Telling-the-Truth Gesture
Honest, I swear I didn't do it! Photograph courtesy of Vanessa Bonilla-Hernandez and Ariana Bonilla-Hernandez.

The I'm-Telling-the-Truth Gesture

In spite of a mother's insistence not to do so, sometimes when Mexicans want to swear that they are telling the truth, they make a cross with their right thumb and index finger. Then they kiss the cross to show that they are not lying. Given the Roman Catholic influence in Mexico, conservative mothers often teach their children that it is disrespectful to swear in the name of God. Yet in fact, many Roman Catholics in other cultures use this gesture as well. For most Mexicans, the I'm-telling-the-truth gesture is not so much a sign of disrespect as it is simply a way to say that they are telling the truth (photograph 6.8).

The Silence Gesture

In the United States, as in many other parts of the world, when people raise their fists, most understand the gesture as a symbol of solidarity and strength. Throughout the years, this gesture has become a signal of resistance. The raised fist has been linked to the Black Power movement, labor unions, civil rights, and feminist activists. However, in Mexico, after the devastating earthquakes in 2017, this gesture became better known as the silence gesture. Rescue workers used it as a sign to the waiting crowds to immediately fall silent. They signaled others to be quiet so

6.9 The Silence Gesture
A raised fist signifying silence.

they could listen for sounds of life. Photograph 6.9 shows our Canadian-born author demonstrating the silence gesture.

AFFECT DISPLAY

Affect display refers to how much a given culture shows emotional feelings in a public way. It is important to remember that a happy person from Monterrey may feel the same level of happiness as a person from Minneapolis but may simply show that emotion differently. People who openly display their happiness in public may not actually be any happier than a reserved person who holds those emotions from public display. Our affect display is both individually and culturally distinct. And this applies to subcultures as well. Most Anglophone Canadians express greater discomfort with displays of emotion—especially public displays of emotion—than do Francophone Canadians, or for that matter members of most US language groups.[2]

In Mexico there is a traditional devotion to family and friends, which is accompanied by open expressions of emotions in public, with hugging, kissing, caressing, and touching others. Many displays of affection—including embracing, holding hands, and kissing—are accepted as public behaviors in Mexico.

These same actions might more appropriately be private in US and Canadian settings. When in Mexico, look around to observe typical patterns. Mostly, we find that small towns are more conservative than large cities; but as a general rule, people feel comfortable showing their emotions in public.

One caution: Be aware that Mexican culture allows for the display of positive emotions, such as happiness, passion, and excitement. However, Mexicans show much more restraint in displaying negative emotions, such as anger, sadness, and frustration. These should be managed with care. Remember that Mexicans try to avoid direct confrontations, and they make efforts to save face and maintain dignity. A Mexican who is angry is still angry, even if he or she does not openly express that anger. Remember, too, that in general it is still a taboo for men to cry in public. Most men keep their suffering private, and macho men are less likely to reveal such feelings.

OCULESICS

Oculesics refers to the way people use their eyes to communicate. This includes direct or indirect eye contact, staring, blinking, gazing, looking away from others, and other ways in which we show emotions with our eyes. Considering what we have already mentioned regarding Mexican affect display, it may not be all that surprising to say that in Mexico, much is communicated with a person's eyes. For example, in Mexico people do not like to point at others with their fingers, which is considered by many to be rude. Instead, they signal direction with their eyes or their chin.

As to looking directly at someone, when Mexicans talk with someone of equal social rank, chances are that they will look directly at another's eyes. However, there are three situations where lowering one's eyes is a sign of respect. First, there may be interactions between people from different social classes. For example, a man shining shoes may avoid contact with a client who is perceived to be from a higher social class. Second, people from rural regions tend to lower their eyes more than people from urban areas. This, for example, may be evident when entering local shops and stores. And third, women may break eye contact or a direct gaze with men, either as a sign of demureness or to cut off flirtation. In the United States and Canada, conversely, lowering one's eyes indicates the opposite of showing respect. It either indicates that the person is lying or shows a lack of self-confidence. Both have negative associations and are far from displays of respect or humility.

DRESS AND APPEARANCE

Another category of nonverbal behavior that can be culturally based is dress and appearance. At a certain level, weather and climate influence the way people dress. A lawyer in Downtown Manhattan in December will certainly dress differently from a person in Miami in July. Dress and appearance are also affected by the formality of the situation—think a casual afternoon at the beach in Southern California versus a formal wedding in Chicago. Likewise, in Mexico, location, weather, climate, and formality all affect the way people dress. Dress and appearance are also major factors in the way people express themselves. Our choice of clothing, makeup, and accessories all make a nonverbal statement.

When it comes to dress and adornment, Mexico brings together an interesting blend of influences. At one end, there are influences from the country's indigenous cultural roots. At the other end, there are styles that come from Europe, from the United States, and from other popular centers of fashion from around the world. What we can say is that in formal business and professional settings, especially in large cities, Mexican dress and appearance can be more formal and conservative than what is normally seen among Americans and Canadians—with the possible exception of Quebec. That is to say, men often wear long-sleeve shirts, a tie, a suit coat, and dress shoes. There are situations where Americans have started to wear running shoes in professional environments, but in Mexico it is still more common to see shoes that can be polished, and keeping them polished is noticed. Women wear dresses, pantsuits, jackets, skirts, and heeled shoes, and they have on more accessories and makeup than in the United States and Canada. People consider social class and gender when choosing an appropriate wardrobe, and they judge what is appropriate clothing depending on the social expectations for a particular context. A good rule of thumb is that in the United States and Canada, informal styles begin with a general sense of comfort. In Mexico, more formal styles begin with a sense of respect. The balance between comfort and respect simply reflects different starting points.

Keep in mind, however, that Mexico is a large county, and depending on regional customs, choices regarding wardrobe can change drastically. For example, in Mexico City and in colonial towns, like Puebla or Guanajuato, people dress more modestly than in beach destinations such as Cancún, Los Cabos, or Puerto Vallarta. In the workplace of large magnet cities—such as Mexico City, Monterrey, and Guadalajara—people are more formal than in the cities of southern Mexico, such as Oaxaca and Chiapas. In the big magnet cities, dark suits and ties for men and a classic suit for women create a good impression. In small towns, a casual and modest outfit is a better choice.

Often, regional variations in dress and appearance reflect the environment where Mexicans live. For example, northern Mexico is hot and dry. The typical clothing of village people in the North comes in earth-tone colors, such as beige, brown, and dark green. Hats and boots are often worn in sunny northern states such as Chihuahua, Coahuila, and Nuevo Léon. On the contrary, clothing in the Center and South of Mexico is colorful. Women's clothing in the southern Mexico states includes all types of regional floral designs. There, *huaraches* (sandals) are more common than boots.

When making decisions about their wardrobe, Mexicans consider the weather and the season. As mentioned above, the weather in Chihuahua and Sonora can be extreme—very hot during the summer, and cold during the winter. In the regions near the Gulf of Mexico (e.g., Veracruz), the cities can be rainy and humid. In the high-altitude cities in the Center of Mexico—for example, in Toluca—the weather is very cool in the morning and at night but warm during the rest of the day. Dress and appearance are affected by all these factors. Mexican cities often have buildings that do not have central heating. Therefore, when it is cold outside, Mexicans expect it to also be colder inside buildings. They know this and dress accordingly.

Dress in Professional Environments

In the workplace, Mexicans generally want to dress upwardly, opting to dress at a higher social station. At the office, men are supposed to wear a conservative dark suit and a tie. Classic lines and tailoring in gray or navy with white or light blue shirts are always appropriate. Expensive suits send a message of status and power. Offices in big cities are usually equipped with air conditioning, and men's suits are made of lightweight and breathable fabrics, such as cotton or linen. Women wear business suits, dresses, slacks, skirts, and blouses. Classic lines in basic colors such as gray, white, and ivory are acceptable. Hosiery and conservative high heels are proper business attire. Makeup and jewelry should be worn, but discreetly. Mexican women prefer defined, intense, and vivid makeup colors. They often choose red tones for blush and lipstick as well as colorful shades to enhance their eyes.

In Mexico's tropical cities, professional attire is less formal. Instead of a dark suit, men and women wear slacks (or skirts) and button-down shirts (or blouses) in neutral and light colors such as light blue, white, gray, and ivory. For men, a *guayabera* (i.e., a traditional lightweight shirt) is perfect and is worn over one's pants. *Guayaberas* are fresh and versatile, and they have been worn in Mexico for more than two hundred years. These are comfortable options in restaurants, too, because many require men to wear long pants and closed shoes. We recommend that jeans, or tight, low-cut clothing, is never appropriate for business in Mexico.

Hidden Meanings in Traditional Mexican Clothing

It is also worth mentioning that beyond functional convenience in the choice of clothing, in Mexico "traditional" clothing may have less obvious hidden meanings related to social and economic status, moods, religious beliefs, places of origin, and customs.

6.10 A Clothing Store Selling *Huipil* and *Guayabera*
On your next trip to Mexico, try these fresh and comfortable garments. Photograph courtesy of Vanessa Bonilla-Hernandez.

Even before Europeans arrived in Mexico, people's identity was
associated with their clothing. In Aztec times, there were strict
laws about what one could wear based on their position in society.
Common people wore simple clothing, while nobles had sophisticated garments (e.g., beautiful and rare feathers) and accessories (e.g., earrings, necklaces, and other piercing). The garments
of warriors used to evoke mystical animals because the belief
was that they would give them the energy and strength to fight.

Mayan people also dressed according to their daily routine
and their level in society. For example, Mayans believe that a
woman who wears her *huipil* (i.e., an ornate Mayan tunic) looks
like an adult butterfly, displaying her beauty. Her head represents
the sun, the ribbons at the front symbolize the sunlight, and the
ribbons at the back characterize the rain. The large brocade represents the rainbow, and the white space in the tunic symbolizes
the final stage of life or death. In general, this garment represents
the different cycles of the butterfly (see photograph 6.10).

We find another example of hidden messages in clothing
in Mexican *zarapes*, which were originally worn by farmers and
shepherds in the highland regions of the country. A woman who
knitted a sophisticated and ornate *zarape* for her loved one was

also sending a message that this man had a wife at home, one who cared for and loved him. The knitted *zarape* was a subtle warning to stay away from her man.

Although most people in Mexico today buy their clothing in modern stores, clothing continues to convey hidden messages. Brand names, expensive clothing, and fashionable accessories make a statement about power and influence. Modest clothing may symbolize a preference for equality and humility. A necklace with a crucifix or an image of the Virgin Mary provides a symbol of devotion to God or Catholicism. There are also handcrafted garments with embroidered flowers, and Mexican symbols like the golden eagle, that send a message of appreciation for nature and Mexican indigenous roots. Additionally, boots and hats tell others of connections to rural areas in the country. And suits and ties—as well as fashionable blouses, skirts, and slacks—tell others of professional behavior. In some ways, all these contain hidden meanings.

Other Traditional Mexican Clothing Styles

Mexico's rich cultural and regional diversity have resulted in many other traditional clothing styles. For example, we see *charro* and *mariachi* suits in the central and western regions; the *China poblana* dress, which was originally associated with Puebla; the Ranchera ribbon dress (e.g., the *escaramuza* dresses from Jalisco); the elegant white Veracruz dress, with its embroidery and lace; the embroidery designs of the Tabasco dress; and the Chiapas dress, with its stunning floral patterns. All are exquisite pieces and are worn exclusively nowadays for celebrations and special occasions, but they are unique in ways that emphasize the diversity of Mexico (photograph 6.11).

Outside large city centers, we still find village people who wear casual Maya *huipiles*, *guayaberas*, and embroidered blouses and dresses. Other accessories include the *rebozo*, *poncho*, and *zarape*. The *rebozo* is the modern take on the *tilmátli*, an ancient Aztec cloak. It can be worn over clothing as a shawl, blouse, shroud, or a cape. The *poncho* is intended to keep the wearer warm and dry, even in the wettest of climates. The *zarape* can be worn as a shawl, blanket, or poncho. Some of these pieces are

6.11 A *Mariachi* Ribbon Dress
The Mariachi Ribbon Dress is just one of many different regional styles. Source: Photograph by Gail Williams, CC BY-ND 2.o.

also common in other Latin American cultural groups. Other well-known Mexican accessories include items like the Baja jacket (which was often worn and popularized by hippies in the United States) and sombreros. And leather cowboy boots might just as accurately be called Mexican boots, with all their various styles, colors, elongated toes, and exotic animal skins. As we have seen, dress and adornment in Mexico have both professional and business applications as well as cultural and traditional implications.

HAPTICS

Haptics refers to how people communicate through physical touch. In every culture, a certain type of touching will be interpreted as professional, social, friendly, or intimate. The challenge comes when a touch from someone in one culture to someone in another culture indicates a distinct level of relationship. This is especially important when dealing with people from Mexico—when, for example, a given pattern of touching is misinterpreted as friendly when it was intended to convey a professional relationship.

There are four occasions when touching becomes part of the exchange when dealing with Mexicans in professional or semiprofessional situations: the greeting or handshake, the kiss, the *abrazo* (hug), and touching while conversing.

The Greeting or Handshake

Let us begin with the handshake. Mexicans are expressive in their emotions. You will find that they greet people with a lot of energy compared with their US and Canadian counterparts. The professional handshake among men is firm, accompanied with a smile, and continues throughout the introduction to the person who is speaking. When men are introduced to women in a professional situation, similarly, a greeting with a handshake is sufficient. Perhaps in a more informal setting or after a number of visits, a man may give a woman a kiss on the cheek as well. In general, however, during initial professional visits, a general handshake is all that is required. Likewise, in a formal, professional setting, a woman will initially give a handshake to another woman. And we should add that in larger groups, or when there is a mixture of people standing and sitting, a simple nod to say hello is acceptable. In informal situations, especially among the younger generation, one also comes across alternative, elaborate handshakes where people personalize the handshake to fit a style. And finally, in special situations of deep emotion, one receives two-handed, double handshakes, which are somewhere between a regular handshake and the *abrazo*.

The Kiss

In addition to the handshake, in more casual situations, even in professional settings, men and women may give each other a kiss on the cheek. Unlike in other countries, this is just one kiss, and it is almost always on the right cheek. Kisses in Mexico are in the air, with one cheek touching the cheek of the other person. That is to say, it would be inappropriate to actually touch one's lips to a woman's cheek. In social situations, especially among younger individuals, men and women also give each other a kiss on the cheek.

The *Abrazo*

Among men, understanding the dynamics of the Mexican *abrazo* is a little more complicated. If Americans or Canadians add a hug to their handshake greeting, chances are that they will use their right hand for the handshake, maintain hold of the hand,

and then extend their left arm to the shoulder of the person receiving the hug. Mexicans, however, generally shake hands first, then release the handshake, and then raise their right arm to the shoulder or back of the person receiving the hug. Additionally, the hug is often accompanied by a few pats on the back. Once you get the hang of it, things become much simpler; but initially, the right versus left side is confusing.

Touching while Conversing

As to touching while conversing, it is socially acceptable for men to touch the shoulder or hold another's arm in a friendly manner. This is simply a gesture of kindness. Women likewise may interlock arms when chatting. We might also add that it is impolite in Mexico to keep your hands in your pockets. Similarly, if a person stands with their hands on their hips, it might come across as looking aggressive.

PROXEMICS

Proxemics refers to the interpersonal distance that people maintain around themselves—in other words, how close or how far away we stand or sit from others when talking together. In Mexico, conversations often take place at a closer physical distance than in the United States. If you are one of two North Americans standing across from each other in a normal conversation, you should be able to extend your arm fully and then be able to place your thumb in the other person's ear (roughly 1.5 feet, or 46 centimeters). The difference in Mexico may just be a couple of inches; still, the typical American and Canadian might feel uncomfortable standing that much closer.

Our recommendation, while communicating with people in Mexico, is to simply try to adapt. If you find yourself feeling uncomfortable, simply adjust your position a little, perhaps by moving side to side.

You will similarly want to follow the Mexican lead with waiting in public lines. Look around and adjust your distance from others based on what they are doing.

In addition to the nonverbal communication behaviors that we have discussed so far in this chapter, there are others that we call passive, nonverbal communication because they refer to the stimuli in the environment around us. These are things to which we respond, for example, colors and symbols.

Colors

As to colors, in Mexico colorful living is common practice. Bold and lively shades coexist in Mexican architecture, painting, sculpture, clothing, ornaments, pottery, leather work, food, and textiles. Color runs rampant in Mexican houses, both outdoors and indoors. One can see parallel stucco walls painted in contrasting hues, like purple paired with yellow or orange. These shades of colors differ greatly from those to which Americans and Canadians might be accustomed. However, for Mexicans vivid colors are the norm, with specific associations to nature or to indigenous influences (photograph 6.12).

6.12 Colorful Houses
A bold and vivid look is the norm! Photograph courtesy of Vanessa Bonilla-Hernandez.

6.13 Huichol Folk Art and Handicrafts
Amazing patience, don't you think? Colorful Huichol designs using beadwork.

In the same way that Americans respond to red, white, and blue, Mexicans have similar feelings about green, red, and white. These are the most important symbolic colors in Mexico, and they are reflected in the Mexican flag. For Mexicans, the green is associated with hope and independence, the white symbolizes faith and religion, and the red represents the blood of the soldiers who defended Mexico's sovereignty. And yes, the *tequila bandera* combines these three colors—lime, *tequila*, and *sangrita*.

Vivid shades that reflect nature also have an impact on the Mexican sense of color. Indigenous influences add symbolism to red (anger and strength), yellow (power), green (the harvest), and blue (innocence). (And for the Mayan people, blue was also associated with sacrifice.) Photograph 6.13 illustrates the use of color in Huichol art. The Huichol are an indigenous group from the mountainous regions of northern and central Mexico. They are famous for their decorative designs, amazing beadwork, yarn pieces, and paintings.

Symbols

National symbols are accompanied by strong emotional ties, and this applies to Mexico as well. Even the name of the country, the coat of arms, and the national anthem all elicit patriotic associations. The name of the country, "Mexico," means the button of the Moon or center of the Moon. Tenochtitlán, now Mexico City, was in the center of Lake Texcoco. Aztecs called Lake Texcoco the Lake of the Moon. This is the place were the Aztecs settled in 1325. The legend says that the Aztecs (i.e., the Mexicans), which are a nomadic tribe, left home looking for a place to start a new life. God told them to find a lake, where an eagle with a snake in its beak would stand on a nopal cactus. This would be the place to build the new city. The Mexican coat of arms, a national emblem, features a golden eagle eating a snake on top of a cactus, symbolizing the origin of Tenochtitlán (i.e., Mexico). The national anthem alludes to Mexican victories in the heat of battle and cries of defending the homeland. Our recommendation is that patriotism not be thought of as a winner-take-all type of competition. It is perfectly legitimate for Americans, Canadians, and Mexicans to all equally have a sense of patriotism that does not diminish the others' sense of nationalism.

There are other Mexican symbols that have indigenous origins as well. All Mexicans identify with the Aztec calendar, which is dedicated to the Sun God. It represents their understanding of time and space. Symbols associated with Mayan astronomy bring to mind their knowledge about the Sun, Moon, and planets. The Jaguar is a symbol representing the fierce and brave elite Aztec warriors. Chocolate is a symbol of nobility, not to mention sensuality and decadence. The owl also has symbolic meanings in Mexico. It represents dark, shamanic forces. Aztecs feared the owl and believed it could bring death. Maize (i.e., corn), which is crucial for survival, was a gift from the god Quetzalcoatl, and as such it carries symbolic meanings. Corn was part of many festivities and offerings. Mexicans relate to all these symbols that have indigenous roots, even if they themselves have no direct indigenous ties.

We also see symbolic meanings in other Mexican folk art pieces. For example, *alebrijes* and skulls are seen everywhere. *Alebrijes* are colorful papier maché or wood sculptures of exotic animals or creatures. They symbolize fantasy, creativity, and magic (photograph 6.14). We have already mentioned skulls and

6.14 *Alebrijes*
Admit it. You thought of the movie *Coco*, right?

the symbolism of death. Because, for Mexicans, death is not the final stage in one's existence, all look forward to a rebirth. Skulls honor the return of a spirit. When Mexicans decorate a grave with skulls, flowers, and foods, they do not do it with morbid associations, but more to symbolize life.

RECOMMENDATIONS

As we mentioned at the beginning of this chapter, cultural differences in nonverbal communication can be difficult to interpret, because many times we are simply unaware of their existence. The topics addressed in this chapter are designed to assist you in becoming a better observer. In doing so, we gain an appreciation for the meaning behind nonverbal cues.

Our first recommendation is precisely this: Try to actively observe nonverbal communication patterns. This will not only help you to interpret hidden messages but will also help you to become aware of your own nonverbal kinesics, emblems, gestures, affect display, and oculesics. Mexicans feel comfortable showing their positive emotions. Look around and identify the norms in particular locations.

Second, we encourage you to adopt specific gestures as you interact with Mexicans. Before you know it, you will be indicating that something is expensive, that it is time to go eat, and that somebody is stingy. There is something delightfully satisfying about using gestures that are new to you but are made totally subconsciously by others.

Third, by understanding haptics and proxemics, you become instantly more comfortable around people physically. Our recommendation is not necessarily that you adopt all the aspects of physical touch and distance described in this chapter but that you become aware that your initial feelings may not successfully interpret your Mexican counterpart's intent.

With respect to dress and clothing, we recommend that you consider the location, weather, type of event, daily activities, and the gender and social class of those with whom you are dealing. Remember that Mexicans are conservative and formal in their dress. Also keep in mind that expensive clothing and accessories are indicators of sophistication, power, reach, and influence. And finally, take time to appreciate the associations that Mexicans make with colors and symbols. These teach us a lot about Mexicans' thoughts and emotions.

Be flexible and forgiving. Chances are that your first reactions will not be accurate. Over time, the nonverbal cues that differ between the United States, Canada, and Mexico will become easier to recognize and easier to accommodate.

NONVERBAL SUMMARY AND CHAPTER 6 HIGHLIGHTS

Kinesics:

- Thank-you gesture
- "Yes" and "no" gestures
- Share-it gesture
- A-lot-of gesture
- Let's-go-eat gesture
- Fear gesture
- Hurry-up gesture
- Stingy gesture

- *Más o menos* gesture
- However gesture
- Cheated-on gesture
- Make-it-short gesture
- I'm telling-the-truth gesture
- Silence gesture

Affect display:

- Public display of affection
- Public display of emotions (e.g., anger)

Oculesics:

- Looking directly at another's eyes to show respect—equal social class
- Not looking directly at another's eyes to show respect—not equal social class
- Breaking direct eye contact with the opposite sex

Dress and appearance:

- Formal and professional
- Conservative dark suit and tie for men
- Business suits, dresses, slacks, and skirts and blouses for women
- Regional differences, influenced, e.g., by weather and climate

Hidden meaning in traditional Mexican clothing:

- Indications of status, mood, religious beliefs, places of origin, and customs
- Indigenous influences
- Rich cultural and regional diversity

Haptics and proxemics:

- Handshakes in professional settings
- Kiss
- *Abrazo*

Passive nonverbal communication:

- Color—bold and lively
- Symbols—*alebrijes*, skulls

Recommendations:

- Actively observe nonverbal communication
- Adopt specific gestures
- Become aware of your feelings about haptics and proxemics
- In formal and professional settings dress conservatively
- Be flexible and forgiving

7

THE MEXICAN
Temporal
Conception

All Our Pasts Are Our Present

Our last subject here—the "T" of the LESCANT approach—
is temporal conception, or how we conceptualize time. Temporal conception refers to the way in which we understand
and use time.

The Mexican conception of time differs from that of its
two northern neighbors in two ways: temporal orientation
and time usage. Temporal orientation deals with the broad
perspective of time, and it corresponds to the nature of how
each culture views what happened in the past and what
is planned for the future. Time usage deals with how we
divide time, adhere to schedules, and approach deadlines.
To explain time usage, we employ the now-classic analysis of
monochronic and *polychronic* time, described nearly fifty years
ago by Edward Hall. In this chapter, we look at both of these
concepts in considerable detail. They differ greatly between
the three cultures, and few things are as absolutely central
for understanding each other.

Mexicans, Canadians, and Americans view both the influence of the past and the conception of the future in profoundly different ways. This is not to say that any of the three lack some influence from the past or the draw of an anticipated future. The three cultures do share things in common with each other, too, but they do so in what we might call a triangulated way. In other words, the things that Mexico and the United States share with each other are not the same things that Mexico and Canada share with each other. Likewise, the things that the United States and Canada share with each other are less emphasized in Mexico. Although views of the past and future may not at first blush seem that significant, in reality few things that we have discussed in this book are more important. This is because the three nations' views of the past and future in many respects define the worldviews of the people belonging to each nation.

The Mexican concept of history is one that informs the present. We will explain what this actually means in much greater detail a bit further on in this chapter. For now, let us contrast this with the view of history in Canada and the United States.

Canadians hold a deep and abiding grasp of their specific histories, but that history is not a nationally shared telling of a common story. Mexicans, like Canadians, share a strong sense of a personal connection to history in their families and in their self-identity. Yet the similarities stop there. As we discussed in chapter 3, the blending of Mexico's mestizo culture forms a strong sense of a unique and unifying Mexican identity. By contrast, in Canada, the mosaic of cultures has very little in the way of a view of a single, unifying history. The Canadian political scientist Robert Latham gets at the heart of this when he explains the wording of the title of his article "What Are We? From a Multicultural to a Multiversal Canada." Latham explains that he uses the word "what" rather than "who" to emphasize

> that when considering ourselves as a collectivity within
> the national social space and political community that

is called Canada, we do so in terms of the question of "what we are" as a Canadian society rather than "who we are" as Canadians, ... [and] to question the possibility of some kind of unified, comprehensive understanding of "we" at all. Indeed, a "what" can be conceived in a highly pluralized and fragmented fashion—an option not easily available in answers to the question "Who we are."[1]

The Canadian sense of the past is, in other words, one of a single strand in a tapestry; the historical experience matters deeply within the ethnic heritage of many cultures rather than a single Canadian history. The Scots of Nova Scotia speak more Gaelic than the Scots of Scotland, and Scottish Canadians hold a deep historical memory of the Jacobite uprisings of 1715 and 1745, the aftermath of which found many of their ancestors forcibly removed from Scotland to Canada. They may share the same language as English-Canadians (i.e., those whose origin is in England), but they do not share the same historical perspective, a point underscored by the separation of Scots from English in the Canadian Census counts. The Québécois represent a national community in a way that Anglophone communities do not. Yet Francophone Canada comprises more than just Quebec, and the Francophone communities of other provinces do not share (at least not entirely) the Québécois identity or its history (at least not necessarily)—and none at all with Francophone Canadians from Haiti, West Africa, or Europe. The First Nations and Inuits in Canada may share a history of displacement in earlier eras, but their histories have little else in common. The same can be said for Canadians of Chinese, Ukrainian, Punjabi, and Italian origin, or most other Canadian communities. In short, for nearly every individual ethnic community in Canada, the historical connection is very strong in a way that is not present at the national level.

The United States shares with Mexico—but not with Canada—a sense of a unifying national identity; but the US perspective of the past influencing the present is almost the exact opposite of the Mexican view of the history. The great US industrialist Henry Ford summarized what is a widely held US view of history when he said, "History is more or less bunk. It's tradition. We don't want tradition. We want to live in the present and the only history that is worth a tinker's dam is the history we make today."[2]

Even when Henry Ford, later in life, created the history park Greenfield Village, the way in which he did so was quintessentially American. Ford had nearly one hundred historical buildings (ranging from the Wright Brothers' bike shop, where they created their first airplane, to the building where Ford himself was born) moved out of their historical context and reconstructed brick by brick in Dearborn, Michigan, in an easily visited theme park. The contrast to Mexico (or Canada) is hard to miss. Be aware, from a Mexican or Canadian perspective, that this description might actually be viewed as sarcastic or somehow condemnatory. It is not. We highly recommend visiting Greenfield Village as a clear example of the US view of history.

How this plays out in day-to-day application can be seen in the example John Condon shared about a US executive in Mexico. The executive told Condon,

> Like many Americans of my day, I came to Mexico impressed with its modern art, its futuristic architecture, and its promise. I always saw Mexico as the land of the future, and history didn't really interest me. Frankly, I thought that history books were for tourists who were afraid to go out and see the real Mexico. Later I came to see that I was the romantic tourist. To really understand Mexico and the US, I realized I had to look more carefully at the past. When I give advice to Americans coming down here to do business, I tell them: Study history. Start with it and continue with it. Apart from the language itself, I don't know of anything that will prepare you better and make you more "respectable" in the eyes of your (Mexican) co-workers. If anybody had told me that 25 years ago, I would have smiled and gone on reading the *Wall Street Journal*. Which, in fact, is just what most Mexicans expect us to do.[3]

What Condon's executive shared was based on twenty-five years of experience—and not much has changed. Condon published *Good Neighbors* in 1955, so the executive was describing what he learned in 1960; but for all intents and purposes, his story could have been told yesterday. Fifty years later, we have heard the same sort of story. The reason is that (though there are exceptions) most Americans do not generally view history as having the sort of impact on the present that Mexicans do. This is neither right nor wrong. It is just different. To Americans, the past is blurry and the present and immediate future are very clear. To Mexicans, the past informs the present.

So what is the Mexican view of history as it affects their self-understanding and day-to-day behavior? In his Nobel Prize speech, Octavio Paz said: "*Los españoles encontraron en México no solo una geografía sino una historia. Esa historia está viva todavía: No es un pasado sino un presente.*" "The Spaniards found in Mexico not only a geography but also a history. That history is still alive; it's not a thing of the past thing but rather a present."[4]

Although Paz is arguably the most eloquent (and most famous) person to express this view, he is far from alone. The novelist and essayist Carlos Fuentes poignantly described how the past infuses the present in Mexico when he wrote in "Kierkegaard en la Zona Rosa," "*Entre nosotros, en cambio, no hay un solo tiempo: todos los tiempos están vivos, todos los pasados son presentes.*" "Among us, there is no single time: All of our times are alive, all of our pasts are present."[5]

Perhaps nowhere is Fuentes's observation more perfectly captured than in Mexico City's Plaza de las Tres Culturas—the Three Cultures Square. At this famous spot, Mexicans truly show what Fuentes meant by "all of our pasts are present." As shown in photograph 7.1, from the Plaza, you can see all at once Aztec ruins, an early seventeenth-century church, and modern office and housing buildings.

Probably no two places are more central to the Mexican identity than Chapultepec and the Basilica of Our Lady of Guadalupe. We already addressed the significance of Our Lady of Guadalupe when we discussed religion in Mexico in chapter 3, so in this chapter we focus our attention on Chapultepec.

Chapultepec is the focal point of all of Mexico's histories, layered one on the next. In a single place, Chapultepec Hill at once

7.1 The Plaza de las Tres Culturas
The Plaza de las Tres Culturas, showing Aztec, early European, and modern influences.

carries reminders of the Aztecs, the Roman Catholic Church, the Spanish Colonial Era, the early Republic, the country's resistance to US and French invasions, and modern Mexican history.

Chapultepec was the residence of the Aztec royalty, which in the 1300s established the Bosque de Chapultepec, the wooded park that stands there still today, the largest park in Latin America, which is often called the "lungs" of Mexico City. After the Spanish Conquest, the Church built a chapel on this site in 1554. Then, at this same site in the 1780s, the Spanish viceroys of Mexico built their summer palace (photograph 7.2).

After Mexico's independence in 1821, the newly formed republic transformed the palace into the residence of Mexican presidents. A little over a decade later, in 1833, the palace was converted into the National Military Academy, which itself became the focal point of the US invasion of Mexico. It was at Chapultepec on September 13, 1847 (still a national holiday), that the Mexicans made their final stand. Significantly, it was here that the six Niños Héroes (the "Boy Heroes") died rather than surrender, with one—Juan Escutia—hurling himself from Chapultepec Hill wrapped in the Mexican flag rather than letting it fall into US hands. This moment is captured on the ceiling above

7.2 Chapultepec Castle in Mexico City
Chapultepec is the focal point of all of Mexico's histories, layered one on the next.

Chapultepec Castle's circular staircase in the famous mural by Gabriel Flores García (photograph 7.3).

A monument with a statue of each boy on a pedestal stands in front of Chapultepec Castle today. The Niños Héroes have ever since represented Mexican resistance to foreign—and especially US—aggression (which is good to know if you are from the United States). So central is this story that, until 1993, the 5,000 peso note (which before the creation of the *nuevos pesos* was more or less equivalent to a US $1 bill or Canadian loonie in usage) featured the Niños Héroes on one side and Chapultepec Castle on the other.

Yet another historical layer was superimposed on Chapultepec during the French invasion of Mexico. Maximilian I made Chapultepec Castle his home when the French invaded Mexico and declared him emperor of Mexico in 1864. Maximilian, by the way, was neither French nor Mexican—he was the brother of the Austrian emperor. His reign was short-lived because the Mexicans forced the French out in 1867, but not before Chapultepec could take on one more layer of resistance to foreign conquest.

After this, Chapultepec became the residence of Mexican presidents, until finally, in 1939, it was transformed yet again. This

7.3 The Niños Héroes
Mural by Gabriel Flores García, on the ceiling of Chapultepec Castle in Mexico City.

time, then–president Lázaro Cárdenas declared the castle to be the site of the National Museum of History, which it remains to this day. The murals of the history of Mexico in Chapultepec Castle are considered among the high points of Mexican mural art.

Chapultepec, though arguably the most important, is just one of many examples of Mexico's rich history. Each city and town is imbued with the presence of history in the present. Likewise, family gatherings and festivals celebrate the blending of personal histories with national history.

In summary, there are deep differences in the way historical memory affects the cultures of Mexico, Canada, and the United States. Mexican history informs the national consciousness in a way that is deeply important and markedly different from the role of history for its northern neighbors, which those traveling to the country from Canada or the United States would do well to keep in mind.

TIME USAGE: POLYCHRONIC AND MONOCHRONIC TIME

Each culture indoctrinates its members with socially reinforced principles regarding time. When the eminent social psychologist

Leonard Doob turned his attention to the subject in his 1971 book *The Patterning of Time*, he explained that "each society provides appropriate information for passing temporal judgment."[6]

We often think of time as being universal, but it really is not. The clock may tick at the same pace, but how you perceive and act on the passing of time that those ticks represent often differs greatly based on how you *prioritize* what is happening.

When we prioritize one thing as "urgent" and another as "I'll get to this when I can," we are actually making a judgment call. It is pretty common to come across situations where something that is urgent to you is not particularly pressing to someone else. This prioritization depends both on our own personal situation and on our culture.

One of the most common observations made by Mexicans when they come to the United States and Canada, and vice versa, is that people seem to see time differently. Mexicans on one hand and Canadians and Americans on the other hand *both* view themselves as having an appropriate balance between punctuality and personalization of relationships. However, most Mexicans and most North Americans set this balance of punctuality and personalization differently. Mexicans often view North Americans as (to use Ned Crouch's term) "slaves of the clock."[7] North Americans, for their part, often view Mexicans as unacceptably lax. These biased assessments do reflect a reality—but only when we choose to judge the other culture in terms of our own. The fact is that Mexican and North American cultures do approach time differently from one another, but each approaches time in a way that is appropriate within their own cultural framework.

In short, how we approach time in each culture is not a matter of somehow being right or wrong—only different. The anthropologist Edward Hall classified cultures as being either *monochronic* or *polychronic* regarding their conception of time. He coined the word *monochronic* from the Greek for "single time," and the word *polychronic* from the Greek for "many or multiple times."

Hall identified *monochronic* cultures as those in which "scheduling is used as a classification system that orders life."[8] Monochronic temporal conception predominates in the United States and Canada, where people organize activities consecutively, attempting to undertake one task at a time. In monochronic cultures, pretty much everything submits to the clock and preset schedules. Most activities have specific, often inflexible, starting and ending times. Monochronic cultures have a strong sense of time as being a limited resource that can be spent well or wasted. As we discuss later in the chapter in more detail, monochronic cultures tend to emphasize keeping to the schedule over personal relationships.

Hall identified *polychronic* cultures as those where tasks are not sequentially handled; instead, many tasks are handled at the same time. Polychronic time predominates in Mexico, where people can bend the schedule enough to accommodate the specifics of what you are doing and, most important, for whom you are doing it.

Hall explained that "for polychronic people, time is seldom experienced as 'wasted,' and is apt to be considered as a point rather than a ribbon or a road, but that point is often sacred."[9] In polychronic cultures such as Mexico, time is often more flexible than in monochronic cultures such as the United States and Canada. People are accustomed to multitasking because they put a priority on ensuring that others have their needs handled. Who you are and the personal relationships you have can bend the schedule. Related to this, personal and work time often blur. Starting and ending times are often adaptable, and people emphasize finishing tasks over strict adherence to preset schedules. Because personal relationships affect who sees whom and when, networking allows you to act quickly if you are adequately connected to others. Conversely, in Mexico it can often be quite hard to get on someone's calendar unless you already have a shared connection.

THE SEESAW: THE SCHEDULE AND
PERSONAL RELATIONSHIPS

When we contrast traditional Mexican to US and Canadian temporal conceptions, we are actually comparing two seemingly unrelated things: adherence to schedules, and personal

relationships. It turns out that these two things are at opposite ends of the same line.

In figure 7.1, this reality is illustrated as a seesaw, with people on one side and a clock on the other. The more we stress the importance of keeping to a schedule, the less we are able to build personalized relationships. Conversely, the more we stress building personal ties with others, the less we can keep to a predetermined schedule.

It turns out that if you adhere to the clock, you cannot truly build up personal relationships. In turn, if you place personal relationships first, you cannot really stick to the schedule.

It is important to keep in mind that in a monochronic culture such as the United States or Canada, people *think* that they have a strong sense of personal relationships. Equally, Mexicans *think* that they have a strong sense of time and scheduling. Only when they find themselves outside their own cultural norms do they realize that they really do not have that sense on the other side of the seesaw.

The Seesaw Tipped to the Clock:
The North American Perspective
To better understand this, it might help to explain US and Canadian behavior. If you are from one of these countries, what follows should strike you as pretty typical. We ask you to keep in mind, however, that from your Mexican counterpart's point of view, this is all quite foreign.

In North America, you predetermine how long you will meet with another person. You keep a calendar and mark on it where you will be at what time. Although things sometimes go awry, on the whole, you probably do a pretty good job of completing the things you are supposed to do within the time frame you have allotted for them. This is especially true for work tasks. From a North American perspective, if you run out of time, you simply schedule another time to meet. It seems normal to need to rush people out of your office before the task at hand is done so that everyone can keep to the schedule. Unless there is a true emergency, it really does not matter how important or unimportant the issue at hand is. Likewise, your relationship with the other person makes no difference. In principle, at least, if you are a North American, you adhere to the schedule whether you are meeting a customer for the first time or with your brother or sister, with whom you just happen to work. In fact, it is sometimes hard to cut your time off with a relative, which is one of the US and Canadian justifications for not hiring relatives. Similarly, we have heard many North Americans warn about getting too close to other people at work because it will begin to affect your impartiality (which, in US or Canadian terms, means showing no favoritism regarding the schedule). In any case, in North America, you make a sharp distinction between personal and work time.

If you are from the United States or Canada, you might adhere to this most strongly in the workplace, but you will find it also affecting all sorts of other settings. For example, you likely will think nothing of ending lunch with a friend at a specific time so that you will not be late for your next appointment—or just to set a time, even if you have nowhere else to go.

You probably do not think twice about any of this because everyone around you sees this as quite normal as long as you stay within the United States or Canada. It almost never occurs to you that anyone would think that you are acting at all impersonally. In short, it may seem strange to think that Mexicans find all this to be strange and foreign.

The Seesaw Tipped to People: The Mexican Perspective
If you are a Mexican, this seesaw perspective comes from the other direction. Personal relationships are simply stronger than in North America, and adherence to the clock is consequently

weaker. This is not to say that Mexicans have no concept of punctuality or that Mexicans are not offended if someone is late. They do, and they are. The difference is that in the United States and Canada, the notion of what you consider to be late depends on some more-or-less absolute point on a clock. By contrast, in Mexico what you consider to be late depends on personal relationships—and with it, the understanding of the context of a particular event. As Mexican observers explain, "In summary, in Mexico, decisions about how to manage time depend on the situation, the relationships, and the individual's role."[10]

This becomes particularly noticeable in observing how North Americans and Mexicans approach social events. In general, professional events in Mexico basically begin and end as scheduled, or at least *are intended* to do so. In all three countries, the expectation is that meetings at work or classes at school are supposed to follow the preset schedule—even if, in practice, timing in Mexico may end up becoming notably more flexible than north of the border when it comes to accommodating people whom you know well and handling unexpected situational circumstances without rescheduling. By contrast, social events in Mexico do not adhere to such scheduling and—unlike things taking place in professional settings—are not intended to do so. They begin at times based on the context rather than the clock, and there is no way to say when they will end.

Because the situation and relationship have less influence in the US and Canada, meetings for social events still follow the clock more or less as they do for business or other nonsocial events, with understood (and usually stated) starting and ending times. In Mexico, it is the opposite. Mexicans *do* allow the situation (social rather than business) and relationships (friends rather than acquaintances) to establish the timing. As one Mexican longtime resident of the United States notes, "After living in the US for more than twenty-eight years, I have never understood the American way of enforcing their party hours. I am . . . still amused to this day to see the hours for the beginning and ending of a get-together on an invitation."[11]

As a Mexican, you may start each day thinking that you will keep to the schedule—and you will stay on that schedule, more or less. That said, as a Mexican, you know that every person you meet has individual needs and that each situation you face really depends on whom you are dealing with. From a Mexican perspective, if you get involved in a complex situation, you cannot just rush the person with whom you are meeting out of your office. It is all right if you run overtime a little (or even a lot), depending on the situation. If the next two people on the schedule must wait a little, they will understand (or at least tolerate the delay), because they know that you will do the same for them (getting you even *more* off schedule).

In Mexico, most people recognize that some matters are more important than others, and that we are not able always to predict their relative importance in advance. As a Mexican, you also recognize that when you are dealing with someone you do not know well, it takes more time to figure out what they are really saying (i.e., to build a context). In any case, as a Mexican, you recognize that people who know each other well can trust one another, and that this will speed things up. As a result, basically every Mexican knows that it is much harder to predict how long a first meeting with a new customer will take than it would be to predict how long it will take to answer a quick question from a brother or sister who happens to work at your company. Conversely, in Mexico, the better you know someone, the less likely it will be that you will ask him or her to leave, because in the end your friendship (let alone your family relationship) is more important than getting home at a specific time. Because of this, as a Mexican, you do not see that great a difference between personal time and work time. From a Mexican perspective, if you are building relationships the right way at work, then your work relationships blur into your personal relationships. For Mexicans, all this comes as second nature as long as they stay in Mexico. It is hard for most Mexicans to fully grasp how foreign—and frustrating—this can be for most North Americans.

The main point here is that whether you do all these things from a North American point of view or from a Mexican one, you probably do not think twice about any of this. As long as you stay within your own culture, this all seems normal. It may even seem strange to you to think that people from the other culture could do things another way. If you are a North American, it may never occur to you that you are acting at all impersonally and that, from a Mexican perspective, you have a very weak sense of personal ties. If you are a Mexican, it may never occur to you that you are at all unusual in how you handle your schedule and that, from a US or Canadian perspective, you have a very weak sense of time.

EXCEPTIONS WITHIN CULTURAL NORMS

At this point, we want to warn that no culture—and certainly no individual person—falls strictly into a monochronic or polychronic pigeonhole. This is particularly true here. It is not really possible to say that *all* people from Canada and the United States or Canada are monochronic or that *all* Mexicans are polychronic. Sometimes, technology and multitasking may affect the way people understand and use time. Frequent demands at work or in an individual's personal life can make even the most monochronic people look as if they were polychronic. This is particularly the case when these individuals use electronic devices. However, polychronicity is an individual characteristic that tends to be stable throughout life, while multitasking is more dynamic. In short, it is not really possible to say that *all* people from Canada and the United States are monochronic or that *all* Mexicans are polychronic.

Four factors in particular affect just how monochronic or polychronic any particular American, Canadian, or Mexican actually is likely to be: (1) ethnic diversity, (2) regional variation, (3) personal exigency, and (4) cross-cultural and global experience.

Ethnic Diversity
The wide ethnic array of both the United States and Canada means that there is marked—sometimes extreme—*ethnic* variation in how time is handled. Though it is true that monochronic temporal conception is the general norm, this is really only in

the shared multicultural arena. By contrast, there can be great variations in the personal and business practices of those living within the confines of their own ethnic heritage. In other words, North Americans with an immigrant background or a strong ethnic heritage may well follow the polychronic norms of their individual cultures when dealing with each other, while switching to a more monochronic norm when dealing with people in a mixed cultural setting. Importantly, this is not that great a factor in Mexico because ethnic diversity and immigration are not major factors there. Indeed, because widespread ethnic diversity is comparatively absent in Mexico, as with other issues where ethnic diversity comes into play, it is often puzzling for Mexicans to see the wide range of US and especially Canadian cultural differences in affecting behavior.

Even though the United States and Canada share similarly diverse societies as well as high levels of immigration, the two countries differ in the degree to which the pressure to confirm to a uniform standard may also be stronger in the United States and Mexico than in Canada. In other words, because Canada promotes cultural diversity more than its two southern neighbors, Canadians belonging to polychronic cultures (e.g., Punjabi, Arab, or, yes, Mexican) may resist assimilating to the monochronic norm of the dominant societies. This may be particularly true for groups living in concentrated subcultural enclaves or among First Nation and Inuit peoples, for whom adhering to traditional norms is seen as contributing to the true diversity of the Canadian mosaic.

Regional Variation

Mexico and the United States show considerable regional variation in time conception. Canada does not.[12] The farther southeast one goes in the United States, the slower is the pace of life and the more polychronic is the culture. Likewise, the closer one gets to either the Mexico City region or to the northern states of Mexico, the faster is the pace of life and the more monochronic is the culture. Nevertheless, no matter how slow the pace is in, say, Jackson, Mississippi, in the US Deep South, it would be reasonable to expect its residents to still appear to be clearly monochronic—even to the most monochronic resident of Querétaro. In other words, regardless of the region, you can expect most people in the United States to be monochronic when compared with Mexicans; likewise, you can expect most people in Mexico to be polychronic when compared with Americans. Still, you can safely expect that people in New York or Chicago in the American North or Midwest will be more monochronic than people in Mobile or Houston in the Deep South or Texas. Likewise, you can safely expect that people in the Yucatán or Chiapas will be more polychronic than people in Mexico City or Monterrey.

Personal Exigency

Some aspects of time are personal. This holds true in all three countries. It is a common experience to "lose track of time," whether you live in Mexico, Canada, or the United States. We can be so wrapped up in a project that we look up to find that hours have passed without our even realizing it. This is one aspect of the personalization of time.

If you have ever been in a hospital emergency room, you have probably experienced another form of personalization—individual perspective. If you are the one with the medical emergency, waiting even 5 minutes before you are treated can seem like forever. If you are the hospital admitting staff, however, you have a different perspective on how long it takes to get a patient to the right medical provider. You could be setting records for how quickly you have acted processing a patient—only 5 minutes rather than the usual 15 or 20—because you know the patient is in pain. If you are the patient experiencing this pain, you are unlikely to recognize—let alone appreciate—that the admitting staff person has processed you faster than usual. It is the same 5 minutes, but your personal urgency affects your perception in such a situation.

You do not need to go to a hospital waiting room to see how we perceive the same time span differently from someone else. If you have sat through a presentation—even an interesting one—you probably view the elapsed time differently from the person actually giving the presentation.

Other issues can also affect how you prioritize time. Take the phrase "as soon as possible." What this phrase means depends on who is requesting it and the situation. Let us imagine, for instance, that you are a midlevel manager at a large company, and the chief executive of your company speaks with you in person for the first time in your career and then asks you to provide an answer to a question "as soon as possible." Now let us imagine that in this same situation, one of the people who reports to you asks for input on a project "as soon as possible." Which of these would you get to first? Does how you perceive authority conception affect the meaning of "as soon as possible" for you? The culture is at play because authority conception is affected by culture.

Cross-Cultural and Global Experience

Cultures do not exist in a vacuum. When we interact with others from different cultures, we affect them and they affect us. As our understanding of others increases, so does our ability to accommodate cultural differences. This is the premise of this book as a whole, and this premise holds particularly true with regard to temporal conception.

Exposure to other cultures, and familiarity with global business practices, influences the way we approach time. When Mexicans deal with monochronic cultures, they may—indeed, they probably *should*—behave more monochronically. If a Mexican multinational corporation deals primarily with monochronic clients and markets, its whole corporate culture may become more monochronic than the overall Mexican norm. Likewise, when people from the United States and Canada deal with polychronic cultures, they may—indeed, they probably *should*—behave more polychronically. If a US or Canadian multinational corporation deals primarily with polychronic clients or markets, its whole corporate culture may become more polychronic than overall US or Canadian norms.

The problem with this—and there *is* a problem—is when one system is viewed as somehow better than the other. Monochronic and polychronic temporal conceptions are equally valid. Neither is somehow right or wrong. However, when a US company sets up an operation in Mexico and demands that it operate on monochronic time, *that is* actually wrong. That this often happens says less about the need for global standards than about US companies' lack of cultural adaptability in Mexico.[13] It does not allow the Mexican employees of that company to maximize the strengths of their own cultural approach.

It is possible to confuse globalization standards with cultural ethnocentrism. Global business communication has *no* cultural standard if the businesses involved take a truly geocentric approach (as many successful multinationals do). When powerful companies come into foreign markets, they bring with them jobs, tax revenues, and development that can be very enticing. This is by no means limited to US companies imposing their values on Mexico and other nations. Indeed, ethnocentric Japanese and German companies in the US are as likely to impose their values on the United States. The problem is that it is not uncommon for countries to mistake as somehow a global expectation what is essentially the cultural ethnocentrism of powerful companies. The United States, Germany, the United Kingdom, and Japan—among other countries—all have large, well-established business cultures, and all are monochronic in orientation.[14] Because of the success of these business cultures, many people from the countries in which they set up operation may begin to view the monochronic way as somehow being the global way of doing business. But it is not. An executive from Banorte, one of Mexico's four largest commercial banks, embodied this in an interview when she said that "before globalization, ... to be late was like nothing happens, they had to wait for us, this attitude has changed as people these days are faced with the fact that they have to gain more clients and that being late can cause us to lose our place in business."[15] The executive here expressed a view shared by many in Mexico. To do business globally, one needs to behave in a monochronic way. In other words, approaching business in a traditionally Mexican way (e.g., "before globalization") was somehow "wrong," and the imposed value of monochronic clients was thus somehow "right." One *might* argue that such accommodation might be valuable in dealing with monochronic clients—say, those US or Canadian clients who are *in* the

United States or Canada. We say *might* rather than *is* because this presumes that the US or Canadian clients could not accommodate to Mexican norms if they were advantageous. Conversely, insisting that "this attitude has changed" suggests that Mexicans should adopt a monochronic approach when doing business within Mexico itself. Such a view overlooks the value of what the polychronic approach brings as a successful system in itself. It also negates the value of a polychronic approach when doing business globally in other polychronic cultures—such as Brazil, Italy, India, Indonesia, and Saudi Arabia.

We want to emphasize that it is not your job—or any foreigner's job—to demand that Mexico transform into a monochronic society. This last point is particularly important to note with Mexico, where the North American presence is so strong that it is possible to find many Mexicans who buy into the demand to adhere to a monochronic view of time in professional settings, as if this were some sort of prerequisite for working with US or Canadian companies. This is a dangerous situation because it leads to operating in an ethnocentric bubble. Hiring only top-level employees who have chosen to accommodate monochronic behavior does not adapt to the cultural norms of the actual Mexico outside this accommodating elite. This is no different than presuming that because a North American company has hired only people fluent in English, everyone else in Mexico is equally comfortable in English. Though we hope that few people would actually make this mistake about language proficiency, we have seen many people assume that time conception is somehow different. In short, we have seen many companies that send an expatriate or even visiting technical expert to work with a Mexican subsidiary or branch with the stated purpose of improving quality control, technical skills, efficiency, and the like. In principle, there is nothing wrong with this. Nevertheless, as part of that assignment, there is a fine line between teaching employees to effectively improve quality, use new machines, or the like and that of misunderstanding the valid reasons why Mexicans do things the way they do. In any country—Mexico or anywhere else—short-term visitors and expatriate visitors rarely understand how the locals work with suppliers, factory workers, union representatives, government agencies, and local police enforcement. In other words, even if you can force people to accept monochronic values in a foreign-owned workplace, that is counterproductive in dealing with the world outside that artificially imposed, foreign view of time.

All this is to say that we should approach cultural accommodation of temporal conception differences just as we do any other area of cross-cultural interaction. Doing so is not a global necessity but a choice. US and Canadian companies doing business in Mexico (or other polychronic cultures) should embrace the benefits of polychronic orientation in terms of the personalization and related speed when connected. Mexican companies doing business in the US and Canada should equally embrace the benefits of monochronic orientation when there. Neither monochronic nor polychronic should be rejected out of hand, however, regardless of the norms of the culture where that business or any interaction takes place. For that matter, switching between time systems as the relationship and situation require is something many people consider doing when working with both cultures at the same time.

RECOMMENDATIONS

Our recommendations here are threefold: the role of the past, taking into consideration polychronic versus monochronic time conceptions, and recognizing the presence of different forms of punctuality. First, be aware that the past influences Mexican behavior in a way that simply has little counterpart in the United States and Canada. History defines Mexican self-identity in a way that goes far beyond what most North Americans expect. History—both national and personal—matters more in Mexico. We recommend that you, too, make it matter for you while you are there.

Second, keep in mind that Mexican polychronic time conception emphasizes personal relationships over the clock. Here we offer a word of warning. All too often, people who have more of a monochronic way of looking at things fall into the smug illusion that their view of time is somehow superior to that of those who hold a polychronic view. This is shared not only by many US and Canadian visitors but also even by Mexicans who have (we feel mistakenly) concluded that globalization somehow demands a monochronic worldview. It does not. Relatedly, we find it more productive to avoid the misunderstanding that is common among many North Americans who are for the first time experiencing a culture with a polychronic time conception. Due to their lack of understanding of time as a cultural value, these North Americans confuse polychronic thinking with "laziness." It is not. You will find that Mexicans work diligently, often putting in longer hours to complete the task at hand, where their US and Canadian counterparts would more likely leave at the scheduled day's end. Both polychronic and monochronic time conception are effective, efficient, and entirely workable systems that result in successful outcomes. Neither is better or worse than the other. They are just different.

Our third recommendation is to be aware that time *does* matter in Mexico; it just matters in a way that differs from that in the United States and Canada. Mexicans differentiate time by various factors, ranging from regional differences to work-versus-social settings to personal relationships and situational exigencies. Schedules in the banks and multinational corporations of Monterrey and Mexico City are more tightly followed than in the oil fields of Chiapas or the mining towns of Michoacán. What is considered late in Mexico in a business meeting or university classroom is different for a social gathering—even if all this may seem more flexible than they would be in many North American settings. Finally, the absence of significant cultural diversity means that the ethnic differences attendant on time in the United States and especially in Canada may be confusing to Mexicans in North America.

TIME SUMMARY AND CHAPTER 7 HIGHLIGHTS

The past informing the present:

- Mexicans carry a different sense of the influence of past events than North Americans.

- History—both in broad social terms and in a personal sense—affect views of the present in Mexico.

Monochronic time (US and Canadian norms):

- Activities are undertaken one thing at a time.
- There are clear starting and ending times.
- Schedules are closely adhered to, with little influence of personal or situational specifics.
- Personal relationships are subordinate to the schedule.
- Enhances the ability to measure the number of units per hour.
- Time is seen as highly tangible. Time can be lost, saved, gained, or squandered.

Polychronic time:

- Multiple tasks are handled simultaneously; multitasking is common.
- Beginning and ending times are not always clear.
- Personal relationships and situational specifics affect timing.
- The use of time is more flexible, and the clock is subordinate to the personal relationship or specific needs.

Schedule versus personal relationships:

- Temporal conception is really more of a balance between time given to the clock versus time given to people.
- In North America, the clock mandates how long we spend with people.
- In Mexico, relationships with people mandate how we manipulate the clock.

Social events:

- Professional events in Mexico basically begin and end as scheduled, with some flexibility, although with notable variation due to region.
- Social events in Mexico begin at times based on the context rather than the clock, and there is no way to say when they will end.

Recommendations:

- Be cautious about thinking that somehow monochronic time is superior to polychronic time. Both have advantages and disadvantages.
- Do not mistake polychronic time values as having no respect for time and schedules.

Case Study

*When Being Bicultural Is
More than Being Bilingual*

Our objective in applying the LESCANT approach to the analysis of intercultural communication in Mexico has been to provide a context for learning about and appreciating the differences in US, Canadian, and Mexican culture, especially in professional settings. In this final chapter, we present a brief cultural vignette—a cultural case study—that provides a chance to apply what we have learned to a real-life Mexican–US interaction. We have changed the names of the company, people, and locations, but the events and details in the vignette represent actual events. The case describes the story of Marta Nieves, a bilingual corporate lawyer who works for Hutchison & Vaile LLP (hereafter, H&V), a full-service law firm with offices in Texas, California, and Mexico. Marta works in their Houston office, where she mainly represents US clients who hope to expand operations in Mexico. She has extensive experience in international trade and immigration law, with specific expertise in foreign investment restrictions and cross-border acquisitions. She also helps clients to navigate through cross-border tax and import/export compliance. What follows is her story and examples of some of her experiences.

After the case, we provide feedback and observations from three Mexican and three US executives who have experience working in similar professional situations. These comments represent their actual opinions, and these are the real names of these people, who have graciously offered to share their opinions. We also add a few of our own comments and observations about the case. The opinions of these six executives add depth and perspective to the case scenario.

We add a few comments and observations about the case as well. After reading the vignette, you will find a final section with questions and topics to help you assess the cultural issues about this case and come up with your own solutions and insights.

THE CASE SCENARIO

Suppose you want to hire a law firm that deals with cross-border transactions between the United States and Mexico. Of course you want a law firm that can deal with foreign investments, especially in restricted areas. You will need someone who understands the bureaucracy of Mexican business practices and knowledge of their legal system, political system, and tax structure—not to mention an understanding of the cultural and social issues that come into play. Your lawyer is also going to have to maneuver negotiations that include the bilateral and cross-border movement of goods, including all the issues related to customs and shipping. At times, your projects will also include issues related to labor laws. And because we are making a wish list, you might also want a lawyer who is also fluent in both Spanish and English.

This is a tall order! If it seems nearly impossible to fill, we have a recommendation for you. Houston-based H&V is a law firm with extensive experience negotiating with counterparties from Mexican businesses. They mainly work with North American clients, but they also have some inbound Mexican clients, assisting them in understanding US business practices. H&V has specific experience in working with mergers and acquisitions and with Mexican joint venture partners, customs and import regulations, and international tax planning. Among those on the International Team, Marta Nieves has been with the firm for over fifteen years.

Marta Nieves: Personal Background

Before we talk about Marta's work experience specifically, we take a moment to introduce her and give her background. She was actually born in Mexico City and lived there until she was five years old. Her mother, Ana Cecilia, a medical doctor, was also born, raised, and had always lived in Mexico City. Her father, Garrett, a Texan, went to Mexico for the first time as a graduate student when he received a grant to conduct fieldwork in medical anthropology. Marta's parents were married in Mexico and had planned on living there permanently. However, as the years rolled on, Ana Cecilia took advantage of opportunities for additional medical training in the United States. In the end, Marta's family moved back and forth between Mexico and Texas a number of times. They finally settled in Corpus Christi, where Marta completed high school in the late 1970s. Subsequently, she enrolled in Texas A&M University Corpus Christi. Later, upon enrolling in law school at the University of Houston in 1989, she met her future husband, Carter. Carter's family comes from the Midwest, and they are all monolingual speakers of English. They have two sons who are currently in their late twenties. All four (with various levels of basic Spanish) frequently return to Mexico to reconnect with relatives. At home, however, English has been the language for family communication, as only Marta speaks with comfortable fluency in both languages. Professionally, Marta toyed with the idea of practicing law in both Mexico and the United States, but given her degree program in the US system, it seemed to make sense to stick to the US side of things.

Marta connects with her maternal Mexican and paternal American US roots—both loved, quite inseparable, but distinct nonetheless. The fact that she comes from a home with an American father and a Mexican mother affects every part of how she reacts to experiences around her. She is comfortable with her bicultural background and cannot always define where one begins and the other ends. She has observed, "I have been blessed with amazing US clients, always understanding, polite, respectful of others, willing to bend culturally, and gentle in their interactions." And she has a similar admiration for the Mexican counterparties with whom she has worked. With this introduction to Marta, let us now look at some of her professional experiences.

Marta Nieves: Professional Experiences

As an example of what it is like to work for an American law firm that also conducts business operations in Mexico, Marta recalls an experience about ten years ago with an American client who owned a small grocery store chain and part of a family-owned food storage business in the American Midwest, perhaps a $100 million–$200 million operation. Bob and Alex King were brothers and owners of King's Food World. They wanted to expand to Mexico and had been in negotiations with a Mexican family that also owned a small grocery chain in Mexico. The two sides had been negotiating for months, and Bob and Alex had assumed they were getting close to the final stages before they brought Marta into the negotiations.

It was at this point that Bob and Alex were referred to H&V, which they hired for its translation services. (Up to this point, all oral and written communication had been conducted only in English.) Initially, they asked Marta to simply prepare a Spanish-language translation of the term sheet. As Marta translated the term sheet, she also took time to assess and anticipate the potential issues, problems, and reasons behind the clauses of the term sheet. In doing so, she was able to better understand what the US client was hoping to accomplish.

After Marta completed the translation, Bob and Alex asked her to accompany the US team to Mexico to finalize the negotiations, which they supposed would take less than one day. The US travel team was made up of the two US owners, Bob and Alex, their lawyer, and Marta. The Mexican side was made up of the owner, his two brothers, and two lawyers from a large Mexican firm. Admittedly, Marta had been brought on to the team late in the game, and the parties had already been working together for some time. Within minutes of arriving, however, Marta could tell that the last round of negotiations was not going well. As she put it, "This was no meeting of the minds."

Marta sensed immediately that the Mexican team members were giving indications of their disapproval. Often, a Mexican team member would say something like, "It would be difficult to implement XYZ," to which an American team member would inappropriately offer words of encouragement: "We know it is difficult, but you can do it!" Marta knew from similar experiences in the past that the Mexican team was not going to come out and strike down the deal directly. The problem was, however, that the American team never took the hints of disapproval. It was not until the Mexican counterparts were unwilling to sign that the America group realized that something must be wrong.

By this time, it was time to break for lunch. The Mexican group did not even invite the US team to join them for lunch. Both parties went their separate ways to strategize separately. At lunch, Marta interjected and told the US contingent that the Mexicans simply did not agree with the terms and conditions. It was like a light bulb had gone on: "No way! We had no idea! Really? They don't agree with these terms?" Marta recognized the syndrome. She had seen it many times before in US–Mexican negotiations. The two sides were so far apart, and yet the US team had not even realized that there was a disagreement.

The next day, everyone tried again, but the deal never did go through. Basically, in the end it became clear that the Mexican side was hoping to gain cash for its operations but was unwilling to give up any control. The Mexican owner wanted to maintain his family business under the control of his family, with hopes that his own children would carry on with the family business someday. He and his family wanted to hold on, as Marta explained, "to their little kingdom." The US team members wanted to expand into a new market, with all of Mexico's promise of a young, vibrant, and growing population. They were hoping to introduce modern technology and equipment, increase efficiency, strengthen buying power, and lower prices.

They had suggestions for new ways to keep food refrigerated and how to better store and transport foodstuffs. In essence, they were hoping to create a more US-style—what they called "more modern"—grocery chain. From the Mexican side, they did not want to lose the intimate feel and sense of community of a neighborhood store, even if it meant less selection and higher costs. In short, while the US side wanted to create a national chain, the Mexican side was unwilling to chance a "fragmented" family business.

Marta uses this example to show that it is easy to blame "language" for miscommunications, when in reality there are other values and priorities that go deeper than just the use of Spanish or English. Not to oversimplify, but in this case, in using the term "family business," the North Americans were emphasizing a cut-and-dry, impersonal approach, which they saw as the ideal business practice, and the Mexicans were emphasizing a family, relational approach, which they just as equally saw as the ideal business practice. Each side did so to the detriment of the other, and in the end this is what killed the deal.

In a second example, Marta recalls an experience when she represented Evan Mardsen, the acquisition officer of Brownsville Finishing, a Texas company working with *maquiladoras* along the US–Mexican border that specialize in metal plating, mainly zinc, silver, gold, and nickel. Brownsville Finishing needed to merge with a restricted (i.e., limited to a specific purpose for which it was incorporated) company in Mexico. Because of this, the Texas company was looking for a Mexican majority-owner partner. Marta could see right away that Brownsville Finishing ran its operations in the impersonalized manner widespread as a norm throughout the United States and Canada. With this in mind, she asked Evan how he planned to describe himself and his company to their potential Mexican partners. He replied, "Well, for starters I would like to tell them that Brownsville Finishing is a 'no-nonsense company' and runs itself in a 'very professional' manner." Evan continued by telling Marta that "I can guarantee that Brownsville Finishing understands the financial and economic aspects of doing business in Mexico extremely well—and that's what we really want them to know."

Evan was taken aback when Marta explained that this might not be the best approach to describing Brownsville Finishing and himself to many—and perhaps even most—potential Mexican partners. "I don't doubt for a minute that Brownsville Finishing may believe it understands the financial and economic aspects of doing business, all right," Marta told him, "but there's more to doing business than the numbers on the page." Even after this, Evan seemed surprised, and so he asked her why she had warned him about this. Marta answered Evan's question with another question: "How would *you* define 'no-nonsense' or 'professional'?" Only as he was answering Marta's question did it finally start to dawn on Evan that his definition meant "in a standard North American way." Implicit in his comments, he realized, was the fact that the quick timelines and short-term, bottom-line monetary results were based on his own cultural values, as if getting to know others and spending time with each other were somehow *un*professional—rather than just a different (and equally effective) way to conduct business.

With this, Evan said that he felt "it was ironic" to be telling Marta this, but that he could tell her "from my own experience" that Brownsville Finishing actually prides itself on being "very gentle, people-focused, and approachable" and a company that "showed care for individuals."

And this was exactly what Evan shared with each of Brownsville Finishing's potential partners. Evan, and in fact the entire Brownsville Finishing team, enjoyed the merger process, took advantage of opportunities to be in Mexico, and demonstrated an interest in Mexico. They were, as Marta explained, "systematic in their approach, but humanistic in their interactions."

When Brownsville Finishing's merger team finally formed their Mexican partnership, at the very initial phase of working together, they even opened up a Mexico office to create a local presence. Their interactions included many dinners and social activities. They attended local sporting activities, participated in holidays and religious ceremonies, and connected with the community. Evan's merger team included people from both the United States and Mexico, and together they engaged well with their new Mexican partners. The merger went off without a hitch, and it looked as though things were going to progress smoothly. However, within three years the collaboration died, and the merger was dissolved. How did things die so quickly when the negotiation process had gone so positively? Marta surmises that the American and Mexican partners had drastically different perceptions about the type of follow-up that happens after negotiations.

From the American side, after the contracts were signed, there was no more reason for the American group to maintain the Mexican office. Evan himself left after the merger was firmly in place, even though he had nurtured the initial relationships on which Brownsville Finishing had built the foundation for its Mexican partnership. From the perspective of Brownsville Finishing, Marta explained, they were simply moving on to the next project. They trusted their Mexican partner and were willing to pass on the day-to-day operations to them. However, from the other side, the Mexicans had supposed that the US company would continue to be linked together with its partners for joint decisions and continued collaboration. At this point, Marta reminds us that the stereotype about Americans is that they come to Mexico to use Mexican resources, make money, take what benefits them, and then disappear without any concern for those on the Mexican side. The stereotype does not hold true for all US companies by any means, but it has had centuries of historical foundation, so many Mexicans remain justifiably alert to this scenario as a possibility. In this case, when the US company pulled out, it simply reinforced the old stereotype of Americans who only care about themselves. From the US team members' perspective, once the merger had been finalized, their moving on should have been a sign of how much they trusted their Mexican partners. There simply was no need to maintain a Mexico office.

The Mexicans' feelings were so hurt by the abandonment that they could not even attend meetings together anymore. They felt betrayed. Partly because of American informality, Americans sometimes give the impression of being close friends who have created a long-lasting relationship. Unfortunately, the informality appears shallow and less than sincere when it is casually discarded. In this case, the Mexico office created the illusion of a long-term commitment to work together as partners. Marta's word of advice: "If you are going to do business with Mexico, commit to being there for the long haul. Mexicans do not want to feel like they are simply being used by those whose only interest is in making a quick buck and then disappearing from the scene."

Marta's Final Observations and Advice

In addition to the examples given above, Marta adds a couple of other observations and pieces of advice. First, attorneys as a profession—regardless of the culture to which belong—are trained to think about potential problems and figure out how to deal with them, even before they happen. When this lawyerly occupational tendency is combined with the cultural North American trait that places great value on the same characteristic, this results in what might be seen from a Mexican perspective as approaching exaggeration—a lawyer stuck in overdrive. As a result, North Americans do lots of initial research and homework. "In many ways," Marta points out, "this is their strength—deep and detailed preparation and planning." Americans work hard to anticipate every eventuality.

Mexicans see the situation differently, and generally attack problems as they happen, with less emphasis on anticipating things before they happen and more attention on working hard to manage life's uncertainties. In general, many Mexicans approach things more with the attitude that they will deal with today's problems today, and not worry about other issues at this time. There is—at least from a US perspective—more of what Marta calls "a spontaneous attitude." For example, just last week Marta had sent a client to Mexico. And despite dozens of phone calls and e-mails, the Mexico contact never arranged for an English-speaking notary. The local counsel simply did not prepare for that contingency. When you hear people in Mexico say, "I've got it taken care of," realize that many times what this really means is that somebody will take on that problem if and when it really comes up, but in the meantime there is no reason to spend time on something that may not even happen. Prepare for this difference in approach.

Second, Marta observes that because many Mexicans are less that 100 percent fluent in English, they sometimes translate words that may make sense in Spanish but do not make sense in English. For example, in Spanish the word *efectivamente* means "really." As such, a phrase like, *Sí, efectivamente eso es absolutamente correcto* means "Yes, this really is absolutely correct." The problem is that a less-than-fluent speaker will say, in English, "Yes, effectively this is absolutely correct." These types of phrases cause misunderstandings during meetings and complicate negotiations with imprecise language. "And this is especially damaging in a field where precise language is key to contracts and decisions," adds Marta. Only those who speak both Spanish and English fluently will understand the intent of such phrases. And Marta adds, "This rarely happens, because the Spanish fluency of American business professionals is almost zero."

As we mentioned at the beginning, if you are looking to hire a law firm that deals with cross-border transactions between the US and Mexico, we have found the perfect lawyer, Marta Nieves.

OBSERVATIONS AND COMMENTS
FROM AMERICAN EXPERTS

What follows are the personal opinions of three North American experts who share their reactions to this cultural vignette. Ryan Jones, Mitchell Slape, and Juan Creixell all have extensive professional experience working in Mexico and with Mexicans.

Ryan Jones, Continental Automotive, ADAS Mexico— Manager of Sensor Software Development

As I read through the vignette, I couldn't help but smile. Certain themes were quite emotive, as they reminded me of challenges that I've faced while communicating with my Mexican colleagues. Other points were less relevant for me. Still, in all cases I found myself feeling relieved at how realistic the situations felt.

I felt comforted that as I read the sentence "It would be hard to implement XYZ" by a Mexican colleague, I immediately noticed a problem. The key is that my Mexican colleagues will rarely ever tell other colleagues that something will be a challenge. If they can't implement something, they will simply agree to it with a less-than-enthusiastic response. In other words, "hard to implement" implies they feel it is not possible. For many of my Mexican colleagues, this is being direct.

Communication in a Mexico business culture is generally very subtle. I have found this style of communication somewhat challenging, as I communicate in a direct manner. For example, in order to truly understand a colleague's opinion, I feel I must speak with them. When discussing topics in Mexico, I have found that one will learn much less from the words that they say, and much more from the way that they say them. Asking a Mexican colleague if they can meet an objective will almost always result in the affirmative. Listening to how the affirmation is said, as well as subtle concerns, provides much more information about their thoughts.

Similar care should be taken when sharing opinions as well. I have offended my coworkers on multiple occasions by being overly direct. I have found it to be much more effective to share my more direct thoughts in private.

The Brownsville Finishing company example also strikes me as a very important representation of challenges within US–Mexico business relationships. While working in the office in the United States, I became heavily accustomed to a US–German–influenced work culture. Decisions were made with cold, almost emotionless logic. We saw each other as a distribution of job functions, and decisions were made solely based upon the best interest of the company, thus forgetting the human side of business.

In Mexico, the foundation of a business relationship is based upon a personal connection as well as perceived mutual respect. A business connection, though important, will never work without showing that you know about each other on a personal level. In this way, it is the opposite of the United States. We will determine if the business cultures are compatible first, and then perhaps get to know each other along the way.

Maria changed the Brownsville team's approach because it would have immediately demonstrated a clash of philosophy.

A personal connection is not a potential side effect of doing business, it is the first step when doing business. My coworkers invite me to their parties and weddings, ask me out for drinks, and freely discuss aspects of their lives. They also make sure to assist me in my life if at all possible, listening to my challenges and getting involved. I've now been supported in buying a car, finding insurance, getting a bank account, and numerous other activities. They treat me, as well as each other, like family.

If the reader is moving toward working in a Mexican work culture, I would recommend that they do so with openness. Projecting a US work culture will typically end in a poor working relationship. Being open, respectful, and friendly is absolutely critical and has opened my eyes to a different way of thinking.

Mitchell Slape, Executive—Retail Industry

There are several aspects of the vignette with which I identify from my experience working with Mexican business people, both from the US and as an expatriate in Mexico. Those concepts include the extreme importance of family and the depth of relationships in Mexican life and business culture. The vignette also reminded me that American business people tend to be very direct, and we often see this as an admirable quality, whereas Mexican business culture is often characterized by a great deal of indirect communication and often requires recognition of subtleties in interactions. Additionally, I was reminded of the concept that substantial work in understanding your business partners, respecting the legacy of what they have built and building your relationships before you ever get to work on an agreement, is so important. Furthermore, after the agreement is signed, the real work in tending the relationship begins!

My own experiences of working in Mexico were very similar in this regard. Fortunately, I was fluent in Spanish when I was posted to Mexico and had the opportunity to go through an orientation process before arrival, so I was somewhat aware of the cultural aspects of the country and of business life. Early in the process of arriving, I was able to spend time getting to know my team members on a personal level and understand more about their families and lives outside of work. Having these conversations and demonstrating an interest in getting to know and understand people beyond work was one of the most important things I did at the start my assignment.

My interactions with prospective and future business partners were also characterized by these same concepts. In the industry in which I work, families have built businesses over generations. There is a high degree of well-earned pride in what has been built as well as concern about respecting and preserving the company's culture into the future. Investing time to understand the history of the company, the involvement of the family, and the traditions that have been developed is an important part of the process of getting to know your partner. Further, integrating these elements into your business together is a fundamental part of not only respecting the business culture of your partner's company but also of building a successful foundation for your joint business into the future.

In the two scenarios that were presented in the vignette, my recommendation in both cases for the American companies would be to slow down, get to know your partner, develop a strong relationship with them, and make sure that you are fully invested in the relationship for the long run. The key in my mind is to approach these relationships with a strong focus on building a foundation of respect. If respect exists, partners will spend the time to get to know each other and to fully understand what each party has built and brings to the relationship. It will also make it substantially easier to resolve issues in the future as they arise. Although good attorneys like Marta will be able to help draft agreements that take into consideration potential problems that may happen down the road in the business relationship, real problems in the future are only going to be amicably resolved by partners who have a high degree of respect for each other and willingness to work through issues. This is best accomplished on a foundation of respect in the relationship.

Juan Creixell, Executive Director, Head of Investments
for Central and South Texas, Global Investment Bank
As someone who has worked in the same industry in both Mexico and the US, I can attest to the difference in conducting business.

I know, understand, and have lived firsthand the description in the passage of how people in Mexico like to do business. I really identified with the two examples from Marta Nieves's professional experience. I have seen similar situations happen in real life. I also thought that giving her personal background first was very descriptive of the Mexican way of conducting business. The description of how she connects with both sides of her roots and the description of her two sons and their interactions really puts me in a Mexican way of doing business. It touched on the emotional side of Marta, and I can see why someone in Mexico would like to know those things. For most people in the US, a background of her professional accomplishments would have been far more important than her upbringing or her family life.

I know the importance of getting to know the people first. In Mexico, to really earn someone's trust, you need to get to know them; and to get to know them, you must be willing to put yourself out there first. In my business experience in Mexico, people do not care how much you know until they know how much you care. Show interest in the person first and then the business comes easy. Once you have earned someone's trust, then it is a true partnership, where they will stay with you through the good and bad times. In my industry in the US, people are a lot less emotional, and business relationships really come down to a "what have you done for me lately" mentality. The history of a relationship is much less meaningful.

I feel I have been very fortunate to have had an upbringing and background similar to the one Marta has in the vignette, and I know that to be successful doing business in two countries you must know how people like to do business. Do clients want you to ask how their weekend was before you can get to business? Or do they want to get straight to the point, and maybe perhaps you can have some chit chat? The situations described are real. I once had a Mexican client and I had to give up working with him because of a change in my professional assignments. I moved to a different office and the move was a promotion for me and helped my career. Yet he felt betrayed that I had left him, and when he told me this, he added that he "had to get it off his chest." As life would have it, after years I am again working with this person, and it has been very difficult to earn his trust back, and this even though the reason for the changes had nothing to do with me or him, and more to do with the regional alignment of our business.

As to my recommendation for someone in a similar situation who has built a relationship and finds himself in a situation similar to the one in the vignette with Brownsville Finishing, my recommendation is to overcommunicate. That is to say, explain ahead of time exactly what is going to happen and why it will happen. Be honest but gentle in the delivery. Make sure that your business partners know that what will happen is business and not personal, and that you are always there to discuss things. Next, let them know that you are not going away and can always be a resource. Explain why they may see or hear less from you, but make sure they know that it is not for a lack of interest and that you can always get involved as needed. And third, do check in now and again. People in Mexico really appreciate it when you check in with them. It is an important part of the business relationship.

OBSERVATIONS AND COMMENTS
FROM MEXICAN EXPERTS

Alfonso Padilla, Rodrigo Ruy, and María Angélica Pech Ortega are three Mexican executives with extensive experience in dealing with North Americans. Their collective experience provides a unique vantage point from which to provide feedback related to the cultural vignette.

Alfonso Padilla, CoC Product Engineer, ZF North America, Inc.
The thing I most identify with in this vignette is the way Marta dealt with both cultures, specifically in meetings between Mexicans and Americans. Because part of my job involves dealing with the Purchasing Department in Mexico and the Engineering Department in the United States, I also participate in many meetings with people from both countries as well as independent meetings in the United States and in Mexico. I have also learned

how to talk differently to both groups of colleagues. On one hand, when I am in US meetings, for example, I try to be brief and go directly to the point. I have noticed that when I try to explain a problem or issue with many words, my US colleagues get anxious and desperate. They prefer things to be said quickly, and they like you to get to the point as soon as possible and then move on to the next topic of the agenda. On the other hand, when I am in conferences in Mexico, my experience is like what Marta mentions in the vignette. My Mexican colleagues talk with lots of sentences and added ideas, and it takes a long time to say what is going on. Given that I am from Mexico, I was not initially aware of this, because I guess I had been dealing with it daily. Now, however, after having worked in another culture, I can immediately detect the Mexican way of saying things and dealing with problems.

So my experience related to this has been almost the same as Marta's. I try to talk differently, depending on the situation or whom I am dealing with; I know that I approach things differently when I am talking with Mexicans or with Americans. The Mexicans, for example, can approach things slowly and without pressure. They know that they will get to things, but of course there are times when urgency matters. Americans, conversely, want things done quickly and want them well planned. When I have conferences with people in Guadalajara, we always take a few minutes to catch up on things, even though we are not necessarily close friends. This is because they know that I am an expatriate, so they always ask about me and my family. They want to know if everything is OK with me and my life. After that, we get into the issues related to the meeting. In meetings with Americans in Northville, we get to the point immediately. There is no time wasted, and almost all the issues are solved in one meeting. This is not the case in Mexico, where it takes one or two more meetings to get through all the open points on the agenda. And this is due to many factors, such as unpunctuality, absence, and wasting of time.

A good example of this is something that happened just a few days ago. We asked for some materials from the purchasing area in Guadalajara. When we received the materials, the shipment was incomplete. So we had to ask for more samples.

We then scheduled a meeting to find out what happened, and to define a new action plan. Our response from Mexico was slow in coming. When we did finally reach the buyer in Mexico, he explained the situation and told us that he would get in contact with the supplier of these component parts and give us an answer as soon as possible. We waited about an hour, then two, and I finally told my US colleagues that we probably would not be receiving an answer until the next day. The next day, our Mexican colleagues were able to provide us with an answer, but by then we had already come up with a new action plan, which we had worked out during the hours when we had been waiting for their response.

Based on my experience, my recommendation in cases similar to those of Marta's is to explain the behavior of each side. At the beginning of a negotiation between US and Mexico, explain how Americans and Mexicans behave and react to certain situations. Try to explain to the Americans how important the bond is that forms when business is done in Mexico, and explain how this relationship goes beyond just business. In both examples that Marta gave in the vignette, the US company wanted to do business with Mexico. I think the negotiations must respect the Mexican traditions. In addition, I would speak to the Mexicans on how formality works with Americans, and not to take things so personally when Americans go searching for another business after the deal is closed with them.

Rodrigo Ruy Gutiérrez Hernández, Industrial Engineer
in Production, WW Corporate Quality Manager, Asteelflash
Here are some of my observations about the stories in this vignette. First off, as to the grocery store deal, both sides made many wrong assumptions. Why were they even thinking of signing a deal without first defining the rules, the metrics, and the goals? The fact that they would not even have lunch together is a really bad sign that things were very cold. Some of this was due to different cultures and styles for managing business, and they obviously had different long-term visions for their companies. I would say that culture, not language, was the main barrier on being able to sign a deal. Second, as to the Brownsville Finishing

Plant, they had an excellent start with high interaction before and during the merging of the companies. However, a cultural bias sent the wrong messages on both sides, and this affected their ability to maintain a working partnership.

I identify with the challenges in these stories. I cannot pinpoint any exact same scenario in my case, but I know that cultural differences do affect the way we conduct business, and I know that it affects how we work together. Everywhere there is a need for diversity training, for understanding the global melting pot, and for dealing with a multicultural workforce. I have had similar challenges over the years, although of course within a different context. In the end, I believe that in order to connect with people who are working together on projects, we all need to focus on universal values: honesty, respect, treating people with dignity, being humble, and having a desire to help, to serve, and to win. If everyone on both sides has the same values, we can accomplish anything, regardless of the culture or any other type of differences.

At the start of my career, I recall that working in the manufacturing/*maquiladora* industry in the North of Mexico was complex, especially as related to how to deal with Asian cultures. During the 1980s and 1990s, the Japanese economy was doing well and there were many Japanese companies that had invested in Mexico. And there were many South Korean companies too. Especially in the case of the South Korean companies, they made many legal demands that were difficult to understand. There were also significant differences in the way that South Korean management interacted with employees, never yielding and being rather abusive. At the same time, we were also dealing with American companies. In those days, people from the South of Mexico had an even more difficult time because they were less familiar with American culture. Those from the North side of the country had at least grown up watching American TV and movies, and their association with border cities made it easier for them to work with American people. There were indeed cultural differences, but many small *maquiladoras* that started in the early 1980s in the North converted into full manufacturing industries. This was especially true in the automotive and aerospace sectors. Nowadays, and after the lessons learned, many companies with international operations have incorporated cross-cultural training into their teams. Employees are now more successful in the various projects and in working with people from different countries and cultures.

As to my recommendations, in order to be successful in dealing with international issues, cross-cultural training is essential to have the tools and knowledge about how people interact. I believe there are three main factors that contribute to these cultural differences: (1) high- versus low-context cultures; (2) the way that management views time, either sequentially or synchronically; and (3) affect, that is, how people demonstrate emotions. These three areas are crucial when dealing with international teams. Additionally, it is important to prepare with background information on facts and statistics that give you a deep dive into how people conduct business, handle negotiations, and manage themselves during meetings.

Similar to what I already mentioned above, one of the keys to prevailing during any type of negotiation is to focus on universal values: be respectful, honest, humble, open to differences that may arise, work to find common ground, have a "win-win approach." This is the only way to achieve common goals, targets, and objectives for any mission that we pursue. Without this knowledge and understanding, we will not be able to accomplish anything. The key to success and proper communication, especially among different cultures, is to develop a deep understanding and respect for the differences among us.

María Angélica Pech Ortega, Fulbright
Scholar, Guerrero, Mexico
When I read the case scenario, immediately I identified with some Mexican attitudes or ways of thinking. Obviously, I cannot speak for all Mexicans, but my observations come from my own experience, things that I have seen in my family, at work, among friends, and with people that I have known. I am from Mexico and I have lived there most of my life, with a couple of exceptions when I lived and worked in the United States with my brother, who has a small family business. The first time I worked with him for about two years and the second time for less than a year.

There, I witnessed some of the issues that come up when people try to do business the Mexican way in the United States.

With respect to the case scenario, it is true that doing business in Mexico takes time. Even if you have done all the legal paperwork, you still need time to get to know people face to face. And this applies to everything—procedures, meetings, meals, and the like. And the way people express themselves also matters. For example, in the case scenario the American team from King's Food said, "We know it's difficult, but *you* can do it." Already there, I would suggest that it would have been better to say, "We know it's difficult but *we* can do it." Why? Because this simple change expresses commitment, it means that we are all together in this, we are part of the team, the family business. This is not a trivial matter; in Mexico, the concept of a family business implies *family*, and being part of that is a big deal.

I was also interested in the comment in the King's Food story about direct communication: "Martha knew that the Mexican team was not going to come out and strike down the deal directly." This is a very important consideration, because in Mexico, *le damos vueltas a las cosas*, "we take a side trip around things." We do not state things so directly. For us, it sounds a bit rude to say something so straightforwardly. For example, if a friend asks, "How do I look?" and if she does not look very good, we will probably say something like, "I like it, it is a very good color for you. And I really like the other short dress you have, too. It looks great on you." That probably means that we really do not like it all that much. So, although we believe that being a straight shooter is a positive thing, deep down we believe that direct speech comes off a little gruff. My recommendation is to keep this in mind, especially when dealing with small and medium-sized companies in Mexico. With the large corporations, this is perhaps less of an issue; but with the smaller ones, communication will be less direct.

Turning to the second story about the acquisition officer from Brownsville Finishing Company, I agree with Martha's advice: Do not automatically think of the "American way" as the best way. I recommend that one start with the attitude that both the American style and Mexican style, although different, will have their own advantages and disadvantages. As a case in point, the Brownsville Finishing team members closed their Mexican office, thinking it was a sign of how much they trusted their Mexican partner, when, from the Mexican side of things, it was perceived as neglect. How unfortunate. From the US side, I can think of at least two things that Brownville Finishing could have done. First, they should have communicated better the reason for closing the Mexican office. It sounds as if they took it for granted that the Mexican partners knew it, but it should have been emphasized more. Second, the Brownsville Finishing team members should have organized something—some event, some activity—to continue to connect with their Mexican offices. They could have had an event every year to celebrate the founding, or perhaps a Christmas party, something to keep the connections. In my own experience, I know that in Puebla the German automaker Volkswagen stops production for one day every year to celebrate Our Lady of Guadalupe, one of the most important celebrations in Mexico. They open their doors to all the employees and their families. They have a Mass, food, mechanical games, music, and much more. They have been doing this since the early 1960s. This is exactly what Marta was referring to when she talked about the importance of committing to being there for the long haul. Commit to the employees, their families, and their community. Brownsville Finishing could have done something similar.

Finally, one item seemed to be a bit of an exaggeration to me. I did not totally agree with the statement that as opposed to preparing beforehand, Mexicans "generally attack problems as they happen." My experience is that this is not always the case, and a lot of effort goes into foreseeing eventualities as well. On balance, however, I agree with Marta, and of course it is important to have someone who understands both the language and the culture.

OBSERVATIONS AND COMMENTS FROM THE AUTHORS

Each of the guest executives, both those from the United States and those from Mexico, emphasizes the importance of getting to know your partners, getting to know them in face-to-face meetings, and building authentic relationships. Mitchell Slape referred to this as a need to add depth to the relationship, with a strong focus on building a foundation of respect. Juan Creixell describes this as a willingness to put yourself out there. This is not just a corny cliché: "People don't care how much you know until they know how much you care." It is real, it is the "bond" that Alfonso Padilla mentions in his comments.

Another area on which each of the guest executives agreed was their observations about the direct, blunt style of communication among the North Americans and the implicit, indirect style among the Mexicans. Ryan Jones says that his Mexican colleagues rarely tell others that something will be a challenge; it is not *what* they say but *how* they say it. Jones observes that they simply agree less than enthusiastically. In chapter 4, we mentioned that relatively low-context North Americans are more direct in stating opinions overtly. Our experience coincides with these opinions. Furthermore, the North American colleagues simply are frequently less adept at taking the hint, waiting instead to hear the direct communication. Our recommendation is simple: Take time to assess how things are communicated. Think about what is *not* being said.

It is interesting that among Juan Creixell's comments, he mentioned how much he appreciated reading about Marta's background. It helped to understand her history, much more than simply knowing that she is a lawyer for Hutchison & Vaile. That personal side of business dealings counts. We appreciate his story about having to give up on a Mexican client, who then felt betrayed, and how even years later after reconnecting, he is still struggling to regain the trust that was lost. His advice is poignant; let people know that you are not going away, and check in with them now and again.

There are a few other comments from the guest executives that we highlight. Alfonso Padilla mentions that he has learned to literally talk differently to both groups of colleagues. He understands that his American colleagues get anxious when he uses too many words. They prefer an approach of getting to the point as soon as possible. In Mexico he spends more time to give added details and ideas. It is a tough concept to grasp, but we appreciate his advice to other Mexican professionals, to not take things so personally when Americans move on to other topics and other projects. We also appreciated Rodrigo's advice that cross-cultural and diversity training is essential. He notes that we all share universal values, which although expressed differently, put us in a position to work together, find common ground, and "accomplish anything." The tendency in Mexico is to hint at opinions implicitly. As Jones says, share direct thoughts only in private, not in front of others. And we value María Angélica's example of Volkswagen, which for years has supported its employees and their families in the celebration of Our Lady of Guadalupe. This is a wonderful example of how a company can keep the connections with its Mexican offices.

Finally, there are a couple of items that our guest executives did not mention that we would like to highlight. Marta mentioned that Evan Mardsen from Brownsville Finishing had assumed that a definition of a "no-nonsense company" and a "very professional manner" would be interpreted the same way by everyone. It was a revelation to him to find out that even these terms were culturally based. Our recommendation is that all benefit from taking time to define what terms, values, concepts, and expressions mean to others. Often, we all value similar concepts, but we simply use different words to describe these values. Other times, we use similar words, but we do so thinking of different concepts. It is actually a difficult task to assess when our concepts and our words coincide. Our recommendation is to take time to think about this and the implications for professional interactions in cross-cultural scenarios.

For readers who want to discuss these issues further, consider the following topics and questions for discussion:

1. In what ways do you think that Brownsville Finishing could have maintained the business operations with its Mexican partner and still have been able to move on to new projects in other areas? What category of the LESCANT approach comes into play in this scenario?

2. Mitchell Slap recommends that negotiators slow down when working with Mexican partners. He suggests that

people take time to know their partner and show that one is fully invested in the relationship for the long run. How can one follow this advice when perhaps others in the US home office do not appreciate this perspective?

3. Juan Creixell made the observation that Mexican partners want to know that "you are not going away and can always be a resource." How does this tie in to the LESCANT approach, and why is it important?

4. To what do you think Rodrigo was referring when he said that both sides of the grocery store deal had made wrong assumptions? What were some of those wrong assumptions, and what were their implications?

5. María Angélica mentions that in Mexico an important consideration is that *le damos vueltas a las cosas*, "we take a side trip around things." To what is she referring, and how does it fit into the LESCANT approach?

6. Among Marta's final observations, she states that one of the Americans' strengths is their deep and detailed preparation and planning, their hard work to anticipate every eventuality. Would you not suppose that this would universally be a positive thing? Why is it, from the Mexican perspective, that this "strength" does not always work?

7. From a linguistic point of view, Marta observed that sometimes words do not translate directly, and this causes misunderstandings when speakers are not completely fluent. She used the example of the word *efectivamente* in Spanish, which does not really mean "effectively" in English but something more like "really." What other examples can you think of where English and Spanish words do not translate as directly as one would hope?

CHAPTER 1

1. US Central Intelligence Agency, *CIA Factbook*, www.cia.gov/library /publications/the-world-factbook/.

2. Jens Manuel Krogstad, "5 Facts about Mexico and Immigration to the US," Fact Tank, Numbers in the News, Pew Research Center, Washington, 2016, www.pewresearch.org/fact-tank/2016/02/11 /mexico-and-immigration-to-us/.

3. "English Language 2018 Proficiency Index, Mexico." EF, Cambridge, MA, https://www.ef.edu/epi/regions/latinoamerica/mexico.

4. Kate Palmer, "75% of Americans Have No Second Language," YouGov.com, Redwood City, CA, 2013, https://today.yougov.com /news/2013/07/31/75-americans-have-no-second-language/.

5. Renee Stepler and Anna Brown, "Statistical Portrait of Hispanics in the United States." Hispanic Trends, Pew Research Center, Washington, 2016, www.pewhispanic.org/2016/04/19/statistical -portrait-of-hispanics-in-the-united-states-key-charts/.

6. US Census Bureau, "National Population Projections Tables, Population by Nativity for the United States: 2015 to 2060," 2014, www.census.gov/data/tables/2014/demo/popproj/2014-summary -tables.html.

7. Calculated from data in "Los Extranjeros en México," Instituto Nacional de Estadística y Geografía (INEGI), 17, 2007, www.beta .inegi.org.mx/app/biblioteca/ficha.html?upc=702825006465. The total population of Mexico in the 2000 census was 102.8 million. The total number of immigrants living in Mexico in 2000 was 492,617. Of these, 69.7 percent were from the United States, 1.2 percent were from Canada, and 0.5 percent were from England. Assuming that all these were native English speakers (which is unlikely, especially from Canada and the United States), this would make a total of 71.4 percent of the total 492,617 immigrants, or 351,729. Calculating 352 as a percentage of 102.8 gives a percentage of 0.34 percent.

8. In the 2011 Census of Canada, Spanish was listed as the mother tongue by 410,670. Out of a total population of 33.12 million, this comes to 1.237 percent. Data from "Selected Demographic and Language Characteristics," 2011 Census of Canada, Statistics Canada, 2011, www12.statcan.gc.ca/census-recensement/2011/dp-pd/tbt-tt /Rp-eng.cfm?APATH=3&DETAIL=0&DIM=0&FL=A&FREE=0&

GC=0&GID=0&GK=0&GRP=1&LANG=E&PID=107988&PRID=
10&PTYPE=101955&S=0&SHOWALL=0&SUB=0&THEME=90&
Temporal=2011&VID=0&VNAMEE=&VNAMEF.

9. "Los Extranjeros en México," INEGI, 10, 2007. For Canadian data, see Jean-Dominique Morency, Éric Caron Malenfant, and Samuel MacIsaac, "Immigration and Diversity: Population Projections for Canada and Its Regions, 2011 to 2036," Statistics Canada, January 25, 2017, www.statcan.gc.ca/pub/91-551-x/91-551-x2017001-eng.htm. For US data, see "Projections of the Population by Nativity for the United States: 2015 to 2060, US Census Bureau, 2017, www.census.gov /data/tables/2017/demo/popproj/2017-summary-tables.html.

10. This was calculated as 44 percent of 38 million. In turn, 16.7 million is 5.2 percent of 318.9 million.

11. Ana Gonzalez-Barrera and Mark Hugo Lopez, "A Demographic Portrait of Mexican Origin Hispanics in the United States," Hispanic Trends, Pew Research Center, Washington, 2013, www .pewhispanic.org/2013/05/01/a-demographic-portrait-of-mexican -origin-hispanics-in-the-united-states/.

12. British Council, Education Intelligence, "English in Mexico: An Examination of Policy, Perception, and Influencing Factors," London, May 2015, https://ei.britishcouncil.org/sites/default/files /latin-america-research/English%20in%20Mexico.pdf.

13. Isabel Becerril, "En México sólo 5 percent de la población habla inglés: IMCO," El Financiero, April 27, 2015, www.elfinanciero.com .mx/economia/en-mexico-solo-de-la-poblacion-habla-ingles-imco .html.

14. British Council, "English in Mexico: An Examination of Policy, Perceptions and Influencing Factors," 7, May 2015, https:// ei.britishcouncil.org/sites/default/files/latin-america-research /English%20in%20Mexico.pdf.

15. Instituto Nacional de Estadística y Geografía (INEGI), "Presentación de la Encuesta Intercensal 2015: Principales Resultados," 75, 2015, www.inegi.org.mx/est/contenidos/proyectos/encuestas /hogares/especiales/ei2015/doc/eic_2015_presentacion.pdf.

16. INEGI, 74.

17. Judith E. Liskin-Gasparro, ETS Oral Proficiency Testing Manual (Princeton, NJ: Educational Testing Service, 1982).

CHAPTER 2

1. Baja California Sur has a population density of 25 people per square mile (= 7 square kilometers), and Nevada has 26 per square mile. These states are Nebraska, at 24.3 people per square mile; Idaho, 19.5; New Mexico, 17.2; South Dakota, 11.1; North Dakota, 10.5; Montana, 7.0; Wyoming, 6.0; and Alaska, 1.3. These data are from the US Census Bureau. In Canadian terms, however, only four provinces are more densely populated.

2. Population counts vary notably, depending on the source. We have chosen "The World's Cities in 2016," UN Department of Economic

and Social Affairs, 2016, www.un.org/en/development/desa
/population/publications/pdf/urbanization/the_worlds_cities_in
_2016_data_booklet.pdf. This is a reliable source, with data all coming from the same year (many other measures have data combined
from different years). The UN also maintain reliable counts historically for every five-year increment. That said, to keep the most
current data, we have included the most recent statistics from "The
World's Cities in 2016."

3. Delhi, Shanghai, São Paulo, Mumbai, and Beijing now rank second
   through sixth, respectively. UN Department of Economic and Social
   Affairs, "World Urbanization Prospects, 2014 Revision," 314–15,
   https://esa.un.org/unpd/wup/publications/files/wup2014-report
   .pdf.

4. One of these—Ecatepec—has 1.655 million people, making it the
   country's second-largest city after Mexico City itself.

5. Mexico's government has officially demarcated this as a region since
   1996. The Spanish literally means "Crown region of the center of
   Mexico."

6. Although Mexico, as of 2019, is the world's fifteenth-largest economy, it has historically broken the top ten—for instance, reaching
   ninth-largest in 2000. Source: "Gross Domestic Product Constant Prices, Report for Selected Countries and Subjects, World
   Economic Outlook Database," April 2019, International Monetary
   Fund, https://www.imf.org/en/data

7. To be exact, 27.24 times. Source: "Gross Domestic Product Per Capita, Report for Selected Countries and Subjects, World Economic
   Outlook Database," April 2019, International Monetary Fund,
   https://www.imf.org/en/data

8. Income inequality is measured with something called the Gini coefficient. The Gini coefficient ranges from 0.0, where everyone would
   have exactly the same income, to 1.0, where one person would own
   all the income. The mean Gini coefficient for all the countries that
   belong to the Organization for Economic Cooperation and Development is 0.318. Canada, at 0.307, is very near that mean. The United
   States, at 0.391, ranks fourth; and Mexico has a Gini coefficient of
   0.458, the OECD's highest disparity. "Income Inequality," Organization for Economic Cooperation and Development, 2017, https://
   data.oecd.org/inequality/income-inequality.htm

9. Average wages, "Organization for Economic Cooperation and Development," 2017, https://data.oecd.org/earnwage/average-wages.htm

10. Mexico is 761,610 square miles (21,972,550 square kilometers);
    the United States is 3,119,885 square miles (8,080,464 square
    kilometers).

11. The US–Mexico border is 1,52 miles long (3,141 kilometers).

12. For agricultural products, Mexico is in the top ten producers of
    lemons (second), chiles (second), strawberries (third), blueberries
    (third), asparagus (third), grapefruit (third), vanilla (fourth), string
    beans (fourth), oranges (fifth), raspberries (fifth), mangos (fifth),

papayas (fifth), cauliflower and broccoli (fifth), sugar cane (sixth), squash (seventh), chickpeas/garbanzos (eighth), coconuts (eighth), pineapples (ninth), lettuce (ninth), and tomatoes (tenth). For animal products, Mexico is in the top ten for eggs (fifth), honey (sixth), chicken (seventh), beef (eighth), leather (eighth), beeswax (eighth), and pigs (ninth). All these data are from Food and Agricultural Organization of the United Nations, FAOSTAT, 2014, www.fao.org /faostat/en/#data.

13. Mexico leads the world in silver production, with 5.36 billion metric tons produced in 2016 alone; that is almost 1.5 billion metric tons more than China, the next-largest producer, at 3.9 billion metric tons. Index Mundi, "Mineral Production Statistics by Country," 2013, www.indexmundi.com/minerals/.

14. Mexico ranks second in the mining of bismuth and fluorite/fluospar; fifth in bentonite, diatomite, lead, and molybdenum; seventh in perlite (used in lead-acid batteries) and industrial grade sand/ gravel; eighth in gold; ninth in zinc; and tenth in copper. All data are from Index Mundi, "Mineral Production Statistics by Country," 2013, www.indexmundi.com/minerals/.

15. Randolph Barker, Christopher A. Scott, Charlotte de Fraiture, and Upali Amarasinghe, "Global Water Shortages and the Challenge Facing Mexico," *Water Resources Development* 16, no. 4 (2000): 525–42, http://udallcenter.arizona.edu/wrpg/Pubs/Barker%20et%20al %202000%20Mexico%20Water%20Scarcity%20IJWRD.pdf.

16. It starts in Colorado and runs through all of New Mexico before it reaches the Mexico-Texas border.

17. Instituto Nacional de Estadística y Geografía, www.inegi.org.mx.

18. Mari N. Jensen, "UA Leading Effort to Evaluate Unprecedented Environmental Flow to Colorado Delta," *UA News*, March 24, 2014, https://uanews.arizona.edu/story/ua-leading-effort-to-evaluate -unprecedented-environmental-flow-to-colorado-delta?utm_source =uanow&utm_medium=email&utm_campaign=biweekly-uanow %3futm_source=uanow&utm_medium=email&utm_campaign= biweekly-uanow.

19. The Sierra Madre chain is more formally called the Trans-Mexican Volcanic Belt, or Eje Volcánico Transversal.

20. This is 140,000 square miles (362,600 square kilometers).

21. A word on "naturally occurring" is needed here. All earthquakes in Mexico are "naturally occurring," as the country prohibits fracking. Indeed, President Andrés Manuel López Obrador in his December 1, 2018 inaugural address specifically banned any future fracking in Mexico. The first tentative steps toward Mexican fracking had begun only a few months earlier in 2018; effectively Mexico has never experienced fracking. See Carlos Ramos Miranda (December 24, 2018), "New president bans fracking," International Law Office, https://www.internationallawoffice.com/Newsletters /Energy-Natural-Resources/Mexico/Hogan-Lovells-BSTL-SC/New -president-bans-fracking#

This is not the case in the United States, where fracking is a major cause of earthquakes. Thus, Oklahoma surpassed California in number of 3.0+ earthquakes. From 1978 to2008, the US Geological Survey (see https://earthquake.usgs.gov/earthquakes/) showed an average of two or less 3.0+ earthquakes per year in Oklahoma. From 2009 to 2018, the average jumped to hundreds per year, peaking with 294 earthquakes of 3.0+ in the state in 2016. Although the US Geological Survey officially published multiple studies indicating that the radical increase in earthquakes in Oklahoma is the result of human- made activities (notably fracking), see, for instance, Jessica Fitzpatrick and Mark Petersen, "Induced Earthquakes Raise Chances of Damaging Shaking in 2016," US Geological Survey, March 28, 2016, www.usgs.gov/ne

22. United Nations, "UN Global Study on Homicide Report," 2014, 15, www.unodc.org/documents/gsh/pdfs/2014_GLOBAL _HOMICIDE_BOOK_web.pdf.

23. Christopher Woody, "The 50 Most Violent Cities in the World," *Business Insider*, April 8, 2017, www.businessinsider.com/most -violent-cities-in-the-world-2017-4/#50-durban-south-africa-had -3443-homicides-per-100000-residents-1.

24. Statistics Canada, "Homicide in Canada 2016," www.statcan.gc.ca /daily-quotidien/161123/dq161123a-eng.htm.

25. Statistics Canada.

26. Statistics Canada.

27. Robberies per 100,000: Mexico, 504.7; Canada, 94.2; United States, 146.4. These aggregates were compiled by NationMaster; see www .nationmaster.com/country-info/stats/Crime/Robberies.

28. Crimes per 1,000 people: Canada, 80.25; the United States, 41.29; Mexico, 14.21. These aggregates were compiled by NationMaster; see www.nationmaster.com/country-info/compare/Mexico/United -States/Crime.

29. Burglaries per 100,000: the United States, 714.4; Canada, 680.9; Mexico, 20.6. These aggregates were compiled by NationMaster; see www.nationmaster.com/country-info/stats/Crime/Burglaries.

30. Automobile thefts per 100,000: the United States, 390.2; Canada, 269.3; Mexico, 136.8. These aggregates were compiled by NationMaster.

31. Rapes per 100,000: Canada, 1.7; the United States, 27.3; Mexico, 13.2. These data are from these sources: for sexual violence and sexual violence against children and rape, United Nations Office on Drugs and Crime. These aggregates were compiled by NationMaster; see www.nationmaster.com/country-info/stats/Crime/Violent -crime/Rapes.

32. Government of Canada Travel Advisory, "Mexico: Safety and Security," December 10, 2018, https://travel.gc.ca/destinations/mexico.

33. United Nations Industrial Development Organization (UNIDO), *Industrial Development Report 2018: The Role of Technology and Innovation in Inclusive and Sustainable Development* (Vienna: UNIDO,

2018), www.unido.org/sites/default/files/files/2017-11/IDR2018
_FULL%20REPORT.pdf. UNIDO defines industrial competitive-
ness as "captures countries' ability to produce and export manu-
factures competitively and to structurally transform" (p. 179). The
rankings are based on data from eight indicators, which demonstrate three main dimensions: (1) the capacity to produce and export
manufactured goods; (2) technological deepening and upgrading;
and (3) global impact on manufacturing value added and trade.

34. Composite scores for the cited countries are as follows: United
States, 0.442; Canada, 0.237; Spain, 0.217; United Kingdom, 0.210;
Mexico, 0.190; Poland, 0.188; Denmark, 0.186; Brazil, 0.112; and
Argentina, 0.089. Mexico is the only Latin America nation in the
top quintile—notably ahead of Brazil, at thirty-sixth, and Argentina,
at forty-sixth, the closest in the region, the only two Latin American nations to reach the second quintile. In fact, Mexico falls just
below Spain (nineteenth) and ranks higher than such industrially
competitive nations as Denmark (twenty-second), Poland (twenty-
third), Finland (twenty-fifth), Israel (twenty-eighth), or Australia
(thirthieth). UNIDO, 1988–99.

35. Ira Brodsky, "How Mexico Went from Telcom Laggard to Mobile
Trailblazer," *Technocrunch*, June 30, 2016, https://techcrunch.com
/2016/06/30/how-mexico-went-from-telecom-laggard-to-mobile
-trailblazer/.

36. After Brazil.

37. Organisation Internationale des Constructeurs d'Automobiles,
"2017 Production Statistics," www.oica.net/category/production
-statistics/2017-statistics/.

38. United Nations Industrial Development Organization, "Industrial Development Report 2016," www.unido.org/resources
/publications/flagship-publications/industrial-development-report
-series/industrial-development-report-2016.

39. TIBA Mexico, "Challenges in Aerospace Logistics," November 9,
2016, www.tibagroup.com/mx/en/aerospace-industry-in-mexico.
The four other states with significant aerospace sectors are Baja
California, Sonora, Chihuahua, and Nuevo Leon.

40. Duncan Tucker, "The Numbers Tell the Story: Mexico's STEM Generation Is Outperforming the USA," *Nearshore Americas*, September 26, 2014, www.nearshoreamericas.com/mexico-offers-money
-alternative-solve-united-states-stem-talent-shortage/.

41. Tucker.

42. Statistics Canada, "Education in Canada: Attainment, Field of Study
and Location of Study," September 15, 2016, www12.statcan.gc.ca
/nhs-enm/2011/as-sa/99-012-x/99-012-x2011001-eng.cfm.

43. Mexico edged past Chile in 2015, the most recent year for which full
data are available.

44. Organization for Economic Cooperation and Development, "Main
Science and Technology Indicators: GERD as a Percentage of GDP,"
https://data.oecd.org/rd/gross-domestic-spending-on-r-d.htm.

45. Octavio Paz, "Critique of the Pyramid," in *The Labyrinth of Solitude and Other Writings* trans. Lysander Kemp (New York: Grove Press, 1985), 284. Paz first published this essay in his 1970 book *Postdata*.
46. Eduardo Bollo, Jaana Remes, Tomás Lajous, James Manyika, Eugenia Ramirez, and Morten Rossé, "A Tale of Two Mexicos: Growth and Prosperity in a Two-Speed Economy," McKinsey Global Institute, March 2014, www.mckinsey.com/global-themes/americas/a-tale-of-two-mexicos.
47. *The Economist*, "The Two Mexicos," September 19, 2015, www.economist.com/news/leaders/21665027-its-combination-modernity-and-poverty-mexico-provides-lessons-all-emerging.
48. Carlos M. Coria-Sánchez, "Mexican Business Culture in Trade Books: Past and Present," in *Mexican Business Culture: Essays on Tradition, Ethics, Entrepreneurship, and Commerce and the State*, edited by John T. Hyatt (Jefferson, NC: McFarland, 2016), 14.
49. Santiago Ramirez, *El Mexican: Psicología de sus motivaciones* (Mexico City: Ed. Grijalbo, 1997), 73. Quoted by Coria-Sánchez, 15.
50. Paz, "Critique."
51. Paz, 286.

CHAPTER 3

1. Pueblo Mágico, or Magical Village, is an initiative of the Mexican Ministry of Tourism and other federal and state agencies to promote a series of towns in Mexico that offer visitors a "magical" experience because of their natural beauty, historical relevance, and traditions. A Magical Village is a place with symbolism. See chapter 6 in this book for more information about them
2. José Vasconcelos, *The Cosmic Race* (Baltimore: Johns Hopkins University Press, 1925; bilingual edition, trans. Didier T. Jaén, 1979).
3. Vasconcelos, 26.
4. Vasconcelos, 9.
5. Quoted by Joseph Bucklin, *Theodore Roosevelt and His Time: Shown in His Own Letter* (New York: Charles Scribner's Sons, 1920), 474.
6. The *Loving v. The State of Virginia* ruling in 1967 overturned laws in sixteen states where whites were prohibited from marrying blacks—Alabama, Arkansas, Delaware, Florida, Georgia, Kentucky, Louisiana, Mississippi, Missouri, North Carolina, Oklahoma, South Carolina, Tennessee, Texas, Virginia, and West Virginia. Four of these states banned whites from marrying any nonwhite (Georgia, South Carolina, Texas, and Virginia). Missouri also banned whites from marrying Asians, and North Carolina and Tennessee banned whites from marrying Native Americans while allowing marriages to other races.
   In addition, five other states repealed their antimiscegenation laws only a few years earlier (or in the case of Maryland, only months before). These laws were repealed in Arizona (1962, banning marriage to blacks, Asians, Filipinos, and East Asians), Maryland (1967, banning marriage of whites to blacks and Filipinos and

also black–Filipino marriages), Nebraska (1963, whites to blacks and Asians), Utah (1963, whites to blacks, Asians, and Filipinos), and Wyoming (1965 whites to blacks, Asians, and Filipinos).

7. Pierre Elliott Trudeau, "Remarks at the Ukrainian-Canadian Congress," October 9, 1971, as cited in *The Essential Trudeau*, edited by Ron Graham (Toronto: McClelland & Stewart, 1988).

8. For census data on Canada, see Statistics Canada, "Immigration and Ethnocultural Diversity in Canada," 2011, www12.statcan.gc.ca /nhs-enm/2011/as-sa/99-010-x/99-010-x2011001-eng.cfm. For US census data, see US Census, "The Foreign-Born Population in the United States: 2010," 2012, www.census.gov/library/publications /2012/acs/acs-19.html.

   For Mexican demographic profiles, see Instituto Nacional de Estadística y Geografía (INEGI), "Perfil sociodemográfico: Estados Unidos Mexicans," http://internet.contenidos.inegi .org.mx/contenidos/productos//prod_serv/contenidos/espanol /bvinegi/productos/censos/poblacion/2010/perfil_socio/uem /702825047610_1.pdf.

9. The data from the Organization for Economic Cooperation and Development on salaries were quoted by Nayeli Meza Orozco, "Buen salario para egresados ¿misión imposible?" *Forbes México*, March 3, 2015, www.forbes.com.mx/buen-salario-para-egresados -mision-imposible/.

10. For data on the Global Gender Gap Index, see World Economic Forum, "Mexico," 2016, http://reports.weforum.org/global-gender -gap-report-2016/economies/#economy=MEX.

11. Although we note that in Canada men are more likely to take on the role of child care. One in ten fathers in Canada are stay-at-home dads; see Statistics Canada, "Changing Profile of Stay-at-Home Parents," 2018, www.statcan.gc.ca/pub/11-630-x/11-630-x2016007-eng .htm.

12. A *maquiladora* is a Mexican assembly plant that operates under a preferential tariff program.

13. Geert Hofstede, *Cultures Consequences: International Differences in Work-Related Values* (Beverly Hills, CA: Sage, 1980), https:// geerthofstede.com/landing-page/.

14. Real Academia Española, "Discutir," 2019, https://dle.rae.es.

15. A *tilma* is a garment similar to a poncho.

16. *Mole* is an ancient thick sauce made with a combination of more than twenty ingredients, including chili peppers and chocolate. This typical dish of Puebla is served on chicken with rice on the side. There are many types of *mole*—black, green, with almonds, and so on. It takes much time to prepare and requires constant supervision.

17. Tamales are a traditional Mesoamerican dish made of a corn-based dough, combined with chicken, pork, beans, and cheese. These are wrapped in a banana leaf (which is discarded before eating).

CHAPTER 4

1. Edward T. Hall, *The Silent Language* (New York: Doubleday, 1959).

CHAPTER 5

1. Erin Meyer, *The Culture Map: Breaking through the Invisible Boundaries of Global Business* (New York: PublicAffairs, 2014), 120.
2. Michael O'Sullivan and John Hecht, "Netflix Orders First Spanish-Language Original," *Hollywood Reporter*, April 23, 2014, www.hollywoodreporter.com/live-feed/netflix-orders-first-spanish-language-698424.
3. David Luhnow, "Mexico's Spoiled Rich Kids: The Entitled Children of the Country's Elite Are Now Coming under Fire," *Wall Street Journal*, June 14, 2013, www.wsj.com/articles/SB10001424127887323734304578543663876242372.
4. "Named and Shamed: Social Media Expose the Ghastliness of Mexico's Entitled Set," *The Economist*, May 17, 2013, www.economist.com/americas-view/2013/05/17/named-and-shamed.
5. Geert Hofstede, *Culture's Consequences: International Differences in Work-Related Values* (Beverly Hills, CA: Sage, 1980).
6. Most notable among these is the GLOBE study edited by Robert J. House, Paul J. Hanges, Mansour Javidan, Peter W. Dorfman, and Vipin Gupta, *Culture, Leadership, and Organizations: The GLOBE Study of 62 Societies* (Thousand Oaks, CA: Sage, 2004). The most recent update of the Globe study was by Jagdeep S. Chhokar, Felix C. Brodbeck, and Robert J. House, eds., *Culture and Leadership across the World: The GLOBE Book of In-Depth Studies of 25 Societies* (New York: Taylor & Francis, 2008).
7. Arnulfo H. Ojeda, Malcom James Ree, and Thomas R. Carretta, "Personality Similarities and Differences between Mexican and American Business Leaders," *Journal of Leadership Studies* 4, no. 5 (2010): 40–47.
8. We should note that leaders in the two countries had more personality traits in common (ten) than unshared (six), which makes the attributes where they differed all the more noteworthy.
9. Ojeda, Ree, and Carretta, "Personality Similarities."
10. See, e.g., John C. Condon, *Good Neighbors: Communicating with the Mexicans* (Yarmouth, ME: Intercultural Press, 1985); Alan Riding, *Distant Neighbors: A Portrait of the Mexicans* (New York: Vintage Books, 1989); and Eva Kras, *Management in Two Cultures* (Yarmouth, ME: Intercultural Press, 1995).
11. Transparency International, "2017 Corruption Perceptions Index," 2017, www.transparency.org/news/feature/corruption_perceptions_index_2017.
12. The score and rank for each of these are Cuba, 47th/62nd; Argentina, 39th/85th; Brazil, 37th/96th; and Bolivia, 33rd/112th.
13. Gabriel Zaid, "Propriedad Privada de las Funciones, Publicas," *Vuelta*, November, 1986, 120.

14. Quoted by Elisabeth Malkin, "Corruption at a Level of Audacity 'Never Seen in Mexico,'" *New York Times*, April 19, 2017, www .nytimes.com/2017/04/19/world/americas/in-mexico-mounting -misdeeds-but-governors-escape-justice.html.

15. Anabella Dávila and Andreas Hartmann, "Tradition and Modern Aspects of Mexican Modern Corporate Culture," *Mexican Business Culture: Essays on Tradition, Ethics, Entrepreneurship and Commerce and the State*, edited by C. M. Coria-Sánchez and J. T. Hyatt (Jefferson, NC: McFarland, 2016), 28.

16. Driss Essabbar, Maria Zrikem, and Marc Zolghadri, "Power Imbalance in Collaboration Relationships," *International Journal of Supply and Operations Management* 2, no. 4 (2016): 1027.

17. See, e.g., María Magdalena Tosoni, "Notas sobre el clientelismo politico en la ciudad de México," *Perfiles Latinoamericans* 14 (2007): 29.

18. Patricia G. Martinez, "Paternalism as a Positive Form of Leadership in the Latin American Context: Leader-Benevolence, Decision-Making, and Human Resource Practices," in *Human Resources in Latin America: An Agenda for International Leaders*, edited by M. M. Elvira and A. Dávila (Oxford: Routledge, 2005), 75–93.

19. Dávila and Hartmann, "Tradition," 27.

20. Robert R. Kaufman, "The Patron–Client Concept and Macro-Politics: Prospects and Problems," *Comparative Studies in Society and History* 16, no. 3 (1974): 284–308. Confusingly, Kaufman referred to what we describe as the Patrón System as "clientelism"; his point was that the role of patron–client relationship had much that was positive, even though, from the US perspective, this was usually only seen as something bad.

21. US "boss machine politics" and Mexican *caciquismo* do, however, differ in two ways. Whereas US boss machine politics was usually limited to major cities (famously, Chicago), Mexican *caciquismo* has its strongest hold in rural areas, particularly among regions with large numbers of indigenous people. Additionally, where US boss machine politics largely ended by the mid-twentieth century, today *caciquismo* continues to thrive in the rural and less-developed regions of Mexico.

22. James D. Cockcroft, *Mexico's Revolution Then and Now* (New York: New York University Press, 2010), 60.

23. This is exemplified by a major collection of scholarly essays on the subject: Alan Knight and Wil Pansters, eds., *Caciquismo in Twentieth-Century Mexico* (London: Institute for the Study of the Americas, 2006).

24. Sarah Childress, "Caciques, Not Cartels, Kill in Mexico This Time," *Public Radio International*, December 11, 2011, www.pri.org/stories /2011-12-16/caciques-not-cartels-kill-mexico-time.

25. Ismael Solis Sánchez, "El caciquismo en México: La otra cara de la democracia mexicana—El caso del caciquismo urbano en el Estado de México," *Estudios Politicos* 37 (January–April 2016): 167–92.

26. Some English speakers have difficulty understanding the term "corporatism" because they think it has something to do with business "corporations." It does not. The term *corporatism* actually comes from the Latin word *corpora*, which means "bodies" or, in this case, special-interest bodies. Corporatism actually came from an initiative of Pope Leo XIII. Because his original encyclical uses the Latin word *corpora* ("bodies") and spread as a concept from there through the Italian equivalent (*corporazioni*), the confusion with the English word was an unintended consequence. So corporatism is a jointly negotiated rule by influential bodies (*corpora*). In North American English, we might call this rule by interest-groupism, but here we stick with the word "corporatism."

27. Though worded in a bit more complicated way, we would probably be incomplete here without quoting the most-cited definition in the literature. This definition comes from the 1974 article "Still the Century of Corporatism?" by Philippe Schmitter: "Corporatism can be defined as a system of interest representation in which the constituent units are organized into a limited number of singular, compulsory, noncompetitive, hierarchically ordered and functionally differentiated categories, recognized or licensed (if not created) by the state and granted a deliberate representational monopoly within their respective categories observing certain controls on their selection of leader and articulation of demands and supports." Philippe C. Schmitter, "Still the Century of Corporatism?" *Review of Politics* 36, no. 1 (1974): 93–95.

28. George W. Grayson, "Mexico, the PRI, and López Obrador: The Legacy of Corporatism," *Orbis* 51, no. 2 (2017): 280.

29. This was the case even if the PRI was in power for seventy-one straight years.

30. Grayson, "Mexico," 281.

31. Paz, "Critique."

32. "Can Mexico Be Americanized?" *New York Times,* June 16, 1865, www.nytimes.com/1865/06/16/archives/can-mexico-be-americanized.html.

33. Joseph Contreras, *In the Shadow of the Giant: The Americanization of Modern Mexico* (New Brunswick, NJ: Rutgers University Press, 2009).

34. When the number of US-owned *maquiladoras* in northern Mexico rapidly increased, claims were made that somehow these northern border states were becoming Americanized. They had not been. When Mexican president Carlos Salinas reached out to US president George H. W. Bush, many assumed that the North American Free Trade Agreement would transform Mexico into a more Americanized nation. It did not. Surely, others claimed, when Ernesto Zedillo came to power as a Mexico's president, Mexican corporatism would disappear—after all, Zedillo grew up in Mexicali just 10 miles (17 kilometers) south of the US border, and he received both his master's and doctoral degrees from Yale University. Mexico,

however, remained implacably Mexican. When the PRI was finally ousted from power after seventy-one years of one-party rule with the election of the probusiness Partido Acción Nacional (National Action Party), many prematurely claimed the death of corporatism; after all, Fox spent a high school study abroad in Wisconsin and had a grandfather from Cincinnati, and his business career as chief executive of Coca Cola Mexico was proof that he knew the United States well (he did) and therefore would choose to eliminate corporatist elements to make Mexico more "American" (he did not).

35. James G. Samstad, "Corporation and Democratic Transition: State and Labor during the Salinas and Zedillo Administrations," *Latin American Politics and Society* 44, no. 4 (2002): 1.

36. Other examples of corporatism gone bad include Argentina's Justicialismo (Peronism) and Portugal's Estado Corporativo (corporatism). Although the populist Juan Perón never used the term "corporatist," his policies reflect the practice in action if not in name. The case is clearer with Portugal. Its dictator António Salazar's own description for the principles of his Estado Novo notes that, though often categorized as a fascist, Salazar himself forcefully rejected the term, explaining instead that the regime practiced "state corporatism." In its more positive forms, corporatism provides the foundation for the Netherlands' tripartite consensus "polder model," Sweden's social democratic *folkhmmet* "people's home," and Turkish kemalist *devletçilik* (the basic "social corporatism")—the *sosyal korporatizm* of modern Turkey's founder Kemal Ataturk.

37. See, in addition to those already cited—Schmitter, "Still the Century"; Grayson, "Mexico"; and Samstad, "Corporation"—support such as that of Wayne A. Cornelius, *Mexican Politicas in Transition* (La Jolla, CA: Center for US-Mexican Studies, 2000); Roger Magazine, "An Innovative Combination of Neoliberalism and State Corporatism: The Case of a Locally Based NGO in Mexico City," *Annals of the American Academy of Political and Social Science* 590 (2003): 243–56; and Armando Barta and Gerardo Otero, "Contesting Neoliberal Globalism and NAFTA in Rural Mexico: From State Corporatism to the Political-Cultural Formation of the Peasantry?" *Journal of Latino–Latin American Studies* 1 (2005): 164–90.

38. See, e.g., Ilán Bizberg, "La crisis del corporativismo méxicano," *Foro Internacional* 30, no. 4 (1990): 695–735; and Trejo Quiroz, José Othon, and Luis Mendez y Berrueta, "Corporativismo, modernidad y autonomía obrera en México," *Sociologica* 6, no. 15 (1991): 159–88.

39. Fredric Jameson, *The Postmodern, or the Cultural Logic of Late Capitalism* (Durham, NC: Duke University Press, 1994).

40. Carlos Monsiváis, "Will Nationalism Be Bilingual?" in *Mass Media and Free Trade: NAFTA and the Cultural Industries*, edited by Emile G. McAnany and Kenton T. Wilkinson (Austin: University of Texas Press, 1997), 247.

41. Monsiváis.

CHAPTER 6

1. For background information on nonverbal behavior, see J. F. Dovidio and M. LaFrance, "Race, Ethnicity, and Nonverbal Behavior," in *Handbooks of Communication Science: Nonverbal Communication*, edited by J. A. Hall and M. L. Knapp (Boston: De Gruyter Mouton, 2013); J. D. Meadors and C. B. Murray, "Measuring Nonverbal Bias through Body Language Responses to Stereotypes," *Journal of Nonverbal Behavior* 38, no. 2 (2014): 209–29; D. C. Albas, K. W. McCluskey, and C. A. Albas, "Perception of the Emotional Content of Speech: A Comparison of Two Canadian Groups," *Journal of Cross-Cultural Psychology* 7, no. 4 (1976): 481–90; and J. Small, S. M. Chan, E. Drance, J. Globerman, W. Hulko, D. O'Connor, and L. Ho, "Verbal and Nonverbal Indicators of the Quality of Communication between Care Staff and Residents in Ethnoculturally and Linguistically Diverse Long-Term Care Settings," *Journal of Cross-Cultural Gerontology* 30, no. 3 (2015): 285–304.

2. For Canadian and US perspectives on affect display, in the Canadian government's own explanation for newcomers of foreigners, it writes: "Many Anglophone Canadians are uncomfortable with strong demonstrations of emotions, particularly if it is with someone they do not know well. In Quebec or in many immigrant communities, emotions may be more freely expressed.... Quebec people may not need as much personal space, and touching is more common. Typically, people from Quebec greet each other using more physical signs such as hugs and kisses and may offer kisses on the cheek to newcomers after a few encounters." Government of Canada–Global Affairs Canada, "Cultural Information: Communication Styles," 2018, www.international.gc.ca/cil-cai/country_insights-apercus_pays/ci-ic_ca.aspx?lang=eng#cn-2. When it comes to public displays of affection, there is considerable regional variation in the United States. In a US government poll on the YouGov site in 2014, the data showed that 23 percent of those in the South founding public kissing inappropriate, 19 percent in the Midwest and West, and just 15 percent in the Northeast. YouGov, "No Petting Please, We're American," 2014, https://today.yougov.com/topics/lifestyle/articles-reports/2014/01/10/no-petting-please-were-american.

CHAPTER 7

1. Robert Latham, "What Are We? From a Multicultural to a Multiversal Canada," *International Journal* 63, no. 1 (Winter 2007): 23.

2. Cited by Clifton Fadiman, ed., *The Little, Brown Book of Anecdotes* (Boston: Little, Brown, 2009). Ford originally made the statement in an interview with Charles Wheeler in the *Chicago Tribune*, May 25, 1916.

3. John C. Condon, *Good Neighbors: Communicating with the Mexicans* (Yarmouth, ME: Intercultural Press, 1985).

4. For an audio recording of Octavio Paz's acceptance speech, see Octavio Paz, "Nobel Lecture: Lá búsqueda del presente," Nobel Media AB, 1990, http://nobelprize.org/nobel_prizes/literature /laureates/1990/paz-lecture-s.html.

5. Carlos Fuentes, "Kierkegaard en la Zona Rosa," in *Tiempo Mexicano*, by Carlos Fuentes (Mexico City: Joaquín Mortiz, 1971), 11.

6. Leonard W. Doob, *Patterning of Time* (New Haven, CT: Yale University Press, 1971), 64–65.

7. Ned Crouch, *Mexicans and Americans: Cracking the Culture Code* (London: Nicholas Brealey International, 2004), 33.

8. Edward T. Hall, *The Dance of Life: The Other Dimensions of Time* (Garden City, NY: Anchor Books, 1983), 48.

9. Hall, 84.

10. Olivia Hernández-Pozas and Sergio Madero-Gómez, "Looking at Time and Business with the Mexican Lens," in *Mexican Business Culture: Essays on Tradition, Ethics, Entrepreneurship and Commerce and the State*, edited by Carlos M. Coria Sánchez and John T. Hyatt), 129.

11. These are the words of Carlos M. Coria Sánchez, quoted by Hernández-Pozas and Madero-Gómez, "Looking at Time," 129.

12. This is with the exception of First Nation reserves or Inuit areas such as Nunavut, which are actually ethnic differences.

13. Although Canadian companies are also guilty of this, it is, quite frankly, more common among US companies, both for cultural reasons (valuing diversity) and economic ones (there are simply more US companies operating in Mexico than Canadian ones).

14. Japan is only partially monochronic—see our other book—but for the purposes here, we can safely call it monochronic. For more on Japan, see Haru Yamada, Orlando R. Kelm and David A. Victor (2019), *The 7 Keys to Communicating in Japan: An Intercultural Approach*, Washington DC: Georgetown University Press.

15. Hernández-Pozas and Madero-Gómez, "Looking at Time," 129.

communication strategies: emotion and language, 19–20; environment and, 59–60; for insider group membership, 20–21; for nonverbal communication, 171–72; social organization and, 97; for speaking English, 15–17, 22; for speaking Spanish, 17–19, 22

¿cómo? (excuse me), 18

compadres, comadres (godparents), 82, *82*

compassion, 114

compliments, 105–6

Condon, John, 178–79

conflict avoidance, 83, 105–6, 159

consonants, emphasis on, 11–12, 16

contexting. *See* communication and contexting

Contreras, Joseph, 143

conversations, 20, 107, 166–67

coral reefs, 40–41

Coria-Sánchez, Carlos, 58

Corona Regional del Centro de México, 27, 225n3

corporate culture, 192–95, 209, 211

corporatism, xvii, 122*f*, 123, 138–44, 147, 233nn26–27, 233–34n34, 234n36

corruption, 127–28, 134–35, 141, 144, 146

córtale (make-it-short), 156

country size, 28–30, 29*f*, 225n10

courteous communication, 106. *See also* formal language use

credit cards, 47

Creixell, Juan, 211–13, 220

crime and safety issues, 44–51; burglaries, 47, 227n29; *caciquismo* (rule by local strongmen), xvii, 131–32, 134–38, 146, 232n21; driving, 47–49; recommendations regarding, 60; robberies, 46–47, 49, 227n27; security guards and

locked entrances, 44, *45*; summary, 61; transportation and, 47–51, *51*; violent crime and, 45–47, 137, 227nn27–31. *See also* corruption

Cristero War (1926–29), 88

cronyism, 133–34, 146

cross-cultural and global experience, 192–95, 216–17, 221

Crouch, Ned, 183

crying, 159

cultural blending. *See mestizaje* and *mestizo*

cultural mosaic concept, xv, 67–70, 68*t*

cultures: collectivist, 82–83; cross-cultural and global experience, 192–95, 216–17, 221; high-context, xvi, 103–4, 220; individualistic, 82–83; low-context, xvi, 103–4, 220; monochronic, 182–84, 195–96; polychronic, 182–84, 195–96; "two Mexicos" concept and, 57–59, 125, 137. *See also* case study; social organization

currency, 181

dams, 34–35

Dávila, Anabella, 128, 131

Daylight Savings Time, 30

death: *calaveritas* (mock obituaries), 111, *112*; *Día de los Muertos* (Day of the Dead), 87, *88*, *112*; folk symbolism of, 170–71, *171*; funerals and graves, 87, 111, 171

decir (to say), 83

dehydration, 60

democracy, 142, 143

desert and arid regions, 24, 31–32

DF (Distrito Federal), Mexico City, 26

Día de los Muertos (Day of the Dead), 87, *88*, *112*

dialects, 10–11

Díaz, Porfirio, 140

skulls and skeletons: *alebrijes* (animal sculptures), 170–71, *171*; Calavera Catrina, 87, *88*, *112*

slang expressions, 15

Slape, Mitchell, 210–11, 220

smartphones, 54

soccer (*fútbol*), 96, *96*

social events, 187, 197. *See also* holidays and festivals; leisure time

social groups, 70–74

social media, 126

social organization, 63–100; authority and power, 125–26; of Aztec people, 163; caste and class system, 72–74, 125–26; communication strategies and, 97; education, 74–77, *76*; family and kinship, 81–82, 81–84, *83f*, *84*; gender roles, 77–81, 79–80; leisure time, 89–90, 89–96, *92–96*; multiculturalism and, 64–70, *68t*; overview, xv–xvi; regional diversity, 70–71; religion, 84–89, *86*, *88*

socioeconomic status: English language use, 9; "two Mexicos" concept, 57–59, 125, 137; wealth gap, 27–28, 57–59, 72–74

Solís Sánchez, Ismael, 138

Spanish-accented English, 16

Spanish language, 1–22; borrowed words from English, 13–14, *14*; characteristics in Mexico, 10–14, 22; communication strategies, 15–21; emotion and subtlety, 18, 19–20; English as status symbol, 8–10; English borrowing words from, 2; English speakers in Mexico, 5, 8, 208; English speaking strategies, 15–17; *fuerte consonantismo* (emphasis on consonants), 11–12; Heritage and nonnative speakers of, 6–7; indigenous

borrowings in, 12–13, *13*, 21; insider status and, 20–21; learning process for, 21; overview, xiv–xv; regional variations in, 10–11; Spanish speakers in United States and Canada, 4–5; Spanish speaking strategies, 17–19. *See also* communication and contexting; Spanish phrases and terms

Spanish phrases and terms: *abogado* (lawyer), 11; *abrazo* (hug), 166–67; *amiguismo* (protectionist cronyism), 133–34; *apúrate* (hurry up), 154, *154*; *bueno* (good), 20; *caciquismo* (rule by local strong-men), 131–32, 134–38; *cantado* (sung), 11; *Chamba/chamba* (American Chamber of Commerce/work), 14; *clásico* (soccer game between rivals), 96; *comenzar* (to commence), 17; *córtale* (make-it-short), 156; *decir* (to say), 83, *83f*; *dichos* (proverbs), 105–8, *108*; *discutir* (to discuss/argue), 83, *83f*, 105; *estos* (those), 11; *fuerte consonantismo* (emphasis on consonants), 11–12; *fútbol* (soccer), 96, *96*; *jonrón* (home run), 14; *le pusieron los cuernos* (cheated on), 156; *lonche* (lunch), 14; *los compadres, las comadres* (godparents), 82; *¿mande?* (excuse me), 18; *más o menos* (more or less), 155, *156*; *mediadores* (brokers), 130; *móchate, ¿no?* (give me some, share it), 152, *152*; *muy amable* (very kind of you), 151; *nada (nothing)*, 11; *parquear* (to park), 14; *patronismo* (personalized relationship network), 129–30; *¿perdón?* (excuse me), 18; *pocho* (Mexican who emigrated), 6–7; *santo patrono* (patron saint),

Orlando R. Kelm, PhD, is an associate professor of Hispanic linguistics at the University of Texas at Austin, where he teaches courses in Portuguese and Spanish, focusing mainly on business language and the cultural aspects of international business communication. He also serves as the director of the UT Portuguese Flagship Program. His research and publications center on the cultural aspects of international business and pedagogical applications of innovative technologies in language learning, focusing mainly on Latin America and Brazil. Together with coauthor David A. Victor, he published the first volume in this series, *The Seven Keys to Communicating in Brazil: An Intercultural Approach* (Georgetown University Press, 2016). With coauthors David A. Victor and Haru Yamada, he published the second volume in this series, *The Seven Keys to Communicating in Japan: An Intercultural Approach* (Georgetown University Press, 2017).

David A. Victor, PhD, is a professor of management and international business at Eastern Michigan University, as well as a consultant, author, and editor. He teaches courses on managing world business communication, international management, and international business and offers a series of seminars on doing business in various countries. As a consultant, he has run training programs and coached the leaders of more than 200 companies and organizations, ranging from Global 500 companies to government and nongovernmental organizations. He is also editor-in-chief of the *Global Advances in Business Communication Journal*. Among his many publications is the groundbreaking *International Business Communication* (HarperCollins, 1992), which introduced the LESCANT model used as the framework for this book.

Olivia Hernandez-Pozas is an associate professor at Tecnológico de Monterrey in Monterrey, Mexico, and the author of works in international business, cultural intelligence, and management education. She teaches classes on negotiation and intercultural communication. She is also a member of the National Research System of Mexico. She is certified as an advanced cultural intelligence facilitator by the Cultural Intelligence Center. She is a member of the Academy of Management and has served as a board member of its Management Education and Development Division.